EVERY
PRAYER
IN THE BIBLE

edited by
Stig Helgren

Every Prayer of the Bible
© 2010, 2019 TheBiblePeople.com

Scripture marked NIV taken from the HOLY BIBLE, NEW INTERNATIONAL VERSION(R). NIV(R). Copyright (C) 1973, 1978, 1984 by International Bible Society. Used by permission of Zondervan Publishing House. All rights reserved.

Quotations marked NASB are taken from the New American Standard Bible. Scripture taken from the NEW AMERICAN STANDARD BIBLE, (c) Copyright The Lockman Foundation 1960, 1962, 1963, 1968, 1971, 1972, 1973, 1975, 1977, 1995. Used by permission.

Scripture marked NRSV Copyright 1989. Division of Christian Education of the National Council of Churches of Christ in the United States.

Scripture marked NLT are taken from the Holy Bible, New Living Translation, copyright (c) 1996 by Tyndale Charitable Trust. All rights reserved.

Scripture marked NJB are taken from the New Jerusalem Bible. Biblical text (c) 1985 by Darton, Longman & Todd Ltd. and Doubleday Notes and Introductions (c) 1990 by Darton, Longman & Todd Ltd. and Doubleday, a division of Bantam Doubleday Dell Publishing Group, Inc. All rights reserved.

Scripture marked GW are taken from God's Word Translation of the Bible. GOD'S WORD is a copyrighted work of God's Word to the Nations Bible Society, (c) 1995. All rights reserved.

Scripture marked TEV are taken from the Today's English Version Second Edition, Copyright c 1992 by American Bible Society. Used by permission.

Scripture marked CEV are taken from the Contemporary English Version (CEV), (c) 1991, 1995 by American Bible Society. Used by permission.

Scripture marked ESV are taken from The Holy Bible, English Standard Version(TM) Copyright(C) 2000; 2003 by Crossway Bibles, A Division of Good News Publishers, 1300 Crescent Street, Wheaton, Illinois 60187, USA. All Rights Reserved.

Scripture marked NAB are taken from the New American Bible with Revised New Testament and Revised Psalms © 1991, 1986, 1970 Confraternity of Christian Doctrine, Washington, D.C. and are used by permission of the copyright owner. All Rights Reserved.

Scripture quotations marked TLB are taken from The Living Bible: Tyndale House, 1997, c1971 by Tyndale House Publishers, Inc. Used by permission. All rights reserved

Introduction

This is the only book in the marketplace that reprints every prayer from the Bible. The prayers are arranged as they appear in the Bible (Genesis-Revelation) and are without commentary so you can enjoy reflective, undistracted moments with God's word. Simple titles are included that help reader identify each prayer. Categories include:

- Blessing & Benediction
- Confessing Sin
- Making Requests Known
- Praying for Others
- Seeking God's Will
- Thanksgiving & Gratitude
- Praising God
- And other verses about prayer

Rather than favor one Bible translation, we have reprinted these verses from a number of respected translations. We have not adjusted punctuation or capitalization so that you can explore the context of each verse more fully if you desire to do so. We hope this book will be useful to you as you continue your study of God's word.

The Editorial Team
TheBiblePeople.com

The Old Testament

Responding to God
Genesis 4:13 (NIV)
Cain said to the Lord, "My punishment is more than I can bear."

Making Requests Known
Genesis 4:26 (NASB)
To Seth, to him also a son was born; and he called his name Enosh. Then men began to call upon the name of the Lord.

Verses about Prayer
Genesis 5:22-24 (NRSV)
Enoch walked with God after the birth of Methuselah three hundred years, and had other sons and daughters. Thus all the days of Enoch were three hundred sixty-five years. Enoch walked with God; then he was no more, because God took him.

Praising God
Genesis 14:20 (NAB)
And blessed be God Most High,
who delivered your foes into your hand." Then Abram gave him a tenth of everything.

Making Requests Known
Genesis 15:2-3 (NJB)
'Lord Yahweh,' Abram replied, 'what use are your gifts, as I am going on my way childless? ... Since you have given me no offspring,' Abram continued, 'a member of my household will be my heir.'

Seeking God's Will
Genesis 15:8 (NLT)
But Abram replied, "O Sovereign Lord, how can I be sure that you will give it to me?"

Praying for Others
Genesis 17:18 (GWT)
Then Abraham said to God, "Why not let Ishmael be my heir?"

Praying for Others
Genesis 18:23-33 (TEV)
Abraham approached the Lord and asked, "Are you really going to destroy the innocent with the guilty? If there are fifty innocent people in the city, will you destroy the whole city? Won't you spare it in order to save the fifty? Surely you won't kill the innocent with the guilty. That's impossible! You can't do that. If you did, the innocent would be punished along with the guilty. That is impossible. The judge of all the earth has to act justly."

The Lord answered, "If I find fifty innocent people in Sodom, I will spare the whole city for their sake."

Abraham spoke again: "Please forgive my boldness in continuing to speak to you, Lord. I am only a man and have no right to say anything. But perhaps there will be only forty-five innocent people instead of fifty. Will you destroy the whole city because there are five too few?"

The Lord answered, "I will not destroy the city if I find forty-five innocent people."

Abraham spoke again: "Perhaps there will be only forty."

He replied, "I will not destroy it if there are forty."

Abraham said, "Please don't be angry, Lord, but I must speak again. What if there are only thirty?"

He said, "I will not do it if I find thirty."

Abraham said, "Please forgive my boldness in continuing to speak to you, Lord. Suppose that only twenty are found?"

He said, "I will not destroy the city if I find twenty."

Abraham said, "Please don't be angry, Lord, and I will speak only once more. What if only ten are found?"

He said, "I will not destroy it if there are ten." After he had finished speaking with Abraham, the Lord went away, and Abraham returned home.

Praying for Others
Genesis 20:7 (CEV)
Her husband is a prophet. Let her go back to him, and his prayers will save you from death. But if you don't return her, you and all your people will die.

Praying for Others
Genesis 20:17-18 (ESV)
Then Abraham prayed to God, and God healed Abimelech, and also healed his wife and female slaves so that they bore children. For the Lord had closed all the wombs of the house of Abimelech because of Sarah, Abraham's wife.

Praising God
Genesis 21:33 (NIV)
Abraham planted a tamarisk tree in Beersheba, and there he called upon the name of the Lord, the Eternal God.

Responding to God
Genesis 22:1 (NASB)
Now it came about after these things, that God tested Abraham, and said to him, "Abraham!" And he said, "Here I am."

Responding to God
Genesis 22:11 (NRSV)
But the angel of the Lord called to him from heaven, and said, "Abraham, Abraham!" And he said, "Here I am."

Making Requests Known
Genesis 24:12-15 (NAB)
Then he prayed: "LORD, God of my master Abraham, let it turn out favorably for me today and thus deal graciously with my master Abraham. While I stand here at the spring and the daughters of the townsmen are coming out to draw water, if I say to a girl, 'Please lower your jug, that I may drink,' and she answers, 'Take a drink, and let me give water to your camels, too,' let her be the one whom you have decided upon for your servant Isaac. In this way I shall know that you have dealt graciously with my master."

He had scarcely finished these words when Rebekah (who was born to Bethuel, son of Milcah, the wife of Abraham's brother Nahor) came out with a jug on her shoulder.

Praising God
Genesis 24:26-27 (NJB)
Then the man bowed down and worshipped Yahweh saying, 'Blessed be Yahweh, God of my master Abraham, for not withholding his faithful

love from my master. Yahweh has led me straight to the house of my master's brother.'

Making Requests Known
Genesis 24:42-45 (NLT)
"So this afternoon when I came to the spring I prayed this prayer: 'O Lord, the God of my master, Abraham, if you are planning to make my mission a success, please guide me in a special way. Here I am, standing beside this spring. I will say to some young woman who comes to draw water, "Please give me a drink of water!" And she will reply, "Certainly! And I'll water your camels, too!" Lord, let her be the one you have selected to be the wife of my master's son.'

"Before I had finished praying these words, I saw Rebekah coming along with her water jug on her shoulder. She went down to the spring and drew water and filled the jug. So I said to her, 'Please give me a drink.'

Praising God
Genesis 24:48 (GWT)
I knelt, bowing down to the Lord. I praised the Lord, the God of my master Abraham. The Lord led me in the right direction to get the daughter of my master's relative for his son.

Praising God
Genesis 24:52 (TEV)
When the servant of Abraham heard this, he bowed down and worshiped the Lord.

Praying for Others
Genesis 25:21-23 (CEV)
Rebekah still had no children. So Isaac asked the Lord to let her have a child, and the Lord answered his prayer.

Before Rebekah gave birth, she knew she was going to have twins, because she could feel them inside her, fighting each other. She thought, "Why is this happening to me?" Finally, she asked the Lord why her twins were fighting, and he told her:
"Your two sons will become two separate nations.
The younger of the two will be stronger, and the older son will be his servant."

Blessings & Benedictions
Genesis 28:3-4 (ESV)
God Almighty bless you and make you fruitful and multiply you, that you may become a company of peoples. May he give the blessing of Abraham to you and to your offspring with you, that you may take possession of the land of your sojournings that God gave to Abraham!"

Pledge & Commitment
Genesis 28:20-22 (NIV)
Then Jacob made a vow, saying, "If God will be with me and will watch over me on this journey I am taking and will give me food to eat and clothes to wear so that I return safely to my father's house, then the Lord will be my God and this stone that I have set up as a pillar will be God's house, and of all that you give me I will give you a tenth."

Making Requests Known
Genesis 32:9-12 (NASB)
Jacob said, "O God of my father Abraham and God of my father Isaac, O Lord, who said to me, 'Return to your country and to your relatives, and I will prosper you,' I am unworthy of all the lovingkindness and of all the faithfulness which You have shown to Your servant; for with my staff only I crossed this Jordan, and now I have become two companies. "Deliver me, I pray, from the hand of my brother, from the hand of Esau; for I fear him, that he will come and attack me and the mothers with the children. "For You said, 'I will surely prosper you and make your descendants as the sand of the sea, which is too great to be numbered.' "

Seeking God's Will
Genesis 32:24-30 (NJB)
And Jacob was left alone.
Then someone wrestled with him until daybreak who, seeing that he could not master him, struck him on the hip socket, and Jacob's hip was dislocated as he wrestled with him. He said, 'Let me go, for day is breaking.' Jacob replied, 'I will not let you go unless you bless me.' The other said, 'What is your name?' 'Jacob,' he replied. He said, 'No longer are you to be called Jacob, but Israel since you have shown your strength against God and men and have prevailed.' Then Jacob asked, 'Please tell me your name?' He replied, 'Why do you ask my name?' With that, he blessed him there.

Jacob named the place Peniel, 'Because I have seen God face to face,' he said, 'and have survived.'

Praying for Others
Genesis 43:14 (NLT)
May God Almighty give you mercy as you go before the man, that he might release Simeon and return Benjamin. And if I must bear the anguish of their deaths, then so be it."

Praising God
Genesis 47:31 (GWT)
"Swear to me," he said. So Joseph swore to him. Then Israel bowed down in prayer with his face at the head of his bed.

Praying for Others
Genesis 48:15-16 (TEV)
Then he blessed Joseph:
"May God, whom my fathers Abraham and Isaac served, bless these boys!
May God, who has led me to this very day, bless them!
May the angel, who has rescued me from all harm, bless them!
May my name and the name of my fathers Abraham and Isaac live on through these boys!
May they have many children, many descendants!"

Making Requests Known
Genesis 49:18 (CEV)
Our Lord, I am waiting for you to save us.

Making Requests Known
Exodus 2:23 (ESV)
During those many days the king of Egypt died, and the people of Israel groaned because of their slavery and cried out for help. Their cry for rescue from slavery came up to God.

Responding to God
Exodus 3:4 (NIV)
When the Lord saw that he had gone over to look, God called to him from within the bush, "Moses! Moses!"
And Moses said, "Here I am."

Seeking God's Will
Exodus 3:11 (NASB)
But Moses said to God, "Who am I, that I should go to Pharaoh, and that I should bring the sons of Israel out of Egypt?"

Seeking God's Will
Exodus 3:13 (NRSV)
But Moses said to God, "If I come to the Israelites and say to them, 'The God of your ancestors has sent me to you,' and they ask me, 'What is his name?' what shall I say to them?"

Seeking God's Will
Exodus 4:1-2 (NAB)
"But," objected Moses, "suppose they will not believe me, nor listen to my plea? For they may say, 'The LORD did not appear to you.'" The LORD therefore asked him, What is that in your hand? "A staff," he answered.

Responding to God
Exodus 4:10 (NJB)
Moses said to Yahweh, 'Please, my Lord, I have never been eloquent, even since you have spoken to your servant, for I am slow and hesitant of speech.'

Making Requests Known
Exodus 4:13 (NLT)
But Moses again pleaded, "Lord, please! Send someone else."

Praising God
Exodus 4:31 (GWT)
And the people believed them. When they heard that the Lord was concerned about the people of Israel and that he had seen their misery, they knelt, bowing with their faces touching the ground.

Seeking God's Will
Exodus 5:22-23 (TEV)
Then Moses turned to the Lord again and said, "Lord, why do you mistreat your people? Why did you send me here? Ever since I went to the king to speak for you, he has treated them cruelly. And you have done nothing to help them!"

Seeking God's Will
Exodus 6:12 (CEV)
But Moses replied, "I'm not a powerful speaker. If the Israelites won't listen to me, why should the king of Egypt?"

Seeking God's Will
Exodus 6:30 (ESV)
But Moses said to the Lord, "Behold, I am of uncircumcised lips. How will Pharaoh listen to me?"

Praying for Others
Exodus 8:12 (NASB)
Then Moses and Aaron went out from Pharaoh, and Moses cried to the Lord concerning the frogs which He had inflicted upon Pharaoh.

Praying for Others
Exodus 8:29-30 (NRSV)
Then Moses said, "As soon as I leave you, I will pray to the Lord that the swarms of flies may depart tomorrow from Pharaoh, from his officials, and from his people; only do not let Pharaoh again deal falsely by not letting the people go to sacrifice to the Lord."

So Moses went out from Pharaoh and prayed to the Lord.

Praying for Others
Exodus 9:29 (NAB)
Moses replied, "As soon as I leave the city I will extend my hands to the LORD; the thunder will cease, and there will be no more hail. Thus you shall learn that the earth is the LORD'S.

Praying for Others
Exodus 9:33 (NJB)
Moses left Pharaoh and went out of the city. He stretched out his hands to Yahweh and the thunder and hail ceased and the rain stopped pouring down on the earth.

Praying for Others
Exodus 10:18 (NLT)
So Moses left Pharaoh and pleaded with the Lord.

Praising God
Exodus 12:27 (GWT)

You must answer, 'It's the Passover sacrifice in the Lord's honor. The Lord passed over the houses of the Israelites in Egypt and spared our homes when he killed the Egyptians.' "

Then the people knelt, bowing with their faces touching the ground.

Making Requests Known
Exodus 14:10-12 (TEV)

When the Israelites saw the king and his army marching against them, they were terrified and cried out to the Lord for help. They said to Moses, "Weren't there any graves in Egypt? Did you have to bring us out here in the desert to die? Look what you have done by bringing us out of Egypt! Didn't we tell you before we left that this would happen? We told you to leave us alone and let us go on being slaves of the Egyptians. It would be better to be slaves there than to die here in the desert."

Praising God
Exodus 15:1-18 (CEV)

Moses and the Israelites sang this song in praise of the Lord:
I sing praises to the Lord for his great victory!
He has thrown the horses
and their riders into the sea.
The Lord is my strength,
the reason for my song, because he has saved me.
I praise and honor the Lord—
he is my God and the God of my ancestors.
The Lord is his name, and he is a warrior!
He threw the chariots and army
of Egypt's king into the Red Sea,
and he drowned the best of the king's officers.
They sank to the bottom just like stones.

With the tremendous force
of your right arm, our Lord, you crushed your enemies.
What a great victory was yours,
as you defeated everyone who opposed you.
Your fiery anger wiped them out, as though they were straw.
You were so furious
that the sea piled up like a wall,
and the ocean depths curdled like cheese.

Your enemies boasted that they would
pursue and capture us,
divide up our possessions,
treat us as they wished,
then take out their swords and kill us right there.
But when you got furious,
they sank like lead, swallowed by ocean waves.
 Our Lord, no other gods
compare with you— Majestic and holy! Fearsome and glorious! Miracle worker!
When you signaled with your right hand,
your enemies were swallowed deep into the earth.

The people you rescued
were led by your powerful love to your holy place.
Nations learned of this and trembled—
Philistines shook with horror.
The leaders of Edom and of Moab were terrified.
Everyone in Canaan fainted, struck down by fear.
Our Lord, your powerful arm kept them still as a rock
until the people you rescued
for your very own had marched by.

You will let your people settle on your chosen mountain,
where you built your home and your temple.
Our Lord, you will rule forever!

Making Requests Known
Exodus 15:25 (ESV)
And he cried to the Lord, and the Lord showed him a log, and he threw it into the water, and the water became sweet.

There the Lord made for them a statute and a rule, and there he tested them.

Making Requests Known
Exodus 17:4 (NIV)
Then Moses cried out to the Lord, "What am I to do with these people? They are almost ready to stone me."

Verses about Prayer
Exodus 17:10-12 (NASB)

Joshua did as Moses told him, and fought against Amalek; and Moses, Aaron, and Hur went up to the top of the hill. So it came about when Moses held his hand up, that Israel prevailed, and when he let his hand down, Amalek prevailed. But Moses' hands were heavy. Then they took a stone and put it under him, and he sat on it; and Aaron and Hur supported his hands, one on one side and one on the other. Thus his hands were steady until the sun set.

Praising God
Exodus 18:10-11 (NRSV)

Jethro said, "Blessed be the Lord, who has delivered you from the Egyptians and from Pharaoh. Now I know that the Lord is greater than all gods, because he delivered the people from the Egyptians, when they dealt arrogantly with them."

Responding to God
Exodus 19:23 (NAB)

Moses said to the LORD, "The people cannot go up to Mount Sinai, for you yourself warned us to set limits around the mountain to make it sacred."

Making Requests Known
Exodus 22:22-24 (NJB)

You will not ill-treat widows or orphans; if you ill-treat them in any way and they make an appeal to me for help, I shall certainly hear their appeal, my anger will be roused and I shall put you to the sword; then your own wives will be widows and your own children orphans.

Praying for Others
Exodus 32:10-13 (NLT)

Now leave me alone so my anger can blaze against them and destroy them all. Then I will make you, Moses, into a great nation instead of them."

But Moses pleaded with the Lord his God not to do it. "O Lord!" he exclaimed. "Why are you so angry with your own people whom you brought from the land of Egypt with such great power and mighty acts? The Egyptians will say, 'God tricked them into coming to the mountains so he could kill them and wipe them from the face of the earth.' Turn away from your fierce anger. Change your mind about this terrible disaster you are planning against your people! Remember your covenant with your servants—Abraham, Isaac, and Jacob. You swore by your own self, 'I will make your descendants as numerous as the stars of heaven. Yes, I will give them all of this land that I have promised to your descendants, and they will possess it forever.'

Praying for Others
Exodus 32:31-32 (GWT)

So Moses went back to the Lord and said, "These people have committed such a serious sin! They made gods out of gold for themselves. But will you forgive their sin? If not, please wipe me out of the book you have written."

Making Requests Known
Exodus 33:9-13 (TEV)

After Moses had gone in, the pillar of cloud would come down and stay at the door of the Tent, and the Lord would speak to Moses from the cloud. As soon as the people saw the pillar of cloud at the door of the Tent, they would bow down. The Lord would speak with Moses face-to-face, just as someone speaks with a friend. Then Moses would return to the camp. But the young man who was his helper, Joshua son of Nun, stayed in the Tent.

Moses said to the Lord, "It is true that you have told me to lead these people to that land, but you did not tell me whom you would send with me. You have said that you know me well and are pleased with me. Now if you are, tell me your plans, so that I may serve you and continue to please you. Remember also that you have chosen this nation to be your own."

Making Requests Known
Exodus 33:15-16 (CEV)

Then Moses replied, "If you aren't going with us, please don't make us leave this place. But if you do go with us, everyone will know that you are pleased with your people and with me. That way, we will be different from the rest of the people on earth."

Making Requests Known
Exodus 33:18 (ESV)

Moses said, "Please show me your glory."

Making Requests Known
Exodus 34:8-9 (NIV)
Moses bowed to the ground at once and worshiped. "O Lord, if I have found favor in your eyes," he said, "then let the Lord go with us. Although this is a stiff-necked people, forgive our wickedness and our sin, and take us as your inheritance."

Blessings & Benedictions
Numbers 6:24-27 (NASB)
> The Lord bless you, and keep you;
>
> The Lord make His face shine on you,
> And be gracious to you;
>
> The Lord lift up His countenance on you,
> And give you peace.'

"So they shall invoke My name on the sons of Israel, and I then will bless them."

Verses about Prayer
Numbers 7:89 (NRSV)
When Moses went into the tent of meeting to speak with the Lord, he would hear the voice speaking to him from above the mercy seat that was on the ark of the covenant from between the two cherubim; thus it spoke to him.

Making Requests Known
Numbers 10:35-36 (NAB)
Whenever the ark set out, Moses would say,
"Arise, O LORD, that your enemies may be scattered,
  and those who hate you may flee before you."
And when it came to rest, he would say,
"Return, O LORD, you who ride upon the clouds,
  to the troops of Israel."

Praying for Others
Numbers 11:2 (NJB)
The people appealed to Moses who interceded with Yahweh and the fire died down.

Making Requests Known
Numbers 11:10-15 (NLT)

Moses heard all the families standing in front of their tents weeping, and the Lord became extremely angry. Moses was also very aggravated. And Moses said to the Lord, "Why are you treating me, your servant, so miserably? What did I do to deserve the burden of a people like this? Are they my children? Am I their father? Is that why you have told me to carry them in my arms—like a nurse carries a baby—to the land you swore to give their ancestors? Where am I supposed to get meat for all these people? They keep complaining and saying, 'Give us meat!' I can't carry all these people by myself! The load is far too heavy! I'd rather you killed me than treat me like this. Please spare me this misery!"

Seeking God's Will
Numbers 11:21-22 (GWT)

But Moses said, "Here I am with 600,000 foot soldiers around me. Yet, you say, 'I will give them meat to eat for a whole month!' Would they have enough if all the flocks and herds were butchered for them? Would they have enough if all the fish in the sea were caught for them?"

Praying for Others
Numbers 12:13 (TEV)

So Moses cried out to the Lord, "O God, heal her!"

Praying for Others
Numbers 14:13-19 (CEV)

Moses replied:

With your mighty power you rescued your people from Egypt, so please don't destroy us here in the desert. If you do, the Egyptians will hear about it and tell the people of Canaan. Those Canaanites already know that we are your people, and that we see you face to face. And they have heard how you lead us with a thick cloud during the day and flaming fire at night. But if you kill us, they will claim it was because you weren't powerful enough to lead us into Canaan as you promised.

Show us your great power, Lord. You promised that you love to show mercy and kindness. And you said that you are very patient, but that you will punish everyone guilty of doing wrong—not only them but their children and grandchildren as well.

You are merciful, and you treat people better than they deserve. So please forgive these people, just as you have forgiven them ever since they left Egypt.

Making Requests Known
Numbers 16:15 (ESV)
And Moses was very angry and said to the Lord, "Do not respect their offering. I have not taken one donkey from them, and I have not harmed one of them."

Praying for Others
Numbers 16:22 (NIV)
But Moses and Aaron fell facedown and cried out, "O God, God of the spirits of all mankind, will you be angry with the entire assembly when only one man sins?"

Praying for Others
Numbers 21:7 (NASB)
So the people came to Moses and said, "We have sinned, because we have spoken against the Lord and you; intercede with the Lord, that He may remove the serpents from us." And Moses interceded for the people.

Making Requests Known
Numbers 22:10-11 (NRSV)
Balaam said to God, "King Balak son of Zippor of Moab, has sent me this message: 'A people has come out of Egypt and has spread over the face of the earth; now come, curse them for me; perhaps I shall be able to fight against them and drive them out.' "

Making Requests Known
Numbers 23:3-4 (NAB)
Balaam then said to him, "Stand here by your holocaust while I go over there. Perhaps the LORD will meet me, and then I will tell you whatever he lets me see." He went out on the barren height, and God met him.

Praying for Others
Numbers 27:5 (NJB)
Moses took their case before Yahweh,

Praying for Others
Numbers 27:15-17 (NLT)
Then Moses said to the Lord, "O Lord, the God of the spirits of all living things, please appoint a new leader for the community. Give them someone who will lead them into battle, so the people of the Lord will not be like sheep without a shepherd."

Blessings & Benedictions
Deut. 1:11 (GWT)

May the Lord God of your ancestors make you a thousand times more numerous, and may he bless you as he has promised.

Praising God
Deut. 3:23-25 (TEV)

"At that time I earnestly prayed, 'Sovereign Lord, I know that you have shown me only the beginning of the great and wonderful things you are going to do. There is no god in heaven or on earth who can do the mighty things that you have done! Let me cross the Jordan River, Lord, and see the fertile land on the other side, the beautiful hill country and the Lebanon Mountains.'

Verses about Prayer
Deut. 4:5-8 (CEV)

No other nation has laws that are as fair as the ones the Lord my God told me to give you. If you faithfully obey them when you enter the land, you will show other nations how wise you are. In fact, everyone that hears about your laws will say, " That great nation certainly is wise!" And what makes us greater than other nations? We have a God who is close to us and answers our prayers.

Praying for Others
Deut. 9:18-20 (CEV)

I bowed down at the place of worship and prayed to the Lord, without eating or drinking for forty days and nights. You had committed a terrible sin by making that idol, and the Lord hated what you had done. He was angry enough to destroy all of you and Aaron as well. So I prayed for you and Aaron as I had done before, and this time the Lord answered my prayers.

Praying for Others
Deut. 9:20 (ESV)

And the Lord was so angry with Aaron that he was ready to destroy him. And I prayed for Aaron also at the same time.

Praying for Others
Deut. 9:25-29 (NIV)

I lay prostrate before the Lord those forty days and forty nights because the Lord had said he would destroy you. I prayed to the Lord and said,

"O Sovereign Lord, do not destroy your people, your own inheritance that you redeemed by your great power and brought out of Egypt with a mighty hand. Remember your servants Abraham, Isaac and Jacob. Overlook the stubbornness of this people, their wickedness and their sin. Otherwise, the country from which you brought us will say, 'Because the Lord was not able to take them into the land he had promised them, and because he hated them, he brought them out to put them to death in the desert.' But they are your people, your inheritance that you brought out by your great power and your outstretched arm."

Praying for Others
Deut. 21:6-9 (NASB)
"All the elders of that city which is nearest to the slain man shall wash their hands over the heifer whose neck was broken in the valley; and they shall answer and say, 'Our hands did not shed this blood, nor did our eyes see it. 'Forgive Your people Israel whom You have redeemed, O Lord, and do not place the guilt of innocent blood in the midst of Your people Israel.' And the bloodguiltiness shall be forgiven them. "So you shall remove the guilt of innocent blood from your midst, when you do what is right in the eyes of the Lord.

Making Requests Known
Deut. 26:5-15 (NRSV)
You shall make this response before the Lord your God: "A wandering Aramean was my ancestor; he went down into Egypt and lived there as an alien, few in number, and there he became a great nation, mighty and populous. When the Egyptians treated us harshly and afflicted us, by imposing hard labor on us, we cried to the Lord, the God of our ancestors; the Lord heard our voice and saw our affliction, our toil, and our oppression. The Lord brought us out of Egypt with a mighty hand and an outstretched arm, with a terrifying display of power, and with signs and wonders; and he brought us into this place and gave us this land, a land flowing with milk and honey. So now I bring the first of the fruit of the ground that you, O Lord, have given me." You shall set it down before the Lord your God and bow down before the Lord your God. Then you, together with the Levites and the aliens who reside among you, shall celebrate with all the bounty that the Lord your God has given to you and to your house.

When you have finished paying all the tithe of your produce in the third year (which is the year of the tithe), giving it to the Levites, the aliens, the orphans, and the widows, so that they may eat their fill within your towns, then you shall say before the Lord your God: "I have removed the sacred portion from the house, and I have given it to the Levites, the resident aliens, the orphans, and the widows, in accordance with your entire commandment that you commanded me; I have neither transgressed nor forgotten any of your commandments: I have not eaten of it while in mourning; I have not removed any of it while I was unclean; and I have not offered any of it to the dead. I have obeyed the Lord my God, doing just as you commanded me. Look down from your holy habitation, from heaven, and bless your people Israel and the ground that you have given us, as you swore to our ancestors--a land flowing with milk and honey."

Praising God
Deut. 32:1-44 (NAB)

Give ear, O heavens, while I speak;
    let the earth hearken to the words of my mouth!
May my instruction soak in like the rain,
    and my discourse permeate like the dew,
Like a downpour upon the grass,
    like a shower upon the crops.
For I will sing the LORD'S renown.
    Oh, proclaim the greatness of our God!
The Rock--how faultless are his deeds,
    how right all his ways!
A faithful God, without deceit,
    how just and upright he is!
Yet basely has he been treated by his degenerate children,
    a perverse and crooked race!
Is the LORD to be thus repaid by you,
    O stupid and foolish people?
Is he not your father who created you?
    Has he not made you and established you?
Think back on the days of old,
    reflect on the years of age upon age.
Ask your father and he will inform you,
    ask your elders and they will tell you:
When the Most High assigned the nations their heritage,
    when he parceled out the descendants of Adam,
He set up the boundaries of the peoples
    after the number of the sons of God;
While the LORD'S own portion was Jacob,
    His hereditary share was Israel.
He found them in a wilderness,

a wasteland of howling desert.
He shielded them and cared for them,
   guarding them as the apple of his eye.
As an eagle incites its nestlings forth
   by hovering over its brood,
So he spread his wings to receive them
   and bore them up on his pinions.
The LORD alone was their leader,
   no strange god was with him.
He had them ride triumphant over the summits of the land
   and live off the products of its fields,
Giving them honey to suck from its rocks
   and olive oil from its hard, stony ground;
Butter from its cows and milk from its sheep,
   with the fat of its lambs and rams;
Its Bashan bulls and its goats,
   with the cream of its finest wheat;
   and the foaming blood of its grapes you drank.
(So Jacob ate his fill,)
   the darling grew fat and frisky;
   you became fat and gross and gorged.
They spurned the God who made them
   and scorned their saving Rock.
They provoked him with strange gods
   and angered him with abominable idols.
They offered sacrifice to demons, to "no-gods,"
   to gods whom they had not known before,
To newcomers just arrived,
   of whom their fathers had never stood in awe.
You were unmindful of the Rock that begot you,
   You forgot the God who gave you birth.
When the LORD saw this, he was filled with loathing
   and anger toward his sons and daughters.
'I will hide my face from them," he said,
   "and see what will then become of them.
What a fickle race they are,
   sons with no loyalty in them!
"Since they have provoked me with their 'no-god'
   and angered me with their vain idols,
I will provoke them with a 'no-people';
   with a foolish nation I will anger them.
"For by my wrath a fire is enkindled
   that shall rage to the depths of the nether world,

Consuming the earth with its yield,
   and licking with flames the roots of the mountains.
I will spend on them woe upon woe
   and exhaust all my arrows against them:
"Emaciating hunger and consuming fever
   and bitter pestilence,
And the teeth of wild beasts I will send among them,
   with the venom of reptiles gliding in the dust.
"Snatched away by the sword in the street
   and by sheer terror at home
Shall be the youth and the maiden alike,
   the nursing babe as well as the hoary old man.
"I would have said, 'I will make an end of them
   and blot out their name from men's memories,'
Had I not feared the insolence of their enemies,
   feared that these foes would mistakenly boast,
'Our own hand won the victory;
   the LORD had nothing to do with it.'
For they are a people devoid of reason,
   having no understanding.
If they had insight they would realize what happened,
   they would understand their future and say,
"How could one man rout a thousand,
   or two men put ten thousand to flight,
Unless it was because their Rock sold them
   and the LORD delivered them up?"
Indeed, their "rock" is not like our Rock,
   and our foes are under condemnation.
They are a branch of Sodom's vinestock,
   from the vineyards of Gomorrah.
Poisonous are their grapes and bitter their clusters.
Their wine is the venom of dragons
   and the cruel poison of cobras.
"Is not this preserved in my treasury,
   sealed up in my storehouse,
Against the day of vengeance and requital,
   against the time they lose their footing?"
Close at hand is the day of their disaster
   and their doom is rushing upon them!
Surely, the LORD shall do justice for his people;
   on his servants he shall have pity.
When he sees their strength failing,
   and their protected and unprotected alike disappearing,

He will say, "Where are their gods
    whom they relied on as their 'rock'?
Let those who ate the fat of your sacrifices
    and drank the wine of your libations
Rise up now and help you!
    Let them be your protection!
"Learn then that I, I alone, am God,
    and there is no god besides me.
It is I who bring both death and life,
    I who inflict wounds and heal them,
    and from my hand there is no rescue.
"To the heavens I raise my hand and swear:
    As surely as I live forever,
I will sharpen my flashing sword,
    and my hand shall lay hold of my quiver.
"With vengeance I will repay my foes
    and requite those who hate me.
I will make my arrows drunk with blood,
    and my sword shall gorge itself with flesh--
With the blood of the slain and the captured,
    Flesh from the heads of the enemy leaders."
Exult with him, you heavens,
    glorify him, all you angels of God;
For he avenges the blood of his servants
    and purges his people's land.

So Moses, together with Joshua, son of Nun, went and recited all the words of this song for the people to hear.

Praying for Others
Deut. 33:7 (NJB)

Of Judah he said this:
    Listen, Yahweh, to the voice of Judah,
        and bring him back to his people.
    That his hands may defend his rights,
        come to his help against his foes!

Praying for Others
Deut. 33:11-16 (NLT)

"Bless the Levites, O Lord,
    and accept all their work.
Crush the loins of their enemies;

strike down their foes so they never rise again."
Moses said this about the tribe of Benjamin:
"The people of Benjamin are loved by the Lord
and live in safety beside him.
He surrounds them continuously
and preserves them from every harm."

Moses said this about the tribes of Joseph:
"May their land be blessed by the Lord
with the choice gift of rain from the heavens,
and water from beneath the earth;
with the riches that grow in the sun,
and the bounty produced each month;
with the finest crops of the ancient mountains,
and the abundance from the everlasting hills;
with the best gifts of the earth and its fullness,
and the favor of the one who appeared in the burning bush.
May these blessings rest on Joseph's head,
crowning the brow of the prince among his brothers.

Seeking God's Will
Joshua 5:13-15 (GWT)

When Joshua was near Jericho, he looked up and saw a man standing in front of him with a sword in his hand. Joshua went up to him and asked, "Are you one of us or one of our enemies?" He answered, "Neither one! I am here as the commander of the Lord's army." Immediately, Joshua bowed with his face touching the ground and worshiped. He asked, "Sir, what do you want to tell me?" The commander of the Lord's army said to Joshua, "Take off your sandals because this place where you are standing is holy." So Joshua did as he was told.

Seeking God's Will
Joshua 7:6-9 (TEV)

Joshua and the leaders of Israel tore their clothes in grief, threw themselves to the ground before the Lord's Covenant Box, and lay there till evening, with dust on their heads to show their sorrow. And Joshua said, "Sovereign Lord! Why did you bring us across the Jordan at all? To turn us over to the Amorites? To destroy us? Why didn't we just stay on the other side of the Jordan? What can I say, O Lord, now that Israel has retreated from the enemy? The Canaanites and everyone else in the country will hear about it. They will surround us and kill every one of us! And then what will you do to protect your honor?"

Making Requests Known
Joshua 10:12-13 (CEV)

The Lord was helping the Israelites defeat the Amorites that day. So about noon, Joshua prayed to the Lord loud enough for the Israelites to hear:
"Our Lord, make the sun stop in the sky over Gibeon,
and the moon stand still over Aijalon Valley."
So the sun and the moon stopped and stood still
until Israel defeated its enemies.
This poem can be found in The Book of Jashar. The sun stood still and didn't go down for about a whole day.

Seeking God's Will
Judges 1:1 (ESV)

After the death of Joshua, the people of Israel inquired of the Lord, "Who shall go up first for us against the Canaanites, to fight against them?"

Making Requests Known
Judges 3:9 (NIV)

But when they cried out to the Lord, he raised up for them a deliverer, Othniel son of Kenaz, Caleb's younger brother, who saved them.

Making Requests Known
Judges 3:15 (NASB)

But when the sons of Israel cried to the Lord, the Lord raised up a deliverer for them, Ehud the son of Gera, the Benjamite, a left-handed man. And the sons of Israel sent tribute by him to Eglon the king of Moab.

Making Requests Known
Judges 4:3 (NRSV)

Then the Israelites cried out to the Lord for help; for he had nine hundred chariots of iron, and had oppressed the Israelites cruelly twenty years.

Praising God
Judges 5:1-31 (NAB)

On that day Deborah (and Barak, son of Abinoam,) sang this song:
Of chiefs who took the lead in Israel,
    of noble deeds by the people who bless the LORD,
Hear, O kings! Give ear, O princes!

I to the LORD will sing my song,
   my hymn to the LORD, the God of Israel.

O LORD, when you went out from Seir,
   when you marched from the land of Edom,
The earth quaked and the heavens were shaken,
   while the clouds sent down showers.
Mountains trembled
   in the presence of the LORD, the One of Sinai,
   in the presence of the LORD, the God of Israel.
In the days of Shamgar, son of Anath,
   in the days of slavery caravans ceased:
Those who traveled the roads
   went by roundabout paths.
Gone was freedom beyond the walls,
   gone indeed from Israel.
When I, Deborah, rose,
   when I rose, a mother in Israel,
New gods were their choice;
   then the war was at their gates.
Not a shield could be seen, nor a lance,
   among forty thousand in Israel!

My heart is with the leaders of Israel,
   nobles of the people who bless the LORD;
They who ride on white asses,
   seated on saddlecloths as they go their way;
Sing of them to the strains of the harpers at the wells,
   where men recount the just deeds of the LORD,
   his just deeds that brought freedom to Israel.

Awake, awake, Deborah!
   awake, awake, strike up a song.
Strength! arise, Barak,
   make despoilers your spoil, son of Abinoam.
Then down came the fugitives with the mighty,
   the people of the LORD came down for me as warriors.
From Ephraim, princes were in the valley;
   behind you was Benjamin, among your troops.
From Machir came down commanders,
   from Zebulun wielders of the marshal's staff.

With Deborah were the princes of Issachar;
    Barak, too, was in the valley, his course unchecked.

Among the clans of Reuben
    great were the searchings of heart.
Why do you stay beside your hearths
    listening to the lowing of the herds?
Among the clans of Reuben
    great were the searchings of heart!

Gilead, beyond the Jordan, rests;
    why does Dan spend his time in ships?
Asher, who dwells along the shore,
    is resting in his coves.
Zebulun is the people defying death;
    Naphtali, too, on the open heights!

The kings came and fought;
    then they fought, those kings of Canaan,
At Taanach by the waters of Megiddo;
    no silver booty did they take.
From the heavens the stars, too, fought;
    from their courses they fought against Sisera.

The Wadi Kishon swept them away;
    a wadi. . . , the Kishon.
Then the hoofs of the horses pounded,
    with the dashing, dashing of his steeds.

"Curse Meroz," says the LORD,
    "hurl a curse at its inhabitants!
For they came not to my help,
    as warriors to the help of the LORD."

Blessed among women be Jael,
    blessed among tent-dwelling women.
He asked for water, she gave him milk;
    in a princely bowl she offered curds.
With her left hand she reached for the peg,
    with her right, for the workman's mallet.

She hammered Sisera, crushed his head;
  she smashed, stove in his temple.
At her feet he sank down, fell, lay still;
  down at her feet he sank and fell;
where he sank down, there he fell, slain.

From the window peered down and wailed
  the mother of Sisera, from the lattice:
"Why is his chariot so long in coming?
  why are the hoofbeats of his chariots delayed?"
The wisest of her princesses answers her,
  and she, too, keeps answering herself:
"They must be dividing the spoil they took:
  there must be a damsel or two for each man,
Spoils of dyed cloth as Sisera's spoil,
  an ornate shawl or two for me in the spoil."
May all your enemies perish thus, O LORD!
  but your friends be as the sun rising in its might!
And the land was at rest for forty years.

Making Requests Known
Judges 6:6-7 (NJB)
Thus, Midian brought Israel to great distress, and the Israelites cried to Yahweh.

When the Israelites cried to Yahweh because of Midian.

Seeking God's Will
Judges 6:12-13 (NLT)
The angel of the Lord appeared to him and said, "Mighty hero, the Lord is with you!"

"Sir," Gideon replied, "if the Lord is with us, why has all this happened to us? And where are all the miracles our ancestors told us about? Didn't they say, 'The Lord brought us up out of Egypt'? But now the Lord has abandoned us and handed us over to the Midianites."

Seeking God's Will
Judges 6:15 (GWT)
Gideon said to him, "Excuse me, sir! How can I rescue Israel? Look at my whole family. It's the weakest one in Manasseh. And me? I'm the least important member of my family."

Making Requests Known
Judges 6:17-18 (TEV)
Gideon replied, "If you are pleased with me, give me some proof that you are really the Lord. Please do not leave until I bring you an offering of food."

He said, "I will stay until you come back."

Making Requests Known
Judges 6:36-37 (CEV)
Gideon prayed to God, "I know that you promised to help me rescue Israel, but I need proof. Tonight I'll put some wool on the stone floor of that threshing-place over there. If you really will help me rescue Israel, then tomorrow morning let there be dew on the wool, but let the stone floor be dry."

Making Requests Known
Judges 6:39 (ESV)
Then Gideon said to God, "Let not your anger burn against me; let me speak just once more. Please let me test just once more with the fleece. Please let it be dry on the fleece only, and on all the ground let there be dew."

Praising God
Judges 7:15 (NASB)
When Gideon heard the account of the dream and its interpretation, he bowed in worship. He returned to the camp of Israel and said, "Arise, for the Lord has given the camp of Midian into your hands."

Confessing Sin
Judges 10:10 (NRSV)
So the Israelites cried to the Lord, saying, "We have sinned against you, because we have abandoned our God and have worshiped the Baals."

Confessing Sin
Judges 10:15 (NAB)
But the Israelites said to the LORD, "We have sinned. Do to us whatever you please. Only save us this day."

Pledge & Commitment
Judges 11:30-31 (NJB)
And Jephthah made a vow to Yahweh, 'If you deliver the Ammonites

into my grasp, the first thing to come out of the doors of my house to meet me when I return in triumph from fighting the Ammonites shall belong to Yahweh, and I shall sacrifice it as a burnt offering.'

Making Requests Known
Judges 13:8 (NLT)
Then Manoah prayed to the Lord. He said, "Lord, please let the man of God come back to us again and give us more instructions about this son who is to be born."

Making Requests Known
Judges 15:18 (GWT)
Samson was very thirsty. So he called out to the Lord and said, "You have given me this great victory. But now I'll die from thirst and fall into the power of godless men."

Making Requests Known
Judges 16:28-30 (TEV)
Then Samson prayed, "Sovereign Lord, please remember me; please, God, give me my strength just this one time more, so that with this one blow I can get even with the Philistines for putting out my two eyes." So Samson took hold of the two middle columns holding up the building. Putting one hand on each column, he pushed against them and shouted, "Let me die with the Philistines!" He pushed with all his might, and the building fell down on the five kings and everyone else. Samson killed more people at his death than he had killed during his life.

Blessings & Benedictions
Judges 17:2 (CEV)
One day he told his mother, "Do you remember those eleven hundred pieces of silver that were stolen from you? I was there when you put a curse on whoever stole them. Well, I'm the one who did it."

His mother answered, "I pray that the Lord will bless you, my son."

Seeking God's Will
Judges 20:18 (ESV)
The people of Israel arose and went up to Bethel and inquired of God, "Who shall go up first for us to fight against the people of Benjamin?" And the Lord said, "Judah shall go up first."

Praising God
Judges 20:23-26 (NIV)

The Israelites went up and wept before the Lord until evening, and they inquired of the Lord. They said, "Shall we go up again to battle against the Benjamites, our brothers?"

The Lord answered, "Go up against them."

Then the Israelites drew near to Benjamin the second day. This time, when the Benjamites came out from Gibeah to oppose them, they cut down another eighteen thousand Israelites, all of them armed with swords.

Then the Israelites, all the people, went up to Bethel, and there they sat weeping before the Lord. They fasted that day until evening and presented burnt offerings and fellowship offerings to the Lord.

Seeking God's Will
Judges 21:2-3 (NASB)

So the people came to Bethel and sat there before God until evening, and lifted up their voices and wept bitterly. They said, "Why, O Lord, God of Israel, has this come about in Israel, so that one tribe should be missing today in Israel?"

Blessings & Benedictions
Ruth 1:8-9 (NRSV)

But Naomi said to her two daughters-in-law, "Go back each of you to your mother's house. May the Lord deal kindly with you, as you have dealt with the dead and with me. The Lord grant that you may find security, each of you in the house of your husband." Then she kissed them, and they wept aloud.

Blessings & Benedictions
Ruth 2:4 (NAB)

Boaz himself came from Bethlehem and said to the harvesters, "The LORD be with you!" and they replied, "The LORD bless you!"

Blessings & Benedictions
Ruth 2:12 (NJB)

May Yahweh repay you for what you have done, and may you be richly rewarded by Yahweh, the God of Israel, under whose wings you have come for refuge!'

Blessings & Benedictions
Ruth 3:10 (NLT)

"The Lord bless you, my daughter!" Boaz exclaimed. "You are showing more family loyalty now than ever by not running after a younger man, whether rich or poor.

Blessings & Benedictions
Ruth 4:11 (GWT)

All the people who were at the gate, including the leaders, said, "We are witnesses. May the Lord make this wife, who is coming into your home, like Rachel and Leah, both of whom built our family of Israel. So show your strength of character in Ephrathah and make a name for yourself in Bethlehem.

Praising God
Ruth 4:14-15 (TEV)

The women said to Naomi, "Praise the Lord! He has given you a grandson today to take care of you. May the boy become famous in Israel! Your daughter-in-law loves you, and has done more for you than seven sons. And now she has given you a grandson, who will bring new life to you and give you security in your old age."

Pledge & Commitment
1 Samuel 1:10-13 (CEV)

Hannah was brokenhearted and was crying as she prayed, "Lord All-Powerful, I am your servant, but I am so miserable! Please let me have a son. I will give him to you for as long as he lives, and his hair will never be cut."

Hannah prayed silently to the Lord for a long time. But her lips were moving, and Eli thought she was drunk.

Praying for Others
1 Samuel 1:16-17 (ESV)

Do not regard your servant as a worthless woman, for all along I have been speaking out of my great anxiety and vexation." Then Eli answered, "Go in peace, and the God of Israel grant your petition that you have made to him."

Praising God
1 Samuel 1:19 (NIV)

Early the next morning they arose and worshiped before the Lord and then went back to their home at Ramah. Elkanah lay with Hannah his wife, and the Lord remembered her.

Praising God
1 Samuel 1:28-2:10 (NASB)

"So I have also dedicated him to the Lord; as long as he lives he is dedicated to the Lord." And he worshiped the Lord there.

Then Hannah prayed and said,
"My heart exults in the Lord;
My horn is exalted in the Lord,
My mouth speaks boldly against my enemies,
Because I rejoice in Your salvation.
"There is no one holy like the Lord,
Indeed, there is no one besides You,
Nor is there any rock like our God.
"Boast no more so very proudly,
Do not let arrogance come out of your mouth;
For the Lord is a God of knowledge,
And with Him actions are weighed.
"The bows of the mighty are shattered,
But the feeble gird on strength.
"Those who were full hire themselves out for bread,
But those who were hungry cease to hunger.
Even the barren gives birth to seven,
But she who has many children languishes.
"The Lord kills and makes alive;
He brings down to Sheol and raises up.
"The Lord makes poor and rich;
He brings low, He also exalts.
"He raises the poor from the dust,
He lifts the needy from the ash heap
To make them sit with nobles,
And inherit a seat of honor;
For the pillars of the earth are the Lord's,
And He set the world on them.
"He keeps the feet of His godly ones,
But the wicked ones are silenced in darkness;
For not by might shall a man prevail.
"Those who contend with the Lord will be shattered;
Against them He will thunder in the heavens,
The Lord will judge the ends of the earth;

And He will give strength to His king,
And will exalt the horn of His anointed."

Praying for Others
1 Samuel 2:20 (NRSV)
Then Eli would bless Elkanah and his wife, and say, "May the Lord repay you with children by this woman for the gift that she made to the Lord", and then they would return to their home.

Responding to God
1 Samuel 3:4 (NAB)
The LORD called to Samuel, who answered, "Here I am."

Responding to God
1 Samuel 3:6 (NJB)
And again Yahweh called, 'Samuel! Samuel!' He got up and went to Eli and said, 'Here I am, as you called me.' He replied, 'I did not call, my son; go back and lie down.'

Responding to God
1 Samuel 3:8 (NLT)
So now the Lord called a third time, and once more Samuel jumped up and ran to Eli. "Here I am," he said. "What do you need?"

Then Eli realized it was the Lord who was calling the boy.

Responding to God
1 Samuel 3:10 (GWT)
The Lord came and stood there. He called as he had called the other times: "Samuel! Samuel!" And Samuel replied, "Speak. I'm listening."

Confessing Sin
1 Samuel 7:6 (TEV)
So they all gathered at Mizpah. They drew some water and poured it out as an offering to the Lord and fasted that whole day. They said, "We have sinned against the Lord." (It was at Mizpah where Samuel settled disputes among the Israelites.)

Praying for Others
1 Samuel 7:9 (CEV)
Samuel begged the Lord to rescue Israel, then he sacrificed a young lamb to the Lord. Samuel had not even finished offering the sacrifice

when the Philistines started to attack. But the Lord answered his prayer and made thunder crash all around them. The Philistines panicked and ran away.

Praying for Others
1 Samuel 8:6 (ESV)
But the thing displeased Samuel when they said, "Give us a king to judge us." And Samuel prayed to the Lord.

Praying for Others
1 Samuel 8:21 (NIV)
When Samuel heard all that the people said, he repeated it before the Lord.

Seeking God's Will
1 Samuel 10:22 (NASB)
Therefore they inquired further of the Lord, "Has the man come here yet?" So the Lord said, "Behold, he is hiding himself by the baggage."

Confessing Sin & Making Requests Known
1 Samuel 12:10 (NRSV)
Then they cried to the Lord, and said, 'We have sinned, because we have forsaken the Lord, and have served the Baals and the Astartes; but now rescue us out of the hand of our enemies, and we will serve you.'

Praying for Others
1 Samuel 12:18-19 (NAB)
Samuel then called to the LORD, and the LORD sent thunder and rain that day.

As a result, all the people dreaded the LORD and Samuel. They said to Samuel, "Pray to the LORD your God for us, your servants, that we may not die for having added to all our other sins the evil of asking for a king."

Praying for Others
1 Samuel 12:23 (NJB)
For my part, far be it from me to sin against Yahweh by ceasing to pray for you or to instruct you in the good and right way.

Seeking God's Will
1 Samuel 14:37 (NLT)
So Saul asked God, "Should we go after the Philistines? Will you help us defeat them?" But God made no reply that day.

Making Requests Known
1 Samuel 14:41 (GWT)
Then Saul said to the Lord, "O God of Israel, why didn't you answer me today? If this sin is mine or my son Jonathan's, Lord God of Israel, {let the priest} draw Urim. But if it is in your people Israel, {let him} draw Thummim." Jonathan and Saul were chosen, and the people were freed {from guilt}.

Praying for Others
1 Samuel 15:11 (TEV)
"I am sorry that I made Saul king; he has turned away from me and disobeyed my commands." Samuel was angry, and all night long he pleaded with the Lord.

Praising God
1 Samuel 15:31 (CEV)
Samuel followed Saul back, and Saul worshiped the Lord.

Seeking God's Will
1 Samuel 16:2 (ESV)
And Samuel said, "How can I go? If Saul hears it, he will kill me." And the Lord said, "Take a heifer with you and say, 'I have come to sacrifice to the Lord.'

Praying for Others & Seeking God's Will
1 Samuel 22:10 (NIV)
Ahimelech inquired of the Lord for him; he also gave him provisions and the sword of Goliath the Philistine."

Seeking God's Will
1 Samuel 23:2 (NASB)
So David inquired of the Lord, saying, "Shall I go and attack these Philistines?" And the Lord said to David, "Go and attack the Philistines and deliver Keilah."

Seeking God's Will
1 Samuel 23:4 (NRSV)

Then David inquired of the Lord again. The Lord answered him, "Yes, go down to Keilah; for I will give the Philistines into your hand."

Seeking God's Will
1 Samuel 23:10-12 (NAB)

David then said: "O LORD God of Israel, your servant has heard a report that Saul plans to come to Keilah, to destroy the city on my account. Will they hand me over? And now: will Saul come down as your servant has heard? O LORD God of Israel, tell your servant." The LORD answered, "He will come down." David then asked, "Will the citizens of Keilah deliver me and my men into the grasp of Saul?" And the LORD answered, "Yes."

Thanksgiving & Gratitude
1 Samuel 25:32 (NJB)

David said to Abigail, 'Blessed be Yahweh, God of Israel, who sent you to meet me today!

Thanksgiving & Gratitude
1 Samuel 25:39 (NLT)

When David heard that Nabal was dead, he said, "Praise the Lord, who has paid back Nabal and kept me from doing it myself. Nabal has received the punishment for his sin." Then David wasted no time in sending messengers to Abigail to ask her to become his wife.

Seeking God's Will
1 Samuel 28:6-7 (GWT)

He prayed to the Lord, but the Lord didn't answer him through dreams, the Urim, or prophets. Saul told his officers, "Find me a woman who conjures up the dead. Then I'll go to her and ask for her services."

His officers told him, "There is a woman at Endor who conjures up the dead."

Seeking God's Will
1 Samuel 30:8 (TEV)

David asked the Lord, "Shall I go after those raiders? And will I catch them?"

He answered, "Go after them; you will catch them and rescue the captives."

Seeking God's Will
2 Samuel 2:1 (CEV)

Later, David asked the Lord, "Should I go back to one of the towns of Judah?"

The Lord answered, "Yes."

David asked, "Which town should I go to?"

"Go to Hebron," the Lord replied.

Blessings & Benedictions
2 Samuel 2:5-6 (ESV)

David sent messengers to the men of Jabesh-gilead and said to them, "May you be blessed by the Lord, because you showed this loyalty to Saul your lord and buried him. Now may the Lord show steadfast love and faithfulness to you. And I will do good to you because you have done this thing.

Seeking God's Will
2 Samuel 5:19 (NIV)

So David inquired of the Lord, "Shall I go and attack the Philistines? Will you hand them over to me?"

The Lord answered him, "Go, for I will surely hand the Philistines over to you."

Seeking God's Will
2 Samuel 5:23 (NASB)

When David inquired of the Lord, He said, "You shall not go directly up; circle around behind them and come at them in front of the balsam trees.

Praising God
2 Samuel 6:14 (NRSV)

David danced before the Lord with all his might; David was girded with a linen ephod.

Praising God
2 Samuel 6:16 (NAB)

As the ark of the LORD was entering the City of David, Saul's daughter Michal looked down through the window and saw King David leaping and dancing before the LORD, and she despised him in her heart.

Praising God
2 Samuel 7:18-29 (NJB)
King David then went in, sat down in Yahweh's presence and said:

'Who am I, Lord Yahweh, and what is my lineage, for you to have led me as far as this? Yet, to you, Lord Yahweh, this seemed too little, and now you extend your promises for your servant's family into the distant future. Such is human destiny, Lord Yahweh. What more can David say to you, since you, Lord Yahweh, know all about your servant? Because of your promise and since you were so inclined, you have had the generosity to reveal this to your servant. That is why you are great, Lord Yahweh; there is no one like you, no God but you alone, as everything that we have heard confirms. Is there another people on earth like your people, like Israel, whom a god proceeded to redeem, to make them his people and to make a name for himself by performing great and terrible things on their behalf, by driving out nations and their gods before his people?— for you constituted your people Israel your own people for ever and you, Yahweh, became their God.

'Now, Yahweh God, may the promise which you have made for your servant and for his family stand firm forever as you have said, so that your name will be exalted for ever and people will say, "Israel's God is Yahweh Sabaoth." Your servant David's dynasty will be secure before you, since you, Yahweh Sabaoth, the God of Israel, have disclosed to your servant, "I am going to build you a dynasty." Hence, your servant has ventured to offer this prayer to you. Yes, Lord Yahweh, you are God indeed, your words are true and you have made this generous promise to your servant. What is more, you have deigned to bless your servant's dynasty, so that it may remain for ever before you; for you, Lord Yahweh, have spoken; and may your servant's dynasty be blessed with your blessing for ever.'

Praying for Others
2 Samuel 12:16-17 (KJV)
David therefore besought God for the child; and David fasted, and went in, and lay all night upon the earth. And the elders of his house arose, and went to him, to raise him up from the earth: but he would not, neither did he eat bread with them.

Praising God
2 Samuel 12:20 (NLT)
Then David got up from the ground, washed himself, put on lotions, and changed his clothes. Then he went to the Tabernacle and worshiped the Lord. After that, he returned to the palace and ate.

Praying for Others
2 Samuel 14:17 (GWT)
I thought that you would reassure me. You are like God's Messenger, who is able to distinguish right from wrong. May the Lord your God be with you!"

Making Requests Known
2 Samuel 15:31 (TEV)
When David was told that Ahithophel had joined Absalom's rebellion, he prayed, "Please, Lord, turn Ahithophel's advice into nonsense!"

Making Requests Known
2 Samuel 21:1 (CEV)
While David was king, there were three years in a row when the nation of Israel could not grow enough food. So David asked the Lord for help, and the Lord answered, "Saul and his family are guilty of murder, because he had the Gibeonites killed."

Making Requests Known
2 Samuel 21:14 (ESV)
And they buried the bones of Saul and his son Jonathan in the land of Benjamin in Zela, in the tomb of Kish his father. And they did all that the king commanded. And after that God responded to the plea for the land.

Praising God
2 Samuel 22:1-51 (NIV)
David sang to the Lord the words of this song when the Lord delivered him from the hand of all his enemies and from the hand of Saul. He said:
"The Lord is my rock, my fortress and my deliverer;
   my God is my rock, in whom I take refuge,
   my shield and the horn of my salvation.
He is my stronghold, my refuge and my savior--
   from violent men you save me.
I call to the Lord, who is worthy of praise,
   and I am saved from my enemies.

"The waves of death swirled about me;
   the torrents of destruction overwhelmed me.
The cords of the grave coiled around me;
   the snares of death confronted me.
In my distress I called to the Lord;

I called out to my God.
From his temple he heard my voice;
   my cry came to his ears.

"The earth trembled and quaked,
   the foundations of the heavens shook;
   they trembled because he was angry.
Smoke rose from his nostrils;
   consuming fire came from his mouth,
   burning coals blazed out of it.
He parted the heavens and came down;
   dark clouds were under his feet.
He mounted the cherubim and flew;
   he soared on the wings of the wind.
He made darkness his canopy around him--
   the dark rain clouds of the sky.
Out of the brightness of his presence
   bolts of lightning blazed forth.
The Lord thundered from heaven;
   the voice of the Most High resounded.
He shot arrows and scattered the enemies,
   bolts of lightning and routed them.
The valleys of the sea were exposed
   and the foundations of the earth laid bare
at the rebuke of the Lord,
   at the blast of breath from his nostrils.
"He reached down from on high and took hold of me;
   he drew me out of deep waters.
He rescued me from my powerful enemy,
   from my foes, who were too strong for me.
They confronted me in the day of my disaster,
   but the Lord was my support.
He brought me out into a spacious place;
   he rescued me because he delighted in me.

"The Lord has dealt with me according to my righteousness;
   according to the cleanness of my hands he has rewarded me.
For I have kept the ways of the Lord;
   I have not done evil by turning from my God.
All his laws are before me;
   I have not turned away from his decrees.
I have been blameless before him
   and have kept myself from sin.

The Lord has rewarded me according to my righteousness,
  according to my cleanness in his sight.

"To the faithful you show yourself faithful,
  to the blameless you show yourself blameless,
to the pure you show yourself pure,
  but to the crooked you show yourself shrewd.
You save the humble,
  but your eyes are on the haughty to bring them low.
You are my lamp, O Lord;
  the Lord turns my darkness into light.
With your help I can advance against a troop;
  with my God I can scale a wall.

"As for God, his way is perfect;
  the word of the Lord is flawless.
He is a shield
  for all who take refuge in him.
For who is God besides the Lord?
  And who is the Rock except our God?
It is God who arms me with strength
  and makes my way perfect.
He makes my feet like the feet of a deer;
  he enables me to stand on the heights.
He trains my hands for battle;
  my arms can bend a bow of bronze.
You give me your shield of victory;
  you stoop down to make me great.
You broaden the path beneath me,
  so that my ankles do not turn.

"I pursued my enemies and crushed them;
  I did not turn back till they were destroyed.
I crushed them completely, and they could not rise;
  they fell beneath my feet.
You armed me with strength for battle;
  you made my adversaries bow at my feet.
You made my enemies turn their backs in flight,
  and I destroyed my foes.
They cried for help, but there was no one to save them--
  to the Lord, but he did not answer.
I beat them as fine as the dust of the earth;
  I pounded and trampled them like mud in the streets.

"You have delivered me from the attacks of my people;
   you have preserved me as the head of nations.
People I did not know are subject to me,
   and foreigners come cringing to me;
   as soon as they hear me, they obey me.
They all lose heart;
   they come trembling from their strongholds.

"The Lord lives! Praise be to my Rock!
   Exalted be God, the Rock, my Savior!
He is the God who avenges me,
   who puts the nations under me,
   who sets me free from my enemies.
You exalted me above my foes;
   from violent men you rescued me.
Therefore I will praise you, O Lord, among the nations;
   I will sing praises to your name.
He gives his king great victories;
   he shows unfailing kindness to his anointed,
   to David and his descendants forever."

Seeking God's Will
2 Samuel 23:17 (NASB)

And he said, "Be it far from me, O Lord, that I should do this. Shall I drink the blood of the men who went in jeopardy of their lives?" Therefore he would not drink it. These things the three mighty men did.

Confessing Sin
2 Samuel 24:10 (NRSV)

But afterward, David was stricken to the heart because he had numbered the people. David said to the Lord, "I have sinned greatly in what I have done. But now, O Lord, I pray you, take away the guilt of your servant; for I have done very foolishly."

Confessing Sin/Praying for Others
2 Samuel 24:17 (NAB)

When David saw the angel who was striking the people, he said to the LORD: "It is I who have sinned; it is I, the shepherd, who have done wrong. But these are sheep; what have they done? Punish me and my kindred."

Praising God
2 Samuel 24:25 (NJB)
David built an altar to Yahweh and offered burnt offerings and communion sacrifices. Yahweh then took pity on the country and the plague was lifted from Israel.

Blessings & Benedictions
1 Kings 1:36-37 (NLT)
"Amen!" Benaiah son of Jehoiada replied. "May the Lord, the God of my lord the king, decree it to be so. And may the Lord be with Solomon as he has been with you, and may he make Solomon's reign even greater than yours!"

Blessings & Benedictions/Praising God
1 Kings 1:47-48 (GWT)
Furthermore, the royal officials have come {to congratulate} His Majesty King David, saying, 'May your God make Solomon's name more famous than yours and his reign greater than your reign.' The king himself bowed down on his bed and said, 'Praise the Lord God of Israel who has let me see the heir to my throne.' "

Making Requests Known
1 Kings 3:6-9 (TEV)
Solomon answered, "You always showed great love for my father David, your servant, and he was good, loyal, and honest in his relation with you. And you have continued to show him your great and constant love by giving him a son who today rules in his place. O Lord God, you have let me succeed my father as king, even though I am very young and don't know how to rule. Here I am among the people you have chosen to be your own, a people who are so many that they cannot be counted. So give me the wisdom I need to rule your people with justice and to know the difference between good and evil. Otherwise, how would I ever be able to rule this great people of yours?"

Praising God
1 Kings 5:7 (CEV)
Hiram was so happy when he heard Solomon's request that he said, "I am grateful that the Lord gave David such a wise son to be king of that great nation!"

Praising God/Making Requests Known
1 Kings 8:14-61 (ESV)

Then the king turned around and blessed all the assembly of Israel, while all the assembly of Israel stood. And he said, "Blessed be the Lord, the God of Israel, who with his hand has fulfilled what he promised with his mouth to David my father, saying, 'Since the day that I brought my people Israel out of Egypt, I chose no city out of all the tribes of Israel in which to build a house, that my name might be there. But I chose David to be over my people Israel.' Now it was in the heart of David my father to build a house for the name of the Lord, the God of Israel. But the Lord said to David my father, 'Whereas it was in your heart to build a house for my name, you did well that it was in your heart. Nevertheless, you shall not build the house, but your son who shall be born to you shall build the house for my name.' Now the Lord has fulfilled his promise that he made. For I have risen in the place of David my father, and sit on the throne of Israel, as the Lord promised, and I have built the house for the name of the Lord, the God of Israel. And there I have provided a place for the ark, in which is the covenant of the Lord that he made with our fathers, when he brought them out of the land of Egypt."

Then Solomon stood before the altar of the Lord in the presence of all the assembly of Israel and spread out his hands toward heaven, and said, "O Lord, God of Israel, there is no God like you, in heaven above or on earth beneath, keeping covenant and showing steadfast love to your servants who walk before you with all their heart, who have kept with your servant David my father what you declared to him. You spoke with your mouth, and with your hand have fulfilled it this day. Now therefore, O Lord, God of Israel, keep for your servant David my father what you have promised him, saying, 'You shall not lack a man to sit before me on the throne of Israel, if only your sons pay close attention to their way, to walk before me as you have walked before me.' Now therefore, O God of Israel, let your word be confirmed, which you have spoken to your servant David my father.

"But will God indeed dwell on the earth? Behold, heaven and the highest heaven cannot contain you; how much less this house that I have built! Yet have regard to the prayer of your servant and to his plea, O Lord my God, listening to the cry and to the prayer that your servant prays before you this day, that your eyes may be open night and day toward this house, the place of which you have said, 'My name shall be there,' that you may listen to the prayer that your servant offers toward this place. And listen to the plea of your servant and of your people Israel, when they pray toward this place. And listen in heaven your dwelling place, and when you hear, forgive.

"If a man sins against his neighbor and is made to take an oath and comes and swears his oath before your altar in this house, then hear in heaven and act and judge your servants, condemning the guilty by bringing his conduct on his own head, and vindicating the righteous by rewarding him according to his righteousness.

"When your people Israel are defeated before the enemy because they have sinned against you, and if they turn again to you and acknowledge your name and pray and plead with you in this house, then hear in heaven and forgive the sin of your people Israel and bring them again to the land that you gave to their fathers.

"When heaven is shut up and there is no rain because they have sinned against you, if they pray toward this place and acknowledge your name and turn from their sin, when you afflict them, then hear in heaven and forgive the sin of your servants, your people Israel, when you teach them the good way in which they should walk, and grant rain upon your land, which you have given to your people as an inheritance.

"If there is famine in the land, if there is pestilence or blight or mildew or locust or caterpillar, if their enemy besieges them in the land at their gates, whatever plague, whatever sickness there is, whatever prayer, whatever plea is made by any man or by all your people Israel, each knowing the affliction of his own heart and stretching out his hands toward this house, then hear in heaven your dwelling place and forgive and act and render to each whose heart you know, according to all his ways (for you, you only, know the hearts of all the children of mankind), that they may fear you all the days that they live in the land that you gave to our fathers.

"Likewise, when a foreigner, who is not of your people Israel, comes from a far country for your name's sake (for they shall hear of your great name and your mighty hand, and of your outstretched arm), when he comes and prays toward this house, hear in heaven your dwelling place and do according to all for which the foreigner calls to you, in order that all the peoples of the earth may know your name and fear you, as do your people Israel, and that they may know that this house that I have built is called by your name.

"If your people go out to battle against their enemy, by whatever way you shall send them, and they pray to the Lord toward the city that you have chosen and the house that I have built for your name, then hear in heaven their prayer and their plea, and maintain their cause.

"If they sin against you— for there is no one who does not sin—and you are angry with them and give them to an enemy, so that they are carried away captive to the land of the enemy, far off or near, yet if they turn their heart in the land to which they have been carried captive, and repent and plead with you in the land of their captors, saying, 'We have sinned and have acted perversely and wickedly,' if they repent with all their mind and with all their heart in the land of their enemies, who carried them captive, and pray to you toward their land, which you gave to their fathers, the city that you have chosen, and the house that I have built for your name, then hear in heaven your dwelling place their prayer and their plea, and maintain their cause and forgive your people who have sinned against you, and all their transgressions that they have committed against you, and grant them compassion in the sight of those who carried them captive, that they may have compassion on them (for they are your people, and your heritage, which you brought out of Egypt, from the midst of the iron furnace). Let your eyes be open to the plea of your servant and to the plea of your people Israel, giving ear to them whenever they call to you. For you separated them from among all the peoples of the earth to be your heritage, as you declared through Moses your servant, when you brought our fathers out of Egypt, O Lord GOD."

Now as Solomon finished offering all this prayer and plea to the Lord, he arose from before the altar of the Lord, where he had knelt with hands outstretched toward heaven. And he stood and blessed all the assembly of Israel with a loud voice, saying, "Blessed be the Lord who has given rest to his people Israel, according to all that he promised. Not one word has failed of all his good promise, which he spoke by Moses his servant. The Lord our God be with us, as he was with our fathers. May he not leave us or forsake us, that he may incline our hearts to him, to walk in all his ways and to keep his commandments, his statutes, and his rules, which he commanded our fathers. Let these words of mine, with which I have pleaded before the Lord, be near to the Lord our God day and night, and may he maintain the cause of his servant and the cause of his people Israel, as each day requires, that all the peoples of the earth may know that the Lord is God; there is no other. Let your heart therefore be wholly true to the Lord our God, walking in his statutes and keeping his commandments, as at this day."

Praying for Others
1 Kings 13:6 (NIV)

Then the king said to the man of God, "Intercede with the Lord your God and pray for me that my hand may be restored." So the man of God interceded with the Lord, and the king's hand was restored and became as it was before.

Praying for Others
1 Kings 17:20-21 (NRSV)

He cried out to the Lord, "O Lord my God, have you brought calamity even upon the widow with whom I am staying, by killing her son?" Then he stretched himself upon the child three times, and cried out to the Lord, "O Lord my God, let this child's life come into him again."

Making Requests Known
1 Kings 18:36-37 (NAB)

At the time for offering sacrifice, the prophet Elijah came forward and said, "LORD, God of Abraham, Isaac, and Israel, let it be known this day that you are God in Israel and that I am your servant and have done all these things by your command. Answer me, LORD! Answer me, that this people may know that you, LORD, are God and that you have brought them back to their senses."

Praising God
1 Kings 18:39 (NJB)

When all the people saw this they fell on their faces. 'Yahweh is God,' they cried, 'Yahweh is God!'

Making Requests Known
1 Kings 18:42 (NLT)

So Ahab prepared a feast. But Elijah climbed to the top of Mount Carmel and fell to the ground and prayed.

Making Requests Known
1 Kings 19:4 (GWT)

Then he traveled through the wilderness for a day. He sat down under a broom plant and wanted to die. "I've had enough now, Lord," he said. "Take my life! I'm no better than my ancestors."

Responding to God
1 Kings 19:10 (TEV)

He answered, "Lord God Almighty, I have always served you—you alone. But the people of Israel have broken their covenant with you, torn down your altars, and killed all your prophets. I am the only one left—and they are trying to kill me!"

Responding to God
1 Kings 19:14 (CEV)

Elijah answered, "Lord God All-Powerful, I've always done my best to obey you. But your people have broken their solemn promise to you. They have torn down your altars and killed all your prophets, except me. And now they are even trying to kill me!"

Making Requests Known
2 Kings 1:12 (ESV)
But Elijah answered them, "If I am a man of God, let fire come down from heaven and consume you and your fifty." Then the fire of God came down from heaven and consumed him and his fifty.

Praying for Others
2 Kings 4:33-35 (NIV)
He went in, shut the door on the two of them and prayed to the Lord. Then he got on the bed and lay upon the boy, mouth to mouth, eyes to eyes, hands to hands. As he stretched himself out upon him, the boy's body grew warm. Elisha turned away and walked back and forth in the room and then got on the bed and stretched out upon him once more. The boy sneezed seven times and opened his eyes.

Confessing Sin
2 Kings 5:18 (NASB)
"In this matter may the Lord pardon your servant: when my master goes into the house of Rimmon to worship there, and he leans on my hand and I bow myself in the house of Rimmon, when I bow myself in the house of Rimmon, the Lord pardon your servant in this matter."

Praying for Others
2 Kings 6:17-18 (NRSV)
Then Elisha prayed: "O Lord, please open his eyes that he may see." So the Lord opened the eyes of the servant, and he saw; the mountain was full of horses and chariots of fire all around Elisha. When the Arameans came down against him, Elisha prayed to the Lord, and said, "Strike this people, please, with blindness." So he struck them with blindness as Elisha had asked.

Praying for Others
2 Kings 6:20 (NAB)
When they entered Samaria, Elisha prayed, "O LORD, open their eyes that they may see." The LORD opened their eyes, and they saw that they were inside Samaria.

Praying for Others
2 Kings 19:4 (NJB)
May Yahweh your God hear the words of the cupbearer-in-chief whom

his master, the king of Assyria, has sent to insult the living God, and may Yahweh your God punish the words he has heard. Offer your prayer for the remnant still remaining." '

Praising God/Making Requests Known
2 Kings 19:15-19 (NLT)

And Hezekiah prayed this prayer before the Lord: "O Lord, God of Israel, you are enthroned between the mighty cherubim! You alone are God of all the kingdoms of the earth. You alone created the heavens and the earth. Listen to me, O Lord, and hear! Open your eyes, O Lord, and see! Listen to Sennacherib's words of defiance against the living God.

"It is true, Lord, that the kings of Assyria have destroyed all these nations, just as the message says. And they have thrown the gods of these nations into the fire and burned them. But of course the Assyrians could destroy them! They were not gods at all—only idols of wood and stone shaped by human hands. Now, O Lord our God, rescue us from his power; then all the kingdoms of the earth will know that you alone, O Lord, are God."

Making Requests Known
2 Kings 20:1-3 (NLT)

About that time Hezekiah became deathly ill, and the prophet Isaiah son of Amoz went to visit him. He gave the king this message: "This is what the Lord says: Set your affairs in order, for you are going to die. You will not recover from this illness."

When Hezekiah heard this, he turned his face to the wall and prayed to the Lord, "Remember, O Lord, how I have always tried to be faithful to you and do what is pleasing in your sight." Then he broke down and wept bitterly.

Making Requests Known
2 Kings 20:11 (GWT)

Then the prophet Isaiah called on the Lord, and the Lord made the shadow that had gone down on Ahaz's stairway go back up ten steps.

Making Requests Known
1 Chron. 4:10 (TEV)

But Jabez prayed to the God of Israel, "Bless me, God, and give me much land. Be with me and keep me from anything evil that might cause me pain." And God gave him what he prayed for.

Making Requests Known
1 Chron. 5:20 (CEV)

Whenever these soldiers went to war against their enemies, they prayed to God and trusted him to help. That's why the tribes of Reuben, Gad, and East Manasseh defeated the Hagrites and their allies.

Seeking God's Will
1 Chron. 14:10 (ESV)

And David inquired of God, "Shall I go up against the Philistines? Will you give them into my hand?" And the Lord said to him, "Go up, and I will give them into your hand."

Seeking God's Will
1 Chron. 14:14 (NIV)

So David inquired of God again, and God answered him, "Do not go straight up, but circle around them and attack them in front of the balsam trees.

Thanksgiving & Gratitude/Praising God
1 Chron. 16:7-36 (NASB)

Then on that day David first assigned Asaph and his relatives to give thanks to the Lord.

> Oh give thanks to the Lord, call upon His name;
> Make known His deeds among the peoples.
> Sing to Him, sing praises to Him;
> Speak of all His wonders.
> Glory in His holy name;
> Let the heart of those who seek the Lord be glad.
> Seek the Lord and His strength;
> Seek His face continually.
> Remember His wonderful deeds which He has done,
> His marvels and the judgments from His mouth,
> O seed of Israel His servant,
> Sons of Jacob, His chosen ones!
> He is the Lord our God;
> His judgments are in all the earth.
> Remember His covenant forever,
> The word which He commanded to a thousand generations,
> The covenant which He made with Abraham,
> And His oath to Isaac.
> He also confirmed it to Jacob for a statute,

To Israel as an everlasting covenant,
Saying, "To you I will give the land of Canaan,
As the portion of your inheritance."
When they were only a few in number,
Very few, and strangers in it,
And they wandered about from nation to nation,
And from one kingdom to another people,
He permitted no man to oppress them,
And He reproved kings for their sakes, saying,
"Do not touch My anointed ones,
And do My prophets no harm."
Sing to the Lord, all the earth;
Proclaim good tidings of His salvation from day to day.
Tell of His glory among the nations,
His wonderful deeds among all the peoples.
For great is the Lord, and greatly to be praised;
He also is to be feared above all gods.
For all the gods of the peoples are idols,
But the Lord made the heavens.
Splendor and majesty are before Him,
Strength and joy are in His place.
Ascribe to the Lord, O families of the peoples,
Ascribe to the Lord glory and strength.
Ascribe to the Lord the glory due His name;
Bring an offering, and come before Him;
Worship the Lord in holy array.
Tremble before Him, all the earth;
Indeed, the world is firmly established, it will not be moved.
Let the heavens be glad, and let the earth rejoice;
And let them say among the nations, "The Lord reigns."
Let the sea roar, and all it contains;
Let the field exult, and all that is in it.
Then the trees of the forest will sing for joy before the Lord;
For He is coming to judge the earth.
O give thanks to the Lord, for He is good;
For His lovingkindness is everlasting.
Then say, "Save us, O God of our salvation,
And gather us and deliver us from the nations,
To give thanks to Your holy name,
And glory in Your praise."
Blessed be the Lord, the God of Israel,
From everlasting even to everlasting.
Then all the people said, "Amen," and praised the Lord.

Praise
1 Chron. 17:16-27 (NRSV)

Then King David went in and sat before the Lord, and said, "Who am I, O Lord God, and what is my house, that you have brought me thus far? And even this was a small thing in your sight, O God; you have also spoken of your servant's house for a great while to come. You regard me as someone of high rank, O Lord God! And what more can David say to you for honoring your servant? You know your servant. For your servant's sake, O Lord, and according to your own heart, you have done all these great deeds, making known all these great things. There is no one like you, O Lord, and there is no God besides you, according to all that we have heard with our ears. Who is like your people Israel, one nation on the earth whom God went to redeem to be his people, making for yourself a name for great and terrible things, in driving out nations before your people whom you redeemed from Egypt? And you made your people Israel to be your people forever; and you, O Lord, became their God.

"And now, O Lord, as for the word that you have spoken concerning your servant and concerning his house, let it be established forever, and do as you have promised. Thus your name will be established and magnified forever in the saying, 'The Lord of hosts, the God of Israel, is Israel's God'; and the house of your servant David will be established in your presence. For you, my God, have revealed to your servant that you will build a house for him; therefore your servant has found it possible to pray before you. And now, O Lord, you are God, and you have promised this good thing to your servant; therefore may it please you to bless the house of your servant, that it may continue forever before you. For you, O Lord, have blessed and are blessed forever."

Confessing Sin
1 Chron. 21:8 (NAB)

Then David said to God, "I have sinned greatly in doing this thing. Take away your servant's guilt, for I have acted very foolishly."

Confessing Sin/Praying for Others
1 Chron. 21:17 (NJB)

And David said to God, 'Did I not order the people to be counted? I was the one who sinned and actually committed the wrong. But these, the flock, what have they done? Yahweh my God, let your hand lie heavy on me and on my family; but spare your people from the plague!'

Praising God
1 Chron. 21:26 (NLT)

David built an altar there to the Lord and sacrificed burnt offerings and peace offerings. And when David prayed, the Lord answered him by sending fire from heaven to burn up the offering on the altar.

Verses about Prayer
1 Chron. 28:9 (NJB)

'And you, Solomon my son, know the God of your father and serve him with an undivided heart and willing mind; for Yahweh scrutinises all hearts and understands whatever plans they may devise. If you seek him, he will let you find him; but forsake him and he will cast you off for ever.

Praising God
1 Chron. 23:30-31 (GWT)

They were appointed to stand to give thanks and praise to the Lord every morning. They were appointed to do the same thing in the evening. They were appointed to stand in front of the Lord in the required numbers whenever burnt offerings were made—on weekly worship days, at New Moon Festivals, and on appointed annual festivals.

Praising God
1 Chron. 29:10-20 (TEV)

There in front of the whole assembly King David praised the Lord. He said, "Lord God of our ancestor Jacob, may you be praised forever and ever! You are great and powerful, glorious, splendid, and majestic. Everything in heaven and earth is yours, and you are king, supreme ruler over all. All riches and wealth come from you; you rule everything by your strength and power; and you are able to make anyone great and strong. Now, our God, we give you thanks, and we praise your glorious name.

"Yet my people and I cannot really give you anything, because everything is a gift from you, and we have only given back what is yours already. You know, O Lord, that we pass through life like exiles and strangers, as our ancestors did. Our days are like a passing shadow, and we cannot escape death. O Lord, our God, we have brought together all this wealth to build a temple to honor your holy name, but it all came from you and all belongs to you. I know that you test everyone's heart and are pleased with people of integrity. In honesty and sincerity I have willingly given all this to you, and I have seen how your people who are gathered here have been happy to bring offerings to you. Lord God of our ancestors Abraham, Isaac, and Jacob, keep such devotion forever strong in your people's hearts and keep them always faithful to you. Give my son Solomon a wholehearted desire to obey everything that you command and to build the Temple for which I have made these preparations."

Then David commanded the people, "Praise the Lord your God!" And the whole assembly praised the Lord, the God of their ancestors, and they bowed low and gave honor to the Lord and also to the king.

Making Requests Known
2 Chron. 1:8-10 (CEV)

Solomon answered:

Lord God, you were always loyal to my father David, and now you have made me king of Israel. I am supposed to rule these people, but there are as many of them as there are specks of dust on the ground. So keep the promise you made to my father and make me wise. Give me the knowledge I'll need to be the king of this great nation of yours.

Praising God/Making Requests Known/Praying for Others
2 Chron. 6:12-42 (ESV)

Then Solomon stood before the altar of the Lord in the presence of all the assembly of Israel and spread out his hands. Solomon had made a bronze platform five cubits long, five cubits wide, and three cubits high, and had set it in the court, and he stood on it. Then he knelt on his knees in the presence of all the assembly of Israel, and spread out his hands toward heaven, and said, "O Lord, God of Israel, there is no God like you, in heaven or on earth, keeping covenant and showing steadfast love to your servants who walk before you with all their heart, who have kept with your servant David my father what you declared to him. You spoke with your mouth, and with your hand have fulfilled it this day. Now therefore, O Lord, God of Israel, keep for your servant David my father what you have promised him, saying, 'You shall not lack a man to sit before me on the throne of Israel, if only your sons pay close attention to their way, to walk in my law as you have walked before me.' Now therefore, O Lord, God of Israel, let your word be confirmed, which you have spoken to your servant David.

"But will God indeed dwell with man on the earth? Behold, heaven and the highest heaven cannot contain you, how much less this house that I have built! Yet have regard to the prayer of your servant and to his plea, O Lord my God, listening to the cry and to the prayer that your servant prays before you, that your eyes may be open day and night toward this house, the place where you have promised to set your name, that you may listen to the prayer that your servant offers toward this place. And listen to the pleas of your servant and of your people Israel, when they pray toward this place. And listen from heaven your dwelling place, and when you hear, forgive.

"If a man sins against his neighbor and is made to take an oath and comes and swears his oath before your altar in this house, then hear from heaven and act and judge your servants, repaying the guilty by bringing his conduct on his own head, and vindicating the righteous by rewarding him according to his righteousness.

"If your people Israel are defeated before the enemy because they have sinned against you, and they turn again and acknowledge your name and pray and plead with you in this house, then hear from heaven and forgive the sin of your people Israel and bring them again to the land that you gave to them and to their fathers.

"When heaven is shut up and there is no rain because they have sinned against you, if they pray toward this place and acknowledge your name and turn from their sin, when you afflict them, then hear in heaven and forgive the sin of your servants, your people Israel, when you teach them the good way in which they should walk, and grant rain upon your land, which you have given to your people as an inheritance.

"If there is famine in the land, if there is pestilence or blight or mildew or locust or caterpillar, if their enemies besiege them in the land at their gates, whatever plague, whatever sickness there is, whatever prayer, whatever plea is made by any man or by all your people Israel, each knowing his own affliction and his own sorrow and stretching out his hands toward this house, then hear from heaven your dwelling place and forgive and render to each whose heart you know, according to all his ways, for you, you only, know the hearts of the children of mankind, that they may fear you and walk in your ways all the days that they live in the land that you gave to our fathers.

"Likewise, when a foreigner, who is not of your people Israel, comes from a far country for the sake of your great name and your mighty hand and your outstretched arm, when he comes and prays toward this house, hear from heaven your dwelling place and do according to all for which the foreigner calls to you, in order that all the peoples of the earth may know your name and fear you, as do your people Israel, and that they may know that this house that I have built is called by your name.

"If your people go out to battle against their enemies, by whatever way you shall send them, and they pray to you toward this city that you have chosen and the house that I have built for your name, then hear from heaven their prayer and their plea, and maintain their cause.

"If they sin against you— for there is no one who does not sin—and you are angry with them and give them to an enemy, so that they are carried away captive to a land far or near, yet if they turn their heart in the land to which they have been carried captive, and repent and plead with you in the land of their captivity, saying, 'We have sinned and have acted perversely and wickedly,' if they repent with all their mind and with all their heart in the land of their captivity to which they were carried captive, and pray toward their land, which you gave to their fathers, the city that you have chosen and the house that I have built for your name, then hear from heaven your dwelling place their prayer and their pleas, and maintain their cause and forgive your people who have sinned against you. Now, O my God, let your eyes be open and your ears attentive to the prayer of this place.

> "And now arise, O Lord God, and go to your resting place,
>   you and the ark of your might.
> Let your priests, O Lord God, be clothed with salvation,
>   and let your saints rejoice in your goodness.
> O Lord God, do not turn away the face of your anointed one!
>   Remember your steadfast love for David your servant."

Thanksgiving & Gratitude
2 Chron. 7:3 (NIV)
When all the Israelites saw the fire coming down and the glory of the Lord above the temple, they knelt on the pavement with their faces to the ground, and they worshiped and gave thanks to the Lord, saying,
   "He is good;
      his love endures forever."

Thanksgiving & Gratitude
2 Chron. 7:6 (NASB)
The priests stood at their posts, and the Levites also, with the instruments of music to the Lord, which King David had made for giving praise to the Lord—"for His lovingkindness is everlasting"—whenever he gave praise by their means, while the priests on the other side blew trumpets; and all Israel was standing.

Confessing Sin
2 Chron. 7:14 (NRSV)
If my people who are called by my name humble themselves, pray, seek my face, and turn from their wicked ways, then I will hear from heaven, and will forgive their sin and heal their land.

Making Requests Known
2 Chron. 13:14 (NAB)

When Judah turned and saw that they had to battle on both fronts, they cried out to the LORD and the priests sounded the trumpets.

Making Requests Known
2 Chron. 14:11 (NJB)

Asa then called on Yahweh his God and said, 'Yahweh, numbers and strength make no difference to you when you give your help. Help us, Yahweh our God, for, relying on you, we are confronting this horde in your name. Yahweh, you are our God. Human strength cannot prevail against you!'

Pledge & Commitment
2 Chron. 15:10-15 (NLT)

The people gathered at Jerusalem in late spring, during the fifteenth year of Asa's reign. On that day they sacrificed to the Lord some of the animals they had taken as plunder in the battle—seven hundred oxen and seven thousand sheep and goats. Then they entered into a covenant to seek the Lord, the God of their ancestors, with all their heart and soul. They agreed that anyone who refused to seek the Lord, the God of Israel, would be put to death—whether young or old, man or woman. They shouted out their oath of loyalty to the Lord with trumpets blaring and horns sounding. All were happy about this covenant, for they had entered into it with all their hearts. Eagerly they sought after God, and they found him. And the Lord gave them rest from their enemies on every side.

Making Requests Known
2 Chron. 20:4-12 (GWT)

The people of Judah gathered to seek the Lord's help. They came from every city in Judah.

In the new courtyard at the Lord's temple, Jehoshaphat stood in front of the people. He said, "Lord God of our ancestors, aren't you the God in heaven? You rule all the kingdoms of the nations. You possess power and might, and no one can oppose you. Didn't you, our God, force those who were living in this country out of Israel's way? Didn't you give this country to the descendants of your friend Abraham to have permanently? His descendants have lived in it and built a holy temple for your name in it. They said, 'If evil comes in the form of war, flood, plague, or famine, we will stand in front of this temple and in front of you because your name is in this temple. We will cry out to you in our troubles, and you will hear us and save us.'

"The Ammonites, Moabites, and the people of Mount Seir have come here. However, you didn't let Israel invade them when they came out of Egypt. The Israelites turned away from them and didn't destroy them. They are now paying us back by coming to force us out of your land that you gave to us. You're our God. Won't you judge them? We don't have the strength to face this large crowd that is attacking us. We don't know what to do, so we're looking to you."

Praising God
2 Chron. 20:18-19 (TEV)

Then King Jehoshaphat bowed low, with his face touching the ground, and all the people bowed with him and worshiped the Lord. The members of the Levite clans of Kohath and Korah stood up and with a loud shout praised the Lord, the God of Israel.

Thanksgiving & Gratitude
2 Chron. 20:21 (CEV)

Then he explained his plan and appointed men to march in front of the army and praise the Lord for his holy power by singing:
"Praise the Lord! His love never ends."

Making Requests Known
2 Chron. 24:22 (ESV)

Thus Joash the king did not remember the kindness that Jehoiada, Zechariah's father, had shown him, but killed his son. And when he was dying, he said, "May the Lord see and avenge!"

Praising God
2 Chron. 29:27-30 (NIV)

Hezekiah gave the order to sacrifice the burnt offering on the altar. As the offering began, singing to the Lord began also, accompanied by trumpets and the instruments of David king of Israel. The whole assembly bowed in worship, while the singers sang and the trumpeters played. All this continued until the sacrifice of the burnt offering was completed.

When the offerings were finished, the king and everyone present with him knelt down and worshiped. King Hezekiah and his officials ordered the Levites to praise the Lord with the words of David and of Asaph the seer. So they sang praises with gladness and bowed their heads and worshiped.

Praying for Others
2 Chron. 30:18-19 (NASB)

For a multitude of the people, even many from Ephraim and Manasseh, Issachar and Zebulun, had not purified themselves, yet they ate the Passover otherwise than prescribed. For Hezekiah prayed for them, saying, "May the good Lord pardon everyone who prepares his heart to seek God, the Lord God of his fathers, though not according to the purification rules of the sanctuary."

Thanksgiving & Gratitude
2 Chron. 31:2 (NRSV)

Hezekiah appointed the divisions of the priests and of the Levites, division by division, everyone according to his service, the priests and the Levites, for burnt offerings and offerings of well-being, to minister in the gates of the camp of the Lord and to give thanks and praise.

Making Requests Known
2 Chron. 32:20 (NAB)

But because of this, King Hezekiah and the prophet Isaiah, son of Amos, prayed and called out to heaven.

Making Requests Known
2 Chron. 32:24 (NJB)

About then Hezekiah fell ill and was at the point of death. He prayed to Yahweh, who heard him and granted him a sign.

Making Requests Known
2 Chron. 33:12-13 (NLT)

But while in deep distress, Manasseh sought the Lord his God and cried out humbly to the God of his ancestors. And when he prayed, the Lord listened to him and was moved by his request for help. So the Lord let Manasseh return to Jerusalem and to his kingdom. Manasseh had finally realized that the Lord alone is God!

Making Requests Known
2 Chron. 33:18 (GWT)

Everything else about Manasseh—including his prayer to his God and the words that the seers spoke to him in the name of the Lord God of Israel—are in the records of the kings of Israel.

Praising God/Thanksgiving & Gratitude
Ezra 3:11 (TEV)

They sang the Lord's praises, repeating the refrain:
"The Lord is good, and his love for Israel is eternal."
Everyone shouted with all their might, praising the Lord, because the work on the foundation of the Temple had been started.

Praising God
Ezra 4:2 (CEV)

So they went to Zerubbabel and to the family leaders and said, "Let us help! Ever since King Esarhaddon of Assyria brought us here, we have worshiped your God and offered sacrifices to him."

Making Requests Known
Ezra 6:12 (ESV)

May the God who has caused his name to dwell there overthrow any king or people who shall put out a hand to alter this, or to destroy this house of God that is in Jerusalem. I Darius make a decree; let it be done with all diligence."

Praising God
Ezra 7:27-28 (NIV)

Praise be to the Lord, the God of our fathers, who has put it into the king's heart to bring honor to the house of the Lord in Jerusalem in this way and who has extended his good favor to me before the king and his advisers and all the king's powerful officials. Because the hand of the Lord my God was on me, I took courage and gathered leading men from Israel to go up with me.

Making Requests Known
Ezra 8:21-23 (NASB)

Then I proclaimed a fast there at the river of Ahava, that we might humble ourselves before our God to seek from Him a safe journey for us, our little ones, and all our possessions. For I was ashamed to request from the king troops and horsemen to protect us from the enemy on the way, because we had said to the king, "The hand of our God is favorably disposed to all those who seek Him, but His power and His anger are against all those who forsake Him." So we fasted and sought our God concerning this matter, and He listened to our entreaty.

Confessing Sin
Ezra 9:5-10:1 (NRSV)

At the evening sacrifice I got up from my fasting, with my garments and my mantle torn, and fell on my knees, spread out my hands to the Lord my God, and said,

"O my God, I am too ashamed and embarrassed to lift my face to you, my God, for our iniquities have risen higher than our heads, and our guilt has mounted up to the heavens. From the days of our ancestors to this day we have been deep in guilt, and for our iniquities we, our kings, and our priests have been handed over to the kings of the lands, to the sword, to captivity, to plundering, and to utter shame, as is now the case. But now for a brief moment favor has been shown by the Lord our God, who has left us a remnant, and given us a stake in his holy place, in order that he may brighten our eyes and grant us a little sustenance in our slavery. For we are slaves; yet our God has not forsaken us in our slavery, but has extended to us his steadfast love before the kings of Persia, to give us new life to set up the house of our God, to repair its ruins, and to give us a wall in Judea and Jerusalem.

"And now, our God, what shall we say after this? For we have forsaken your commandments, which you commanded by your servants the prophets, saying, 'The land that you are entering to possess is a land unclean with the pollutions of the peoples of the lands, with their abominations. They have filled it from end to end with their uncleanness. Therefore do not give your daughters to their sons, neither take their daughters for your sons, and never seek their peace or prosperity, so that you may be strong and eat the good of the land and leave it for an inheritance to your children forever.' After all that has come upon us for our evil deeds and for our great guilt, seeing that you, our God, have punished us less than our iniquities deserved and have given us such a remnant as this, shall we break your commandments again and intermarry with the peoples who practice these abominations? Would you not be angry with us until you destroy us without remnant or survivor? O Lord, God of Israel, you are just, but we have escaped as a remnant, as is now the case. Here we are before you in our guilt, though no one can face you because of this."

While Ezra prayed and made confession, weeping and throwing himself down before the house of God, a very great assembly of men, women, and children gathered to him out of Israel; the people also wept bitterly.

Confessing Sin/Making Requests Known
Neh. 1:4-11 (NAB)

When I heard this report, I began to weep and continued mourning for several days; I fasted and prayed before the God of heaven.

I prayed: "O LORD, God of heaven, great and awesome God, you who preserve your covenant of mercy toward those who love you and keep your commandments, may your ear be attentive, and your eyes open, to heed the prayer which I, your servant, now offer in your presence day and night for your servants the Israelites, confessing the sins which we of Israel have committed against you, I and my father's house included. Grievously have we offended you, not keeping the commandments, the statutes, and the ordinances which you committed to your servant Moses. But remember, I pray, the promise which you gave through Moses, your servant, when you said: 'Should you prove faithless, I will scatter you among the nations; but should you return to me and carefully keep my commandments, even though your outcasts have been driven to the farthest corner of the world, I will gather them from there, and bring them back to the place which I have chosen as the dwelling place for my name.' They are your servants, your people, whom you freed by your great might and your strong hand. O Lord, may your ear be attentive to my prayer and that of all your willing servants who revere your name. Grant success to your servant this day, and let him find favor with this man"-for I was cupbearer to the king.

Making Requests Known
Neh. 2:4 (NJB)
The king then said to me, 'What would you like me to do?' Praying to the God of heaven,

Making Requests Known
Neh. 4:4-5 (NLT)
Then I prayed, "Hear us, O our God, for we are being mocked. May their scoffing fall back on their own heads, and may they themselves become captives in a foreign land! Do not ignore their guilt. Do not blot out their sins, for they have provoked you to anger here in the presence of the builders."

Making Requests Known
Neh. 4:9 (GWT)
But we prayed to our God and set guards to protect us day and night.

Praising God
Neh. 5:13 (TEV)
Then I took off the sash I was wearing around my waist and shook it out. "This is how God will shake any of you who don't keep your

promise," I said. "God will take away your houses and everything you own, and will leave you with nothing."

Everyone who was present said, "Amen!" and praised the Lord. And the leaders kept their promise.

Making Requests Known
Neh. 5:19 (CEV)
I pray that God will bless me for everything I have done for my people.

Making Requests Known
Neh. 6:9 (ESV)
For they all wanted to frighten us, thinking, "Their hands will drop from the work, and it will not be done." But now, O God, strengthen my hands.

Making Requests Known
Neh. 6:14 (NIV)
Remember Tobiah and Sanballat, O my God, because of what they have done; remember also the prophetess Noadiah and the rest of the prophets who have been trying to intimidate me.

Praising God
Neh. 8:6 (NASB)
Then Ezra blessed the Lord the great God. And all the people answered, "Amen, Amen!" while lifting up their hands; then they bowed low and worshiped the Lord with their faces to the ground.

Confessing Sin/Praising God
Neh. 9:2-3 (NRSV)
Then those of Israelite descent separated themselves from all foreigners, and stood and confessed their sins and the iniquities of their ancestors. They stood up in their place and read from the book of the law of the Lord their God for a fourth part of the day, and for another fourth they made confession and worshiped the Lord their God.

Praising God
Neh. 9:5-37 (NAB)
The Levites Jeshua, Kadmiel, Bani, Hashabneiah, Sherebiah, Hodiah, Shebaniah, and Pethahiah said,
"Arise, bless the LORD, your God,
from eternity to eternity!"

The Israelites answered with the blessing,
"Blessed is your glorious name,
and exalted above all blessing and praise."
Then Ezra said: "It is you, O LORD, you are the only one; you made the heavens, the highest heavens and all their host, the earth and all that is upon it, the seas and all that is in them. To all of them you give life, and the heavenly hosts bow down before you.

"You, O LORD, are the God who chose Abram, who brought him out from Ur of the Chaldees, and named him Abraham. When you had found his heart faithful in your sight, you made the covenant with him to give to him and his posterity the land of the Canaanites, Hittites, Amorites, Perizzites, Jebusites, and Girgashites. These promises of yours you fulfilled, for you are just.

"You saw the affliction of our fathers in Egypt,
you heard their cry by the Red Sea;
You worked signs and wonders against Pharaoh,
against all his servants and the people of his land,
Because you knew of their insolence toward them;
thus you made for yourself a name even to this day.
The sea you divided before them,
on dry ground they passed through the midst of the sea;
Their pursuers you hurled into the depths,
like a stone into the mighty waters.
With a column of cloud you led them by day,
and by night with a column of fire,
To light the way of their journey,
the way in which they must travel.
On Mount Sinai you came down,
you spoke with them from heaven;
You gave them just ordinances, firm laws,
good statutes, and commandments;
Your holy sabbath you made known to them,
commandments, statutes, and law you prescribed for them,
by the hand of Moses your servant.
Food from heaven you gave them in their hunger,
water from a rock you sent them in their thirst.
You bade them enter and occupy the land
which you had sworn with upraised hand to give them.

"But they, our fathers, proved to be insolent; they held their necks stiff and would not obey your commandments. They refused to obey and no longer remembered the miracles you had worked for them. They stiffened their necks and turned their heads to return to their slavery in Egypt. But you are a God of pardons, gracious and compassionate, slow to anger and rich in mercy; you did not forsake them. Though they made for themselves a molten calf, and proclaimed, 'Here is your God who brought you up out of Egypt,' and were guilty of great effronteries, yet in your great mercy you did not forsake them in the desert. The column of cloud did not cease to lead them by day on their journey, nor did the column of fire by night cease to light for them the way by which they were to travel.

"Your good spirit you bestowed on them, to give them understanding; your manna you did not withhold from their mouths, and you gave them water in their thirst. Forty years in the desert you sustained them: they did not want; their garments did not become worn, and their feet did not become swollen. You gave them kingdoms and peoples, which you divided up among them as border lands. They possessed the land of Sihon, king of Heshbon, and the land of Og, king of Bashan.

"You made their children as numerous as the stars of the heavens, and you brought them into the land which you had commanded their fathers to enter and possess. The sons went in to take possession of the land, and you humbled before them the Canaanite inhabitants of the land and delivered them over into their power, their kings as well as the peoples of the land, to do with them as they would. They captured fortified cities and fertile land; they took possession of houses filled with all good things, cisterns already dug, vineyards, olive groves, and fruit trees in abundance. They could eat and have their fill, fatten and feast themselves on your immense good gifts.

"But they were contemptuous and rebellious: they cast your law behind their backs, they slew your prophets who bore witness against them in order to bring them back to you, and they were guilty of great effronteries. Therefore you delivered them into the power of their enemies, who oppressed them. But in the time of their oppression they would cry out to you, and you would hear them from heaven, and according to your great mercy give them saviors to deliver them from the power of their enemies.

"As soon as they had relief, they would go back to doing evil in your sight. Then again you abandoned them to the power of their enemies, who crushed them. Then they cried out to you, and you heard them from heaven and delivered them according to your mercy, many times over. You bore witness against them, in order to bring them back to your law. But they were insolent and would not obey your commandments; they sinned against your ordinances, from which men draw life when they practice them. They turned stubborn backs, stiffened their necks, and would not obey. You were patient with them for many years, bearing witness against them through your spirit, by means of your prophets; still they would not listen. Thus you delivered them over into the power of the peoples of the lands. Yet in your great mercy you did not completely destroy them and you did not forsake them, for you are a kind and merciful God.

"Now, therefore, O our God, great, mighty, and awesome God, you who in your mercy preserve the covenant, take into account all the disasters that have befallen us, our kings, our princes, our priests, our prophets, our fathers, and your entire people, from the time of the kings of Assyria until this day! In all that has come upon us you have been just, for you kept faith while we have done evil. Yes, our kings, our princes, our priests, and our fathers have not kept your law; they paid no attention to your commandments and the obligations of which you reminded them. While they were yet in their kingdom, in the midst of the many good things that you had given them and in the wide and fertile land that you had spread out before them, they did not serve you nor did they turn away from their evil deeds. But, see, we today are slaves; and as for the land which you gave our fathers that they might eat its fruits and good things--see, we have become slaves upon it! Its rich produce goes to the kings whom you set over us because of our sins, who rule over our bodies and our cattle as they please. We are in great distress!"

Thanksgiving & Gratitude
Neh. 11:17 (NJB)

Mattaniah son of Mica, son of Zabdi, son of Asaph, who led the praises and intoned the thanksgiving associated with the prayer, Bakbukiah being his junior colleague; and Obadiah son of Shammua, son of Galal, son of Jeduthun.

Thanksgiving & Gratitude
Neh. 12:31 (NLT)

I led the leaders of Judah to the top of the wall and organized two large choirs to give thanks. One of the choirs proceeded southward along the top of the wall to the Dung Gate.

Thanksgiving & Gratitude
Neh. 12:40 (GWT)

So both choirs stood in God's temple, as did I and the half of the leaders who were with me.

Making Requests Known
Neh. 13:14 (TEV)

Remember, my God, all these things that I have done for your Temple and its worship.

Making Requests Known
Neh. 13:29 (CEV)
I pray that God will punish them for breaking their priestly vows and disgracing the Levi tribe.

Making Requests Known
Neh. 13:31 (ESV)
And I provided for the wood offering at appointed times, and for the firstfruits.
Remember me, O my God, for good.

Praying for Others
Esther 4:14 (NIV)
For if you remain silent at this time, relief and deliverance for the Jews will arise from another place, but you and your father's family will perish. And who knows but that you have come to royal position for such a time as this?"

Praising God
Job 1:20-22 (NASB)
Then Job arose and tore his robe and shaved his head, and he fell to the ground and worshiped. He said,
> "Naked I came from my mother's womb,
> And naked I shall return there.
> The Lord gave and the Lord has taken away.
> Blessed be the name of the Lord."

Through all this Job did not sin nor did he blame God.

Making Requests Known
Job 7:7 (NRSV)
"Remember that my life is a breath;
 my eye will never again see good.

Seeking God's Will/Making Requests Known
Job 7:17-21 (NAB)
What is man, that you make much of him,
 or pay him any heed?
You observe him with each new day
 and try him at every moment!

How long will it be before you look away from me,
    and let me alone long enough to swallow my spittle?
Though I have sinned, what can I do to you,
    O watcher of men?
Why do you not pardon my offense,
    or take away my guilt?
For soon I shall lie down in the dust;
    and should you seek me I shall then be gone.

Seeking God's Will /Making Requests Known
Job 10:1-22 (NJB)

Since I have lost all taste for life,
    I shall give free rein to my complaining;
    I shall let my embittered soul speak out.
I shall say to God, 'Do not condemn me,
    tell me what your case is against me.
Is it right for you to attack me,
    in contempt for what you yourself have made,
    thus abetting the schemes of the wicked?
Are your eyes mere human eyes,
    do you see as human beings see?
Are you mortal like human beings?
    do your years pass as human days pass?
You, who enquire into my faults
    and investigate my sins,
you know very well that I am innocent,
    and that no one can rescue me from your grasp.
Your hands having shaped and created me,
    now you change your mind and mean to destroy me!
Having made me, remember, as though of clay,
    now you mean to turn me back into dust!
Did you not pour me out like milk,
    and then let me thicken like curds,
clothe me with skin and flesh,
    and weave me of bone and sinew?
In your love you gave me life,
    and in your care watched over my every breath.
Yet, all the while, you had a secret plan:
    I know that you were biding your time
to see if I should sin
    and then not acquit me of my faults.
Woe to me, if I am guilty;
    even if I am upright, I dare not lift my head,

so overwhelmed with shame and drunk with pain am I!
Proud as a lion, you hunt me down,
    multiplying your exploits at my expense,
attacking me again and again,
    your fury against me ever increasing,
    your troops assailing me, wave after wave.

Why did you bring me out of the womb?
    I should have perished then, unseen by any eye,
a being that had never been,
    to be carried from womb to grave.
The days of my life are few enough:
    turn your eyes away, leave me a little joy,
before I go to the place of no return,
    to the land of darkness and shadow dark as death,
where dimness and disorder hold sway,
    and light itself is like dead of night.

Making Requests Known
Job 12:4 (NLT)

Yet my friends laugh at me. I am a man who calls on God and receives an answer. I am a just and blameless man, yet they laugh at me.

Making Requests Known
Job 13:20-14:22 (GWT)

    "Please don't do two things to me
        so that I won't have to hide from you:
            Stop oppressing me.
            Don't let your terror frighten me.
        Then call, and I'll answer.
            Otherwise, I'll speak, and you'll answer me.
    How many crimes and sins have I committed?
        Make me aware of my disobedience and my sin.
    Why do you hide your face {from me} and consider me your enemy?
    Are you trying to make a fluttering leaf tremble
        or trying to chase dry husks?
            You write down bitter accusations against me.
            You make me suffer for the sins of my youth.
            You put my feet in shackles.
            You follow my trail by engraving marks on the soles of my feet.

I am like worn-out wineskins,
> like moth-eaten clothes.

"A person who is born of a woman is short-lived
> and is full of trouble.
>> He comes up like a flower; then he withers.
>> He is like a fleeting shadow; he doesn't stay long.
You observe this
> and call me to account to you.

"If only an unclean person could become clean!
> It's not possible.
If the number of his days
> and the number of his months are determined by you,
> and you set his limit,
then he cannot go past it.
Look away from him, and he will cease to be.
> Meanwhile, he loves life as a laborer loves work.
There is hope for a tree when it is cut down.
> It will sprout again.
> Its shoots will not stop sprouting.
If its roots grow old in the ground
> and its stump dies in the soil,
>> merely a scent of water will make it sprout
>> and grow branches like a plant.
But a human dies and is powerless.
A person breathes his last breath, and where is he?
> {As} water drains out of a lake,
>> or {as} a river dries up completely,
>>> so each person lies down
>>>> and does not rise until the heavens cease to exist.
>>> He does not wake up.
>>> He is not awakened from his sleep.
I wish you would hide me in Sheol
> and keep me hidden there until your anger cools.
>> Set a specific time for me when you will remember me.

"If a person dies, will he go on living?
I will wait for my relief to come
> as long as my hard labor continues.
You will call, and I will answer you.
You will long for the person your hands have made.
Though now you count my steps,

you will not keep {a record of} my sins.
My disobedience will be closed up in a bag,
   and you will cover over my sins.
As surely as a mountain falls
   and rocks are dislodged,
{so} water wears away stone,
   floods wash away soil from the land,
      and you destroy a mortal's hope.
You overpower him forever, and he passes away.
You change his appearance and send him away.
      His sons are honored, and he doesn't know it.
         Or they become unimportant, and he doesn't realize it.
         He feels only his body's pain.
         He is only worried about himself."

Responding to God
Job 16:7-8 (TEV)
You have worn me out, God;
   you have let my family be killed.
   You have seized me; you are my enemy.
I am skin and bones,
   and people take that as proof of my guilt.

Making Requests Known
Job 17:3-5 (CEV)
If you, Lord, don't help,
who will pay the price for my release?
My friends won't really listen, all because of you,
and so you must be the one to prove them wrong.
They have condemned me,
just to benefit themselves; now blind their children.

Making Requests Known
Job 22:17 (ESV)
They said to God, 'Depart from us,'
   and 'What can the Almighty do to us?'

Making Requests Known
Job 22:27 (NIV)
> You will pray to him, and he will hear you,
> and you will fulfill your vows.

Making Requests Known
Job 23:3-5 (NASB)
> "Oh that I knew where I might find Him,
> That I might come to His seat!
> "I would present my case before Him
> And fill my mouth with arguments.
> "I would learn the words which He would answer,
> And perceive what He would say to me.

Making Requests Known
Job 30:20 (NRSV)
> I cry to you and you do not answer me;
> I stand, and you merely look at me.

Responding to God
Job 40:3-5 (NAB)
> Then Job answered the LORD and said:
> Behold, I am of little account; what can I answer you?
> I put my hand over my mouth.
> Though I have spoken once, I will not do so again;
> though twice, I will do so no more.

Praising God/Praying for Others
Job 42:1-10 (NJB)
> This was the answer Job gave to Yahweh:
>
> I know that you are all-powerful:
> what you conceive, you can perform.
> I was the man who misrepresented your intentions
> with my ignorant words.
> You have told me about great works that I cannot understand,
> about marvels which are beyond me, of which I know nothing.
> (Listen, please, and let me speak:
> I am going to ask the questions, and you are to inform me.)
> Before, I knew you only by hearsay
> but now, having seen you with my own eyes,

I retract what I have said,
    and repent in dust and ashes.

When Yahweh had finished saying this to Job, he said to Eliphaz of Teman, 'I burn with anger against you and your two friends, for not having spoken correctly about me as my servant Job has done. So now find seven bullocks and seven rams, and take them back with you to my servant Job and make a burnt offering for yourselves, while Job, my servant, offers prayers for you. I shall show him favour and shall not inflict my displeasure on you for not having spoken about me correctly, as my servant Job has done.' Eliphaz of Teman, Bildad of Shuah and Zophar of Naamath went away to do as Yahweh had ordered, and Yahweh listened to Job with favour.

And Yahweh restored Job's condition, while Job was interceding for his friends. More than that, Yahweh gave him double what he had before.

Making Requests Known
Psalm 3:1-8 (NLT)

    O Lord, I have so many enemies;
        so many are against me.
    So many are saying,
        "God will never rescue him!"
Interlude

    But you, O Lord, are a shield around me,
        my glory, and the one who lifts my head high.
    I cried out to the Lord,
        and he answered me from his holy mountain.
        Interlude

    I lay down and slept.
        I woke up in safety,
        for the Lord was watching over me.
    I am not afraid of ten thousand enemies
        who surround me on every side.

    Arise, O Lord!
        Rescue me, my God!
    Slap all my enemies in the face!
        Shatter the teeth of the wicked!

    Victory comes from you, O Lord.

May your blessings rest on your people.
Interlude

Making Requests Known
Psalm 4:1-8 (GWT)
Answer me when I call, O God of my righteousness.
>You have freed me from my troubles.
Have pity on me, and hear my prayer!

>You important people,
>>how long are you going to insult my honor?
>>How long are you going to love what is empty
>>>and seek what is a lie?
>>Selah
>>Know that the Lord singles out godly people for himself.
>>>The Lord hears me when I call to him.
>>Tremble and do not sin.
>>Think about this on your bed and remain quiet.
>>Selah
>>Offer the sacrifices of righteousness
>>>by trusting the Lord.

Many are saying, "Who can show us anything good?"
>Let the light of your presence shine on us, O Lord.
>>You put more joy in my heart
>>>than when their grain and new wine increase.
I fall asleep in peace the moment I lie down
>because you alone, O Lord, enable me to live securely.

Making Requests Known
Psalm 5:1-12 (TEV)
>Listen to my words, O Lord,
>>and hear my sighs.
>Listen to my cry for help,
>>my God and king!
>I pray to you, O Lord;
>>you hear my voice in the morning;
>at sunrise I offer my prayer
>>and wait for your answer.

You are not a God who is pleased with wrongdoing;
>   you allow no evil in your presence.
You cannot stand the sight of the proud;
>   you hate all wicked people.
You destroy all liars
>   and despise violent, deceitful people.

But because of your great love
>   I can come into your house;
I can worship in your holy Temple
>   and bow down to you in reverence.
Lord, I have so many enemies!
>   Lead me to do your will;
>   make your way plain for me to follow.

What my enemies say can never be trusted;
>   they only want to destroy.
Their words are flattering and smooth,
>   but full of deadly deceit.
Condemn and punish them, O God;
>   may their own plots cause their ruin.
Drive them out of your presence
>   because of their many sins
>   and their rebellion against you.

But all who find safety in you will rejoice;
>   they can always sing for joy.
Protect those who love you;
>   because of you they are truly happy.
You bless those who obey you, Lord;
>   your love protects them like a shield.

Making Requests Known
Psalm 6:1-10 (CEV)
Don't punish me, Lord,
or even correct me when you are angry!
Have pity on me and heal my feeble body.
My bones tremble with fear,
and I am in deep distress. How long will it be?

Turn and come to my rescue.
Show your wonderful love and save me, Lord.

If I die, I cannot praise you or even remember you.
My groaning has worn me out.
At night my bed and pillow are soaked with tears.
Sorrow has made my eyes dim,
and my sight has failed because of my enemies.

You, Lord, heard my crying,
and those hateful people had better leave me alone.
You have answered my prayer and my plea for mercy.
My enemies will be ashamed and terrified,
as they quickly run away in complete disgrace.

Making Requests Known
Psalm 7:1-17 (ESV)

O Lord my God, in you do I take refuge;
    save me from all my pursuers and deliver me,
  lest like a lion they tear my soul apart,
    rending it in pieces, with none to deliver.
O Lord my God, if I have done this,
    if there is wrong in my hands,
if I have repaid my friend with evil
    or plundered my enemy without cause,
let the enemy pursue my soul and overtake it,
    and let him trample my life to the ground
    and lay my glory in the dust.
  Selah

Arise, O Lord, in your anger;
    lift yourself up against the fury of my enemies;
    awake for me; you have appointed a judgment.
Let the assembly of the peoples be gathered about you;
    over it return on high.
The Lord judges the peoples;
    judge me, O Lord, according to my righteousness
    and according to the integrity that is in me.
Oh, let the evil of the wicked come to an end,
    and may you establish the righteous—
you who test the minds and hearts,
    O righteous God!
My shield is with God,
    who saves the upright in heart.
God is a righteous judge,

and a God who feels indignation every day.
If a man does not repent, God will whet his sword;
    he has bent and readied his bow;
he has prepared for him his deadly weapons,
    making his arrows fiery shafts.
Behold, the wicked man conceives evil
    and is pregnant with mischief
    and gives birth to lies.
He makes a pit, digging it out,
    and falls into the hole that he has made.
His mischief returns upon his own head,
    and on his own skull his violence descends.
I will give to the Lord the thanks due to his righteousness,
    and I will sing praise to the name of the Lord, the Most High.

Praising God
Psalm 8:1-9 (NIV)
O Lord, our Lord,
    how majestic is your name in all the earth!
You have set your glory
    above the heavens.
From the lips of children and infants
    you have ordained praise
because of your enemies,
    to silence the foe and the avenger.

When I consider your heavens,
    the work of your fingers,
the moon and the stars,
    which you have set in place,
what is man that you are mindful of him,
    the son of man that you care for him?
You made him a little lower than the heavenly beings
    and crowned him with glory and honor.

You made him ruler over the works of your hands;
    you put everything under his feet:
all flocks and herds,
    and the beasts of the field,
the birds of the air,
    and the fish of the sea,
    all that swim the paths of the seas.

O Lord, our Lord,
>how majestic is your name in all the earth!

Praising God
Psalm 9:1-20 (NASB)

I will give thanks to the Lord with all my heart;
I will tell of all Your wonders.
I will be glad and exult in You;
I will sing praise to Your name, O Most High.

When my enemies turn back,
They stumble and perish before You.
For You have maintained my just cause;
You have sat on the throne judging righteously.
You have rebuked the nations, You have destroyed the wicked;
You have blotted out their name forever and ever.
The enemy has come to an end in perpetual ruins,
And You have uprooted the cities;
The very memory of them has perished.

But the Lord abides forever;
He has established His throne for judgment,
And He will judge the world in righteousness;
He will execute judgment for the peoples with equity.
The Lord also will be a stronghold for the oppressed,
A stronghold in times of trouble;
And those who know Your name will put their trust in You,
For You, O Lord, have not forsaken those who seek You.

Sing praises to the Lord, who dwells in Zion;
Declare among the peoples His deeds.
For He who requires blood remembers them;
He does not forget the cry of the afflicted.
Be gracious to me, O Lord;
See my affliction from those who hate me,
You who lift me up from the gates of death,
That I may tell of all Your praises,
That in the gates of the daughter of Zion
I may rejoice in Your salvation.
The nations have sunk down in the pit which they have made;
In the net which they hid, their own foot has been caught.

The Lord has made Himself known;
He has executed judgment.
In the work of his own hands the wicked is snared.
Higgaion Selah.

The wicked will return to Sheol,
Even all the nations who forget God.
For the needy will not always be forgotten,
Nor the hope of the afflicted perish forever.
Arise, O Lord, do not let man prevail;
Let the nations be judged before You.
Put them in fear, O Lord;
Let the nations know that they are but men.
Selah.

Seeking God's Will/Praying for Others
Psalm 10:1-18 (NRSV)

Why, O Lord, do you stand far off?
   Why do you hide yourself in times of trouble?
In arrogance the wicked persecute the poor--
   let them be caught in the schemes they have devised.

For the wicked boast of the desires of their heart,
   those greedy for gain curse and renounce the Lord.
In the pride of their countenance the wicked say, "God will
   not seek it out"; all their thoughts are, "There is no God."

Their ways prosper at all times;
   your judgments are on high, out of their sight;
   as for their foes, they scoff at them.
They think in their heart, "We shall not be moved;
   throughout all generations we shall not meet adversity."

Their mouths are filled with cursing and deceit and oppression;
   under their tongues are mischief and iniquity.
They sit in ambush in the villages;
   in hiding places they murder the innocent.
Their eyes stealthily watch for the helpless;
   they lurk in secret like a lion in its covert;
they lurk that they may seize the poor;
   they seize the poor and drag them off in their net.

They stoop, they crouch,
   and the helpless fall by their might.
They think in their heart, "God has forgotten,
   he has hidden his face, he will never see it."

Rise up, O Lord; O God, lift up your hand;
   do not forget the oppressed.
Why do the wicked renounce God,
   and say in their hearts, "You will not call us to account"?

But you do see! Indeed you note trouble and grief,
   that you may take it into your hands;
the helpless commit themselves to you;
   you have been the helper of the orphan.

Break the arm of the wicked and evildoers;
   seek out their wickedness until you find none.
The Lord is king forever and ever;
   the nations shall perish from his land.

O Lord, you will hear the desire of the meek;
   you will strengthen their heart, you will incline your ear
to do justice for the orphan and the oppressed,
   so that those from earth may strike terror no more.

Making Requests Known/Praying for Others
Psalm 12:1-8 (NAB)

Help, LORD, for no one loyal remains;
   the faithful have vanished from the human race
Those who tell lies to one another
   speak with deceiving lips and a double heart.
May the LORD cut off all deceiving lips,
   and every boastful tongue,
  Those who say, "By our tongues we prevail;
   when our lips speak, who can lord it over us?"
"Because they rob the weak, and the needy groan,
   I will now arise," says the LORD;
   "I will grant safety to whoever longs for it."
The promises of the LORD are sure,
   silver refined in a crucible,
   silver purified seven times.

LORD, protect us always;
  preserve us from this generation.
On every side the wicked strut;
  the shameless are extolled by all.

Making Requests Known
Psalm 13:1-6 (NJB)

How long, Yahweh, will you forget me? For ever?
How long will you turn away your face from me?
How long must I nurse rebellion in my soul,
sorrow in my heart day and night?
How long is the enemy to domineer over me?
Look down, answer me, Yahweh my God!
Give light to my eyes or I shall fall into the sleep of death.

Or my foe will boast, 'I have overpowered him,'
and my enemy have the joy of seeing me stumble.
  As for me, I trust in your faithful love, Yahweh.
Let my heart delight in your saving help,
  let me sing to Yahweh for his generosity to me,
let me sing to the name of Yahweh the Most High!

Seeking God's Will
Psalm 15:1-5 (NLT)

Who may worship in your sanctuary, Lord?
  Who may enter your presence on your holy hill?

Those who lead blameless lives
  and do what is right,
    speaking the truth from sincere hearts.
Those who refuse to slander others
  or harm their neighbors
  or speak evil of their friends.
Those who despise persistent sinners,
    and honor the faithful followers of the Lord
    and keep their promises even when it hurts.
Those who do not charge interest on the money they lend,
    and who refuse to accept bribes to testify against the innocent.
Such people will stand firm forever.

Making Requests Known/Praising God
Psalm 16:1-11 (GWT)

    Protect me, O God, because I take refuge in you.
        I said to the Lord,
            "You are my Lord. Without you, I have nothing good."
    Those who lead holy lives on earth
        are the noble ones who fill me with joy.
    Those who quickly chase after other gods multiply their sorrows.
        I will not pour out their sacrificial offerings of blood
            or use my lips to speak their names.

    The Lord is my inheritance and my cup.
        You are the one who determines my destiny.
        Your boundary lines mark out pleasant places for me.
    Indeed, my inheritance is something beautiful.

    I will praise the Lord, who advises me.
        My conscience warns me at night.
    I always keep the Lord in front of me.
        When he is by my side, I cannot be moved.
            That is why my heart is glad and my soul rejoices.
                My body rests securely
                      because you do not abandon my soul to the grave
                      or allow your holy one to decay.
    You make the path of life known to me.
        Complete joy is in your presence.
            Pleasures are by your side forever.

Making Requests Known
Psalm 17:1-15 (TEV)

    Listen, O Lord, to my plea for justice;
        pay attention to my cry for help!
        Listen to my honest prayer.
    You will judge in my favor,
        because you know what is right.

    You know my heart.
        You have come to me at night;
        you have examined me completely
        and found no evil desire in me.
    I speak no evil, as others do;

I have obeyed your command
and have not followed paths of violence.
I have always walked in your way
and have never strayed from it.

I pray to you, O God, because you answer me;
so turn to me and listen to my words.
Reveal your wonderful love and save me;
at your side I am safe from my enemies.

Protect me as you would your very eyes;
hide me in the shadow of your wings
from the attacks of the wicked.
Deadly enemies surround me;
they have no pity and speak proudly.
They are around me now, wherever I turn,
watching for a chance to pull me down.
They are like lions, waiting for me,
wanting to tear me to pieces.

Come, Lord! Oppose my enemies and defeat them!
Save me from the wicked by your sword;
save me from those who in this life have all they want.
Punish them with the sufferings you have stored up for them;
may there be enough for their children
and some left over for their children's children!

But I will see you, because I have done no wrong;
and when I awake, your presence will fill me with joy.

Praising God
Psalm 18:1-50 (CEV)
I love you, Lord God, and you make me strong.
You are my mighty rock, my fortress, my protector,
the rock where I am safe,
my shield, my powerful weapon, and my place of shelter.

I praise you, Lord!
I prayed, and you rescued me from my enemies.
Death had wrapped its ropes around me,
and I was almost swallowed by its flooding waters.

Every Prayer of the Bible

Ropes from the world
of the dead had coiled around me,
and death had set a trap in my path.
I was in terrible trouble when I called out to you,
but from your temple
you heard me and answered my prayer.

The earth shook and shivered,
and the mountains trembled down to their roots.
You were angry and breathed out smoke.
Scorching heat and fiery flames spewed from your mouth.

You opened the heavens like curtains,
and you came down
with storm clouds under your feet.
You rode on the backs of flying creatures
and swooped down with the wind as wings.
Darkness was your robe;
thunderclouds filled the sky, hiding you from sight.
Hailstones and fiery coals
lit up the sky in front of you.

Lord Most High, your voice thundered from the heavens,
as hailstones and fiery coals poured down like rain.
You scattered your enemies with arrows of lightning.
You roared at the sea,
and its deepest channels could be seen.
You snorted,
and the earth shook to its foundations.

You reached down from heaven,
and you lifted me from deep in the ocean.
You rescued me from enemies,
who were hateful and too powerful for me.
On the day disaster struck,
they came and attacked, but you defended me.
When I was fenced in,
you freed and rescued me because you love me.

You are good to me, Lord, because I do right,
and you reward me because I am innocent.
I do what you want and never turn to do evil.
I keep your laws in mind

and never look away from your teachings.
I obey you completely and guard against sin.
You have been good to me because I do right;
you have rewarded me
for being innocent by your standards.

You are always loyal to your loyal people,
and you are faithful to the faithful.
With all who are sincere, you are sincere,
but you treat the unfaithful as their deeds deserve.
You rescue the humble,
but you put down all who are proud.

You, the Lord God,
keep my lamp burning and turn darkness to light.
You help me defeat armies and capture cities.

Your way is perfect, Lord, and your word is correct.
You are a shield for those who run to you for help.
You alone are God! Only you are a mighty rock.
You give me strength and guide me right.
You make my feet run as fast as those of a deer,
and you help me stand on the mountains.

You teach my hands to fight
and my arms to use a bow of bronze.
You alone are my shield. Your right hand supports me,
and by coming to help me, you have made me famous.
You clear the way for me, and now I won't stumble.

I kept chasing my enemies,
until I caught them and destroyed them.
I stuck my sword through my enemies,
and they were crushed under my feet.
You helped me win victories,
and you forced my attackers to fall victim to me.

You made my enemies run, and I killed them.
They cried out for help, but no one saved them;
they called out to you, but there was no answer.
I ground them to dust blown by the wind,
and I poured them out like mud in the streets.

You rescued me from stubborn people,
and you made me the leader
of foreign nations, who are now my slaves.
They obey and come crawling. They have lost all courage,
and from their fortresses, they come trembling.

You are the living Lord! I will praise you.
You are a mighty rock.
I will honor you for keeping me safe.
You took revenge for me,
and you put nations in my power.
You protected me from violent enemies
and made me much greater than all of them.

I will praise you, Lord,
and I will honor you among the nations.
You give glorious victories to your chosen king.
Your faithful love for David
and for his descendants will never end.

Praising God/Making Requests Known
Psalm 19:1-14 (ESV)

The heavens declare the glory of God,
>   and the sky above proclaims his handiwork.
>   Day to day pours out speech,
>   and night to night reveals knowledge.
>   There is no speech, nor are there words,
>   whose voice is not heard.
>   Their measuring line goes out through all the earth,
>   and their words to the end of the world.
>   In them he has set a tent for the sun,
>   which comes out like a bridegroom leaving his chamber,
>   and, like a strong man, runs its course with joy.
>   Its rising is from the end of the heavens,
>   and its circuit to the end of them,
>   and there is nothing hidden from its heat.
>   The law of the Lord is perfect,
>   reviving the soul;
>   the testimony of the Lord is sure,
>   making wise the simple;
>   the precepts of the Lord are right,

rejoicing the heart;
the commandment of the Lord is pure,
    enlightening the eyes;
the fear of the Lord is clean,
    enduring forever;
the rules of the Lord are true,
    and righteous altogether.
More to be desired are they than gold,
    even much fine gold;
sweeter also than honey
    and drippings of the honeycomb.
Moreover, by them is your servant warned;
    in keeping them there is great reward.
Who can discern his errors?
    Declare me innocent from hidden faults.
Keep back your servant also from presumptuous sins;
    let them not have dominion over me!
Then I shall be blameless,
    and innocent of great transgression.
Let the words of my mouth and the meditation of my heart
    be acceptable in your sight,
    O Lord, my rock and my redeemer.

Praying for Others
Psalm 20:1-9 (NIV)

May the Lord answer you when you are in distress;
    may the name of the God of Jacob protect you.
May he send you help from the sanctuary
    and grant you support from Zion.
May he remember all your sacrifices
    and accept your burnt offerings.
        Selah

May he give you the desire of your heart
    and make all your plans succeed.
We will shout for joy when you are victorious
    and will lift up our banners in the name of our God.
May the Lord grant all your requests.
Now I know that the Lord saves his anointed;
    he answers him from his holy heaven
    with the saving power of his right hand.
Some trust in chariots and some in horses,

but we trust in the name of the Lord our God.
They are brought to their knees and fall,
　　　but we rise up and stand firm.
O Lord, save the king!
　　　Answer us when we call!

Praising God
Psalm 21:1-13 (NASB)

　　　O Lord, in Your strength the king will be glad,
　　　And in Your salvation how greatly he will rejoice!
　　　You have given him his heart's desire,
　　　And You have not withheld the request of his lips.
　　　Selah.
　　　For You meet him with the blessings of good things;
　　　You set a crown of fine gold on his head.
　　　He asked life of You,
　　　You gave it to him,
　　　Length of days forever and ever.
　　　His glory is great through Your salvation,
　　　Splendor and majesty You place upon him.
　　　For You make him most blessed forever;
　　　You make him joyful with gladness in Your presence.

　　　For the king trusts in the Lord,
　　　　　　And through the lovingkindness of the Most High he will not be shaken.
　　　Your hand will find out all your enemies;
　　　Your right hand will find out those who hate you.
　　　You will make them as a fiery oven in the time of your anger;
　　　The Lord will swallow them up in His wrath,
　　　And fire will devour them.
　　　Their offspring You will destroy from the earth,
　　　And their descendants from among the sons of men.
　　　Though they intended evil against You
　　　And devised a plot,
　　　They will not succeed.
　　　For You will make them turn their back;
　　　You will aim with Your bowstrings at their faces.
　　　Be exalted, O Lord, in Your strength;
　　　We will sing and praise Your power.

Making Requests Known
Psalm 22:1-31 (NRSV)

My God, my God, why have you forsaken me?
   Why are you so far from helping me, from the words of my groaning?
O my God, I cry by day, but you do not answer;
   and by night, but find no rest.

Yet you are holy,
   enthroned on the praises of Israel.
In you our ancestors trusted;
   they trusted, and you delivered them.
To you they cried, and were saved;
   in you they trusted, and were not put to shame.

But I am a worm, and not human;
   scorned by others, and despised by the people.
All who see me mock at me; they make mouths at me,
   they shake their heads;
"Commit your cause to the Lord; let him deliver--
   let him rescue the one in whom he delights!"

Yet it was you who took me from the womb;
   you kept me safe on my mother's breast.
On you I was cast from my birth,
   and since my mother bore me you have been my God.
Do not be far from me,
   for trouble is near
   and there is no one to help.

Many bulls encircle me,
   strong bulls of Bashan surround me;
they open wide their mouths at me,
   like a ravening and roaring lion.

I am poured out like water,
   and all my bones are out of joint;
my heart is like wax;
   it is melted within my breast;
my mouth is dried up like a potsherd,
   and my tongue sticks to my jaws;
   you lay me in the dust of death.

For dogs are all around me;

a company of evildoers encircles me.
My hands and feet have shriveled;
I can count all my bones.
They stare and gloat over me;
they divide my clothes among themselves,
   and for my clothing they cast lots.
But you, O Lord, do not be far away!
   O my help, come quickly to my aid!
Deliver my soul from the sword,
   my life from the power of the dog!
Save me from the mouth of the lion!
From the horns of the wild oxen you have rescued me.
I will tell of your name to my brothers and sisters;
   in the midst of the congregation I will praise you:
You who fear the Lord, praise him!
   All you offspring of Jacob, glorify him;
   stand in awe of him, all you offspring of Israel!
For he did not despise or abhor
   the affliction of the afflicted;
he did not hide his face from me,
   but heard when I cried to him.
From you comes my praise in the great congregation;
   my vows I will pay before those who fear him.
The poor shall eat and be satisfied;
   those who seek him shall praise the Lord.
   May your hearts live forever!

All the ends of the earth shall remember
   and turn to the Lord;
and all the families of the nations
   shall worship before him.
For dominion belongs to the Lord,
   and he rules over the nations.
To him, indeed, shall all who sleep in the earth bow down;
   before him shall bow all who go down to the dust,
   and I shall live for him.
Posterity will serve him;
   future generations will be told about the Lord,
and proclaim his deliverance to a people yet unborn,
   saying that he has done it.

Praising God
Psalm 23:1-6 (NAB)
The LORD is my shepherd;
    there is nothing I lack.
In green pastures you let me graze;
    to safe waters you lead me;
    you restore my strength.
You guide me along the right path
    for the sake of your name.
Even when I walk through a dark valley,
    I fear no harm for you are at my side;
    your rod and staff give me courage.
You set a table before me
    as my enemies watch;
You anoint my head with oil;
    my cup overflows.
Only goodness and love will pursue me
    all the days of my life;
I will dwell in the house of the LORD
    for years to come.

Praising God
Psalm 24:1-10 (NJB)
To Yahweh belong the earth and all it contains,
the world and all who live there;
it is he who laid its foundations on the seas,
on the flowing waters fixed it firm.

Who shall go up to the mountain of Yahweh?
Who shall take a stand in his holy place?

The clean of hands and pure of heart,
whose heart is not set on vanities,
who does not swear an oath in order to deceive.

Such a one will receive blessing from Yahweh,
saving justice from the God of his salvation.
Such is the people that seeks him,
that seeks your presence, God of Jacob.
    Pause

Gates, lift high your heads,
raise high the ancient gateways,
and the king of glory shall enter!

Who is he, this king of glory?
It is Yahweh, strong and valiant,
Yahweh valiant in battle.

Gates, lift high your heads,
raise high the ancient gateways,
and the king of glory shall enter!

Who is he, this king of glory?
Yahweh Sabaoth,
he is the king of glory.
    Pause

Making Requests Known/Confessing Sin
Psalm 25:1-22 (NLT)

To you, O Lord, I lift up my soul.
    I trust in you, my God!
Do not let me be disgraced,
    or let my enemies rejoice in my defeat.
No one who trusts in you will ever be disgraced,
    but disgrace comes to those who try to deceive others.

Show me the path where I should walk, O Lord;
    point out the right road for me to follow.
Lead me by your truth and teach me,
    for you are the God who saves me.
    All day long I put my hope in you.

Remember, O Lord, your unfailing love and compassion,
    which you have shown from long ages past.
Forgive the rebellious sins of my youth;
    look instead through the eyes of your unfailing love,
    for you are merciful, O Lord.

The Lord is good and does what is right;
    he shows the proper path to those who go astray.

He leads the humble in what is right,
    teaching them his way.
The Lord leads with unfailing love and faithfulness
    all those who keep his covenant and obey his decrees.

For the honor of your name, O Lord,
    forgive my many, many sins.
Who are those who fear the Lord?
    He will show them the path they should choose.
They will live in prosperity,
    and their children will inherit the Promised Land.
Friendship with the Lord is reserved for those who fear him.
    With them he shares the secrets of his covenant.
My eyes are always looking to the Lord for help,
    for he alone can rescue me from the traps of my enemies.

Turn to me and have mercy on me,
    for I am alone and in deep distress.
My problems go from bad to worse.
    Oh, save me from them all!
Feel my pain and see my trouble.
    Forgive all my sins.
See how many enemies I have,
    and how viciously they hate me!
Protect me! Rescue my life from them!
    Do not let me be disgraced, for I trust in you.
May integrity and honesty protect me,
    for I put my hope in you.

O God, ransom Israel
    from all its troubles.

Making Requests Known
Psalm 26:1-12 (GWT)

Judge me favorably, O Lord,
    because I have walked with integrity
        and I have trusted you without wavering.
Examine me, O Lord, and test me.
Look closely into my heart and mind.
    I see your mercy in front of me.
    I walk in the light of your truth.
    I did not sit with liars,

        and I will not be found among hypocrites.
I have hated the mob of evildoers
        and will not sit with wicked people.
I will wash my hands in innocence.
I will walk around your altar, O Lord,
        so that I may loudly sing a hymn of thanksgiving
        and tell about all your miracles.

O Lord, I love the house where you live,
    the place where your glory dwells.

Do not sweep away my soul along with hardened sinners
    or my life along with bloodthirsty people.
        Evil schemes are in their hands.
        Their right hands are full of bribes.
But I walk with integrity.
    Rescue me, and have pity on me.
My feet stand on level ground.
I will praise the Lord with the choirs in worship.

Making Requests Known
Psalm 27:1-14 (TEV)
The Lord is my light and my salvation;
    I will fear no one.
The Lord protects me from all danger;
    I will never be afraid.

When evil people attack me and try to kill me,
    they stumble and fall.
Even if a whole army surrounds me,
    I will not be afraid;
even if enemies attack me,
    I will still trust God.

I have asked the Lord for one thing;
    one thing only do I want:
to live in the Lord's house all my life,
    to marvel there at his goodness,
    and to ask for his guidance.
In times of trouble he will shelter me;
    he will keep me safe in his Temple
    and make me secure on a high rock.

So I will triumph over my enemies around me.
> With shouts of joy I will offer sacrifices in his Temple;
I will sing, I will praise the Lord.

Hear me, Lord, when I call to you!
> Be merciful and answer me!
When you said, "Come worship me,"
I answered, "I will come, Lord."
> Don't hide yourself from me!
Don't be angry with me;
> don't turn your servant away.
You have been my help;
> don't leave me, don't abandon me,
> O God, my savior.
My father and mother may abandon me,
> but the Lord will take care of me.

Teach me, Lord, what you want me to do,
> and lead me along a safe path,
> because I have many enemies.
Don't abandon me to my enemies,
> who attack me with lies and threats.

I know that I will live to see
> the Lord's goodness in this present life.
Trust in the Lord.
> Have faith, do not despair.
Trust in the Lord.

Making Requests Known
Psalm 28:1-9 (CEV)

Only you, Lord, are a mighty rock!
Don't refuse to help me when I pray.
If you don't answer me, I will soon be dead.
Please listen to my prayer and my cry for help,
as I lift my hands toward your holy temple.

Don't drag me away, Lord, with those cruel people,
who speak kind words, while planning trouble.
Treat them as they deserve! Punish them for their sins.
They don't pay any attention to your wonderful deeds.
Now you will destroy them and leave them in ruin.

I praise you, Lord, for answering my prayers.
You are my strong shield, and I trust you completely.
You have helped me,
and I will celebrate and thank you in song.

You give strength to your people, Lord,
and you save and protect your chosen ones.
Come save us and bless us.
Be our shepherd and always carry us in your arms.

Thanksgiving & Gratitude
Psalm 30:1-12 (ESV)

I will extol you, O Lord, for you have drawn me up
    and have not let my foes rejoice over me.
O Lord my God, I cried to you for help,
    and you have healed me.
O Lord, you have brought up my soul from Sheol;
    you restored me to life from among those who go down to the pit.
    Sing praises to the Lord, O you his saints,
and give thanks to his holy name.
    For his anger is but for a moment,
and his favor is for a lifetime.
    Weeping may tarry for the night,
but joy comes with the morning.
    As for me, I said in my prosperity,
"I shall never be moved."
    By your favor, O Lord,
you made my mountain stand strong;
    you hid your face;
I was dismayed.
To you, O Lord, I cry,
    and to the Lord I plead for mercy:
"What profit is there in my death,
    if I go down to the pit?
Will the dust praise you?
    Will it tell of your faithfulness?
Hear, O Lord, and be merciful to me!
    O Lord, be my helper!"
You have turned for me my mourning into dancing;
    you have loosed my sackcloth
    and clothed me with gladness,

that my glory may sing your praise and not be silent.
O Lord my God, I will give thanks to you forever!

Making Requests Known
Psalm 31:1-24 (NIV)

In you, O Lord, I have taken refuge;
  let me never be put to shame;
  deliver me in your righteousness.
Turn your ear to me,
  come quickly to my rescue;
be my rock of refuge,
  a strong fortress to save me.
Since you are my rock and my fortress,
  for the sake of your name lead and guide me.
Free me from the trap that is set for me,
  for you are my refuge.
Into your hands I commit my spirit;
  redeem me, O Lord, the God of truth.

I hate those who cling to worthless idols;
  I trust in the Lord.
I will be glad and rejoice in your love,
  for you saw my affliction
  and knew the anguish of my soul.
You have not handed me over to the enemy
  but have set my feet in a spacious place.

Be merciful to me, O Lord, for I am in distress;
  my eyes grow weak with sorrow,
  my soul and my body with grief.
My life is consumed by anguish
  and my years by groaning;
my strength fails because of my affliction,
  and my bones grow weak.
Because of all my enemies,
  I am the utter contempt of my neighbors;
I am a dread to my friends--
  those who see me on the street flee from me.
I am forgotten by them as though I were dead;
  I have become like broken pottery.
For I hear the slander of many;
  there is terror on every side;

they conspire against me
  and plot to take my life.

But I trust in you, O Lord;
  I say, "You are my God."
My times are in your hands;
  deliver me from my enemies
  and from those who pursue me.
Let your face shine on your servant;
  save me in your unfailing love.
Let me not be put to shame, O Lord,
  for I have cried out to you;
but let the wicked be put to shame
  and lie silent in the grave.
Let their lying lips be silenced,
  for with pride and contempt
  they speak arrogantly against the righteous.

How great is your goodness,
  which you have stored up for those who fear you,
which you bestow in the sight of men
  on those who take refuge in you.
In the shelter of your presence you hide them
  from the intrigues of men;
in your dwelling you keep them safe
  from accusing tongues.

Praise be to the Lord,
  for he showed his wonderful love to me
  when I was in a besieged city.
In my alarm I said,
  "I am cut off from your sight!"
Yet you heard my cry for mercy
  when I called to you for help.

Love the Lord, all his saints!
  The Lord preserves the faithful,
  but the proud he pays back in full.
Be strong and take heart,
  all you who hope in the Lord.

Praising God
Psalm 32:1-11 (NASB)
How blessed is he whose transgression is forgiven,
Whose sin is covered!
How blessed is the man to whom the Lord does not
 impute iniquity,
And in whose spirit there is no deceit!

When I kept silent about my sin, my body wasted away
Through my groaning all day long.
For day and night Your hand was heavy upon me;
My vitality was drained away as with the fever heat of summer.
Selah.
I acknowledged my sin to You,
And my iniquity I did not hide;
I said, "I will confess my transgressions to the Lord";
And You forgave the guilt of my sin.
Selah.
Therefore, let everyone who is godly pray to You in a time
 when You may be found;
Surely in a flood of great waters they will not reach him.
You are my hiding place; You preserve me from trouble;
You surround me with songs of deliverance.
Selah.

I will instruct you and teach you in the way which you should go;
I will counsel you with My eye upon you.
Do not be as the horse or as the mule which have
 no understanding,
Whose trappings include bit and bridle to hold them in check,
Otherwise they will not come near to you.
Many are the sorrows of the wicked,
But he who trusts in the Lord, lovingkindness shall surround him.
Be glad in the Lord and rejoice, you righteous ones;
And shout for joy, all you who are upright in heart.

Praising God
Psalm 33:22 (NLT)
Let your unfailing love surround us, Lord,
 for our hope is in you alone.

Making Requests Known
Psalm 34:1-22 (TLB)

I will praise the Lord no matter what happens. I will constantly speak of his glories and grace. I will boast of all his kindness to me. Let all who are discouraged take heart. Let us praise the Lord together and exalt his name.

For I cried to him and he answered me! He freed me from all my fears. Others too were radiant at what he did for them. Theirs was no downcast look of rejection! This poor man cried to the Lord--and the Lord heard him and saved him out of his troubles. For the Angel of the Lord guards and rescues all who reverence him.

Oh, put God to the test and see how kind he is! See for yourself the way his mercies shower down on all who trust in him. If you belong to the Lord, reverence him; for everyone who does this has everything he needs. Even strong young lions sometimes go hungry, but those of us who reverence the Lord will never lack any good thing.

Sons and daughters, come and listen and let me teach you the importance of trusting and fearing the Lord. Do you want a long, good life? Then watch your tongue! Keep your lips from lying. Turn from all known sin and spend your time in doing good. Try to live in peace with everyone; work hard at it.

For the eyes of the Lord are intently watching all who live good lives, and he gives attention when they cry to him. But the Lord has made up his mind to wipe out even the memory of evil men from the earth. Yes, the Lord hears the good man when he calls to him for help and saves him out of all his troubles.

The Lord is close to those whose hearts are breaking; he rescues those who are humbly sorry for their sins. The good man does not escape all troubles--he has them too. But the Lord helps him in each and every one. Not one of his bones is broken.

Calamity will surely overtake the wicked; heavy penalties are meted out to those who hate the good. But as for those who serve the Lord, he will redeem them; everyone who takes refuge in him will be freely pardoned.

Making Requests Known
Psalm 35:1-28 (GWT)

O Lord, attack those who attack me.
> Fight against those who fight against me.
> Use your shields, {both} small and large.
> Arise to help me.
> Hold your spear to block the way of those who pursue me.
> Say to my soul, "I am your savior."

Let those who seek my life be put to shame and disgraced.
Let those who plan my downfall be turned back in confusion.
Let them be like husks blown by the wind
   as the Messenger of the Lord chases them.
Let their path be dark and slippery
   as the Messenger of the Lord pursues them.
For no reason they hid their net in a pit.
   For no reason they dug the pit {to trap me}.
Let destruction surprise them.
   Let the net that they hid catch them.
   Let them fall into their own pit and be destroyed.
My soul will find joy in the Lord
   and be joyful about his salvation.
All my bones will say, "O Lord, who can compare with you?
You rescue the weak person from the one who is too strong for
   him and weak and needy people from the one who robs them."

Malicious people bring charges against me.
They ask me things I know nothing about.
I am devastated
   because they pay me back with evil instead of good.
But when they were sick, I wore sackcloth.
I humbled myself with fasting.
When my prayer returned unanswered,
   I walked around as if I were mourning for my friend
   or my brother.
I was bent over as if I were mourning for my mother.

Yet, when I stumbled,
   they rejoiced and gathered together.
   They gathered together against me.
Unknown attackers tore me apart without stopping.
With crude and abusive mockers,
   they grit their teeth at me.
O Lord, how long will you look on?
   Rescue me from their attacks.
   Rescue my precious life from the lions.
   I will give you thanks in a large gathering.
   I will praise you in a crowd {of worshipers}.

Do not let my treacherous enemies gloat over me.
Do not let those who hate me for no reason wink {at me}.
   They do not talk about peace.

Instead, they scheme against the peaceful people in the land.
    They open their big mouths and say about me,
        "Aha! Aha! Our own eyes have seen it."
You have seen it, O Lord.
    Do not remain silent.
O Lord, do not be so far away from me.
    Wake up, and rise to my defense.
    Plead my case, O my God and my Lord.
    Judge me by your righteousness, O Lord my God.
Do not let them gloat over me
    or think, "Aha, just what we wanted!"
Do not let them say, "We have swallowed him up."
Let those who gloat over my downfall
    be thoroughly put to shame and confused.
Let those who promote themselves at my expense
    be clothed with shame and disgrace.
Let those who are happy when I am declared innocent
    joyfully sing and rejoice.
Let them continually say, "The Lord is great.
    He is happy when his servant has peace."
Then my tongue will tell about your righteousness,
    about your praise all day long.

Praising God/Making Requests Known
Psalm 36:5-12 (CEV)
Your love is faithful, Lord,
and even the clouds in the sky can depend on you.
Your decisions are always fair.
They are firm like mountains, deep like the sea,
and all people and animals are under your care.

Your love is a treasure,
and everyone finds shelter in the shadow of your wings.
You give your guests a feast in your house,
and you serve a tasty drink that flows like a river.
The life-giving fountain belongs to you,
and your light gives light to each of us.

Our Lord, keep showing love to everyone who knows you,
and use your power to save all whose thoughts please you.
Don't let those proud and merciless people

kick me around or chase me away.
Look at those wicked people!
They are knocked down, never to get up again.

Making Requests Known
Psalm 37:4-7 (ESV)

    Delight yourself in the Lord,
        and he will give you the desires of your heart.
    Commit your way to the Lord;
        trust in him, and he will act.
    He will bring forth your righteousness as the light,
        and your justice as the noonday.
    Be still before the Lord and wait patiently for him;
        fret not yourself over the one who prospers in his way,
        over the man who carries out evil devices!

Making Requests Known
Psalm 38:1-22 (ESV)

O Lord, rebuke me not in your anger,
    nor discipline me in your wrath!
  For your arrows have sunk into me,
    and your hand has come down on me.
  There is no soundness in my flesh
    because of your indignation;
  there is no health in my bones
    because of my sin.
  For my iniquities have gone over my head;
    like a heavy burden, they are too heavy for me.
  My wounds stink and fester
    because of my foolishness,
  I am utterly bowed down and prostrate;
    all the day I go about mourning.
  For my sides are filled with burning,
    and there is no soundness in my flesh.
  I am feeble and crushed;
    I groan because of the tumult of my heart.
  O Lord, all my longing is before you;
    my sighing is not hidden from you.
  My heart throbs; my strength fails me,
    and the light of my eyes—it also has gone from me.
  My friends and companions stand aloof from my plague,

and my nearest kin stand far off.
Those who seek my life lay their snares;
    those who seek my hurt speak of ruin
    and meditate treachery all day long.
But I am like a deaf man; I do not hear,
    like a mute man who does not open his mouth.
I have become like a man who does not hear,
    and in whose mouth are no rebukes.
But for you, O Lord, do I wait;
    it is you, O Lord my God, who will answer.
For I said, "Only let them not rejoice over me,
    who boast against me when my foot slips!"
For I am ready to fall,
    and my pain is ever before me.
I confess my iniquity;
    I am sorry for my sin.
But my foes are vigorous, they are mighty,
    and many are those who hate me wrongfully.
Those who render me evil for good
    accuse me because I follow after good.
Do not forsake me, O Lord!
    O my God, be not far from me!
Make haste to help me,
    O Lord, my salvation!

Making Requests Known
Psalm 39:1-13 (NIV)

I said, "I will watch my ways
    and keep my tongue from sin;
I will put a muzzle on my mouth
    as long as the wicked are in my presence."
But when I was silent and still,
    not even saying anything good,
    my anguish increased.
My heart grew hot within me,
    and as I meditated, the fire burned;
    then I spoke with my tongue:

"Show me, O Lord, my life's end
    and the number of my days;
    let me know how fleeting is my life.
You have made my days a mere handbreadth;

the span of my years is as nothing before you.
Each man's life is but a breath.
　　Selah
Man is a mere phantom as he goes to and fro:
　He bustles about, but only in vain;
　he heaps up wealth, not knowing who will get it.

"But now, Lord, what do I look for?
　My hope is in you.
Save me from all my transgressions;
　do not make me the scorn of fools.
I was silent; I would not open my mouth,
　for you are the one who has done this.
Remove your scourge from me;
　I am overcome by the blow of your hand.
You rebuke and discipline men for their sin;
　you consume their wealth like a moth--
　each man is but a breath.
　　Selah

"Hear my prayer, O Lord,
　listen to my cry for help;
　be not deaf to my weeping.
For I dwell with you as an alien,
　a stranger, as all my fathers were.
Look away from me, that I may rejoice again
　before I depart and am no more."

Making Requests Known/Praising God
Psalm 40:1-17 (NASB)

I waited patiently for the Lord;
　　And He inclined to me and heard my cry.
　　He brought me up out of the pit of destruction, out of the
　　　miry clay,
　　And He set my feet upon a rock making my footsteps firm.
　　He put a new song in my mouth, a song of praise to our God;
　　Many will see and fear
　　And will trust in the Lord.

　　How blessed is the man who has made the Lord his trust,
　　　And has not turned to the proud, nor to those who lapse
　　　into falsehood.

Many, O Lord my God, are the wonders which You have done,
And Your thoughts toward us;
There is none to compare with You.
If I would declare and speak of them,
They would be too numerous to count.

Sacrifice and meal offering You have not desired;
My ears You have opened;
Burnt offering and sin offering You have not required.
Then I said, "Behold, I come;
In the scroll of the book it is written of me.
I delight to do Your will, O my God;
Your Law is within my heart."

I have proclaimed glad tidings of righteousness in
    the great congregation;
Behold, I will not restrain my lips,
O Lord, You know.
I have not hidden Your righteousness within my heart;
I have spoken of Your faithfulness and Your salvation;
I have not concealed Your lovingkindness and Your truth
    from the great congregation.

You, O Lord, will not withhold Your compassion from me;
Your lovingkindness and Your truth will continually preserve me.
For evils beyond number have surrounded me;
My iniquities have overtaken me, so that I am not able to see;
They are more numerous than the hairs of my head,
And my heart has failed me.

Be pleased, O Lord, to deliver me;
Make haste, O Lord, to help me.
Let those be ashamed and humiliated together
Who seek my life to destroy it;
Let those be turned back and dishonored
Who delight in my hurt.
Let those be appalled because of their shame
Who say to me, "Aha, aha!"
Let all who seek You rejoice and be glad in You;
Let those who love Your salvation say continually,
"The Lord be magnified!"
Since I am afflicted and needy,
Let the Lord be mindful of me.

You are my help and my deliverer;
   Do not delay, O my God.

Making Requests Known
Psalm 41:1-13 (NRSV)

Happy are those who consider the poor;
   the Lord delivers them in the day of trouble.
The Lord protects them and keeps them alive;
   they are called happy in the land.
You do not give them up to the will of their enemies.
The Lord sustains them on their sickbed;
   in their illness you heal all their infirmities.

As for me, I said, "O Lord, be gracious to me;
   heal me, for I have sinned against you."
My enemies wonder in malice
   when I will die, and my name perish.
And when they come to see me, they utter empty words,
   while their hearts gather mischief;
   when they go out, they tell it abroad.
All who hate me whisper together about me;
   they imagine the worst for me.

They think that a deadly thing has fastened on me,
   that I will not rise again from where I lie.
Even my bosom friend in whom I trusted,
   who ate of my bread, has lifted the heel against me.
But you, O Lord, be gracious to me,
   and raise me up, that I may repay them.

By this I know that you are pleased with me;
   because my enemy has not triumphed over me.
But you have upheld me because of my integrity,
   and set me in your presence forever.

Blessed be the Lord, the God of Israel,
   from everlasting to everlasting.
Amen and Amen.

Making Requests Known
Psalm 42:1-11 (NAB)

As the deer longs for streams of water,
   so my soul longs for you, O God.
My being thirsts for God, the living God.
   When can I go and see the face of God?
My tears have been my food day and night,
   as they ask daily,"Where is your God?"
Those times I recall
   as I pour out my soul,
When I went in procession with the crowd,
   I went with them to the house of God,
Amid loud cries of thanksgiving,
   with the multitude keeping festival.
Why are you downcast, my soul;
   why do you groan within me?
Wait for God, whom I shall praise again,
   my savior and my God.
My soul is downcast within me;
   therefore I will remember you
From the land of the Jordan and Hermon,
   from the land of Mount Mizar.
  Here deep calls to deep in the roar of your torrents.
   All your waves and breakers sweep over me.
  At dawn may the LORD bestow faithful love
   that I may sing praise through the night,
   praise to the God of my life.
I say to God, "My rock,
   why do you forget me?
Why must I go about mourning
   with the enemy oppressing me?"
  It shatters my bones, when my adversaries reproach me.
   They say to me daily: "Where is your God?"
Why are you downcast, my soul,
   why do you groan within me?
Wait for God, whom I shall praise again,
   my savior and my God.

Making Requests Known
Psalm 43:1-5 (NJB)

Judge me, God, defend my cause
  against a people who have no faithful love;
from those who are treacherous and unjust,
  rescue me.

For you are the God of my strength;
  why abandon me?
Why must I go around in mourning,
  harrassed by the enemy?

Send out your light and your truth;
  they shall be my guide,
to lead me to your holy mountain
  to the place where you dwell.

Then I shall go to the altar of God,
  to the God of my joy.
I will rejoice and praise you on the harp,
  O God, my God.

Why so downcast,
  why all these sighs?
Hope in God! I will praise him still,
  my Saviour, my God.

Making Requests Known
Psalm 44:1-26 (NLT)

O God, we have heard it with our own ears—
    our ancestors have told us
  of all you did in other days,
    in days long ago:
  You drove out the pagan nations
    and gave all the land to our ancestors;
  you crushed their enemies,
    setting our ancestors free.
  They did not conquer the land with their swords;
    it was not their own strength that gave them victory.
  It was by your mighty power that they succeeded;
    it was because you favored them and smiled on them.

You are my King and my God.
> You command victories for your people.

Only by your power can we push back our enemies;
> only in your name can we trample our foes.

I do not trust my bow;
> I do not count on my sword to save me.

It is you who gives us victory over our enemies;
> it is you who humbles those who hate us.

O God, we give glory to you all day long
> and constantly praise your name.
> Interlude

But now you have tossed us aside in dishonor.
> You no longer lead our armies to battle.

You make us retreat from our enemies
> and allow them to plunder our land.

You have treated us like sheep waiting to be slaughtered;
> you have scattered us among the nations.

You sold us—your precious people—for a pittance.
> You valued us at nothing at all.

You have caused all our neighbors to mock us.
> We are an object of scorn and derision to the nations around us.

You have made us the butt of their jokes;
> we are scorned by the whole world.

We can't escape the constant humiliation;
> shame is written across our faces.

All we hear are the taunts of our mockers.
> All we see are our vengeful enemies.

All this has happened despite our loyalty to you.
> We have not violated your covenant.

Our hearts have not deserted you.
> We have not strayed from your path.

Yet you have crushed us in the desert.
> You have covered us with darkness and death.

If we had turned away from worshiping our God
> or spread our hands in prayer to foreign gods,

God would surely have known it,
> for he knows the secrets of every heart.

For your sake we are killed every day;

we are being slaughtered like sheep.

Wake up, O Lord! Why do you sleep?
    Get up! Do not reject us forever.
Why do you look the other way?
    Why do you ignore our suffering and oppression?
We collapse in the dust,
    lying face down in the dirt.
Rise up! Come and help us!
    Save us because of your unfailing love.

Praising God
Psalm 45:6 (GWT)

Your throne, O God, is forever and ever.
The scepter in your kingdom is a scepter for justice.

Praising God
Psalm 46:1-11 (TEV)

God is our shelter and strength,
    always ready to help in times of trouble.
So we will not be afraid, even if the earth is shaken
    and mountains fall into the ocean depths;
even if the seas roar and rage,
    and the hills are shaken by the violence.

There is a river that brings joy to the city of God,
    to the sacred house of the Most High.
God is in that city, and it will never be destroyed;
    at early dawn he will come to its aid.
Nations are terrified, kingdoms are shaken;
    God thunders, and the earth dissolves.

The Lord Almighty is with us;
    the God of Jacob is our refuge.

Come and see what the Lord has done.
    See what amazing things he has done on earth.
He stops wars all over the world;
    he breaks bows, destroys spears,
    and sets shields on fire.
"Stop fighting," he says, "and know that I am God,

supreme among the nations,
supreme over the world."

The Lord Almighty is with us;
the God of Jacob is our refuge.

Praising God
Psalm 48:1-14 (CEV)
The Lord God is wonderful!
He deserves all praise in the city where he lives.
His holy mountain,
beautiful and majestic, brings joy to all on earth.
Mount Zion, truly sacred, is home for the Great King.
God is there to defend it
and has proved to be its protector.

Kings joined forces to attack the city,
but when they saw it,
they were terrified and ran away.
They trembled all over like women giving birth
or like seagoing ships wrecked by eastern winds.
We had heard about it,
and now we have seen it in the city of our God, the Lord All-Powerful.
This is the city that God will let stand forever.

Our God, here in your temple we think about your love.
You are famous and praised everywhere on earth,
as you win victories with your powerful arm.
Mount Zion will celebrate,
and all Judah will be glad, because you bring justice.

Let's walk around Zion and count its towers.
We will see its strong walls and visit each fortress.
Then you can say to future generations,
"Our God is like this forever and will always guide us."

Verses About Prayer
Psalm 50:7-15 (TLB)
O my people, listen! For I am your God. Listen! Here are my charges against you: I have no complaint about the sacrifices you bring to my

altar, for you bring them regularly. But it isn't sacrificial bullocks and goats that I really want from you. For all the animals of field and forest are mine! The cattle on a thousand hills! And all the birds upon the mountains!

If I were hungry, I would not mention it to you--for all the world is mine and everything in it. No, I don't need your sacrifices of flesh and blood. What I want from you is your true thanks; I want your promises fulfilled. I want you to trust me in your times of trouble, so I can rescue you and you can give me glory.

Making Requests Known
Psalm 51:1-19 (ESV)

Have mercy on me, O God,
    according to your steadfast love;
according to your abundant mercy
    blot out my transgressions.
Wash me thoroughly from my iniquity,
    and cleanse me from my sin!
For I know my transgressions,
    and my sin is ever before me.
Against you, you only, have I sinned
    and done what is evil in your sight,
so that you may be justified in your words
    and blameless in your judgment.
Behold, I was brought forth in iniquity,
    and in sin did my mother conceive me.
Behold, you delight in truth in the inward being,
    and you teach me wisdom in the secret heart.
Purge me with hyssop, and I shall be clean;
    wash me, and I shall be whiter than snow.
Let me hear joy and gladness;
    let the bones that you have broken rejoice.
Hide your face from my sins,
    and blot out all my iniquities.
Create in me a clean heart, O God,
    and renew a right spirit within me.
Cast me not away from your presence,
    and take not your Holy Spirit from me.
Restore to me the joy of your salvation,
    and uphold me with a willing spirit.
Then I will teach transgressors your ways,
    and sinners will return to you.
Deliver me from bloodguiltiness, O God,

O God of my salvation,
    and my tongue will sing aloud of your righteousness.
O Lord, open my lips,
    and my mouth will declare your praise.
For you will not delight in sacrifice, or I would give it;
    you will not be pleased with a burnt offering.
The sacrifices of God are a broken spirit;
    a broken and contrite heart, O God, you will not despise.
Do good to Zion in your good pleasure;
    build up the walls of Jerusalem;
then will you delight in right sacrifices,
    in burnt offerings and whole burnt offerings;
    then bulls will be offered on your altar.

Making Requests Known
Psalm 54:1-7 (NIV)

Save me, O God, by your name;
    vindicate me by your might.
Hear my prayer, O God;
    listen to the words of my mouth.

Strangers are attacking me;
    ruthless men seek my life--
    men without regard for God.
        Selah

Surely God is my help;
    the Lord is the one who sustains me.

Let evil recoil on those who slander me;
    in your faithfulness destroy them.

I will sacrifice a freewill offering to you;
    I will praise your name, O Lord,
    for it is good.
For he has delivered me from all my troubles,
    and my eyes have looked in triumph on my foes.

Making Requests Known
Psalm 55:1-23 (NASB)

Give ear to my prayer, O God;
And do not hide Yourself from my supplication.
Give heed to me and answer me;
I am restless in my complaint and am surely distracted,
Because of the voice of the enemy,
Because of the pressure of the wicked;
For they bring down trouble upon me
And in anger they bear a grudge against me.

My heart is in anguish within me,
And the terrors of death have fallen upon me.
Fear and trembling come upon me,
And horror has overwhelmed me.
I said, "Oh, that I had wings like a dove!
I would fly away and be at rest.
"Behold, I would wander far away,
I would lodge in the wilderness.
Selah.
"I would hasten to my place of refuge
From the stormy wind and tempest."

Confuse, O Lord, divide their tongues,
For I have seen violence and strife in the city.
Day and night they go around her upon her walls,
And iniquity and mischief are in her midst.
Destruction is in her midst;
Oppression and deceit do not depart from her streets.

For it is not an enemy who reproaches me,
Then I could bear it;
Nor is it one who hates me who has exalted himself against me,
Then I could hide myself from him.
But it is you, a man my equal,
My companion and my familiar friend;
We who had sweet fellowship together
Walked in the house of God in the throng.
Let death come deceitfully upon them;
Let them go down alive to Sheol,
For evil is in their dwelling, in their midst.

As for me, I shall call upon God,
And the Lord will save me.
Evening and morning and at noon, I will complain and murmur,
And He will hear my voice.
He will redeem my soul in peace from the battle
   which is against me,
For they are many who strive with me.
God will hear and answer them—
Even the one who sits enthroned from of old—
Selah.
With whom there is no change,
And who do not fear God.
He has put forth his hands against those who were
   at peace with him;
He has violated his covenant.
His speech was smoother than butter,
But his heart was war;
His words were softer than oil,
Yet they were drawn swords.

Cast your burden upon the Lord and He will sustain you;
He will never allow the righteous to be shaken.
But You, O God, will bring them down to the pit of destruction;
Men of bloodshed and deceit will not live out half their days.
But I will trust in You.

Making Requests Known
Psalm 56:1-13 (NRSV)
Be gracious to me, O God, for people trample on me;
   all day long foes oppress me;
my enemies trample on me all day long,
   for many fight against me.
O Most High, when I am afraid,
   I put my trust in you.
In God, whose word I praise,
   in God I trust; I am not afraid;
   what can flesh do to me?

All day long they seek to injure my cause;
   all their thoughts are against me for evil.
They stir up strife, they lurk,

they watch my steps.
As they hoped to have my life,
    so repay them for their crime;
    in wrath cast down the peoples, O God!

You have kept count of my tossings;
    put my tears in your bottle.
    Are they not in your record?
Then my enemies will retreat
    in the day when I call.
    This I know, that God is for me.
In God, whose word I praise,
    in the Lord, whose word I praise,
in God I trust; I am not afraid.
    What can a mere mortal do to me?

My vows to you I must perform, O God;
    I will render thank offerings to you.
For you have delivered my soul from death,
    and my feet from falling,
so that I may walk before God
    in the light of life.

Making Requests Known/Praising God
Psalm 57:1-11 (NAB)

Have mercy on me, God,
    have mercy on me.
    In you I seek shelter.
In the shadow of your wings I seek shelter
    till harm pass by.
  I call to God Most High,
    to God who provides for me.
  May God send help from heaven to save me,
    shame those who trample upon me.
  May God send fidelity and love. Selah
  I must lie down in the midst of lions
    hungry for human prey.
  Their teeth are spears and arrows;
    their tongue, a sharpened sword.
  Show yourself over the heavens, God;
    may your glory appear above all the earth.
They have set a trap for my feet;

my soul is bowed down;
They have dug a pit before me.
    May they fall into it themselves! Selah
My heart is steadfast, God,
    my heart is steadfast.
    I will sing and chant praise.
Awake, my soul;
    awake, lyre and harp!
    I will wake the dawn.
I will praise you among the peoples, Lord;
    I will chant your praise among the nations.
For your love towers to the heavens;
    your faithfulness, to the skies.
Show yourself over the heavens, God;
    may your glory appear above all the earth.

Making Requests Known
Psalm 58:6 (NJB)

God, break the teeth in their mouths,
snap off the fangs of these young lions, Yahweh.

Making Requests Known
Psalm 59:1-17 (NLT)

Rescue me from my enemies, O God.
    Protect me from those who have come to destroy me.
Rescue me from these criminals;
    save me from these murderers.

They have set an ambush for me.
    Fierce enemies are out there waiting,
    though I have done them no wrong, O Lord.
Despite my innocence, they prepare to kill me.
    Rise up and help me! Look on my plight!
O Lord God Almighty, the God of Israel,
    rise up to punish hostile nations.
    Show no mercy to wicked traitors.
    Interlude

They come at night,
    snarling like vicious dogs
    as they prowl the streets.

Listen to the filth that comes from their mouths,
  the piercing swords that fly from their lips.
"Who can hurt us?" they sneer.

But Lord, you laugh at them.
  You scoff at all the hostile nations.
You are my strength; I wait for you to rescue me,
  for you, O God, are my place of safety.
In his unfailing love, my God will come and help me.
  He will let me look down in triumph on all my enemies.

Don't kill them, for my people soon forget such lessons;
  stagger them with your power, and bring them to their knees,
  O Lord our shield.
Because of the sinful things they say,
  because of the evil that is on their lips,
let them be captured by their pride,
  their curses, and their lies.
Destroy them in your anger!
  Wipe them out completely!
Then the whole world will know
  that God reigns in Israel.
  Interlude

My enemies come out at night,
  snarling like vicious dogs
  as they prowl the streets.
They scavenge for food
  but go to sleep unsatisfied.

But as for me, I will sing about your power.
I will shout with joy each morning because of
  your unfailing love.
For you have been my refuge,
  a place of safety in the day of distress.

O my Strength, to you I sing praises,
  for you, O God, are my refuge,
  the God who shows me unfailing love.

Making Requests Known
Psalm 60:1-12 (GWT)
O God, you have rejected us.

You have broken down our defenses.
You have been angry.
   Restore us!
You made the land quake.
You split it wide open.
  Heal the cracks in it
    because it is falling apart.
You have made your people experience hardships.
You have given us wine that makes us stagger.
Yet, you have raised a flag for those who fear you
  so that they can rally to it
    when attacked by bows {and arrows}.
  Selah
  Save {us} with your powerful hand, and answer us
    so that those who are dear to you may be rescued.

God has promised the following through his holiness:
  "I will triumph!
    I will divide Shechem.
    I will measure the valley of Succoth.
    Gilead is mine.
    Manasseh is mine.
    Ephraim is the helmet on my head.
    Judah is my scepter.
    Moab is my washtub.
    I will throw my shoe over Edom.
    I will shout in triumph over Philistia."

Who will bring me into the fortified city?
Who will lead me to Edom?
  Isn't it you, O God, who rejected us?
  Isn't it you, O God, who refused to accompany our armies?

Give us help against the enemy
  because human assistance is worthless.
    With God we will display great strength.
      He will trample our enemies.

Making Requests Known/Praising God
Psalm 61:1-8 (TEV)

Hear my cry, O God;
  listen to my prayer!

In despair and far from home
   I call to you!
Take me to a safe refuge,
   for you are my protector,
   my strong defense against my enemies.

Let me live in your sanctuary all my life;
   let me find safety under your wings.
You have heard my promises, O God,
   and you have given me what belongs to those who honor you.

Add many years to the king's life;
   let him live on and on!
May he rule forever in your presence, O God;
   protect him with your constant love and faithfulness.

So I will always sing praises to you,
   as I offer you daily what I have promised.

Praising God
Psalm 63:1-11 (CEV)
You are my God. I worship you. In my heart, I long for you,
as I would long for a stream in a scorching desert.
I have seen your power
and your glory in the place of worship.
Your love means more
than life to me, and I praise you.
As long as I live, I will pray to you.
I will sing joyful praises
and be filled with excitement like a guest at a banquet.

I think about you before I go to sleep,
and my thoughts turn to you during the night.
You have helped me,
and I sing happy songs in the shadow of your wings.
I stay close to you,
and your powerful arm supports me.

All who want to kill me will end up in the ground.
Swords will run them through, and wild dogs will eat them.

Because of you, our God, the king will celebrate

with your faithful followers, but liars will be silent.

Making Requests Known
Psalm 64:1-10 (ESV)

> Hear my voice, O God, in my complaint;
> > preserve my life from dread of the enemy.
>
> Hide me from the secret plots of the wicked,
> > from the throng of evildoers,
>
> who whet their tongues like swords,
> > who aim bitter words like arrows,
>
> shooting from ambush at the blameless,
> > shooting at him suddenly and without fear.
>
> They hold fast to their evil purpose;
> > they talk of laying snares secretly,
>
> thinking, who can see them?
> > They search out injustice,
>
> saying, "We have accomplished a diligent search."
> > For the inward mind and heart of a man are deep!
>
> But God shoots his arrow at them;
> > they are wounded suddenly.
>
> They are brought to ruin, with their own tongues turned against them;
> > all who see them will wag their heads.
>
> Then all mankind fears;
> > they tell what God has brought about
> > and ponder what he has done.
>
> Let the righteous one rejoice in the Lord
> > and take refuge in him!
>
> Let all the upright in heart exult!

Praising God
Psalm 65:1-13 (NIV)

> Praise awaits you, O God, in Zion;
> > to you our vows will be fulfilled.
>
> O you who hear prayer,
> > to you all men will come.
>
> When we were overwhelmed by sins,
> > you forgave our transgressions.
>
> Blessed are those you choose
> > and bring near to live in your courts!
>
> We are filled with the good things of your house,
> > of your holy temple.

You answer us with awesome deeds of righteousness,
>   O God our Savior,
the hope of all the ends of the earth
>   and of the farthest seas,
who formed the mountains by your power,
>   having armed yourself with strength,
who stilled the roaring of the seas,
>   the roaring of their waves,
>   and the turmoil of the nations.
Those living far away fear your wonders;
>   where morning dawns and evening fades
>   you call forth songs of joy.

You care for the land and water it;
>   you enrich it abundantly.
The streams of God are filled with water
>   to provide the people with grain,
>   for so you have ordained it.
You drench its furrows
>   and level its ridges;
you soften it with showers
>   and bless its crops.
You crown the year with your bounty,
>   and your carts overflow with abundance.
The grasslands of the desert overflow;
>   the hills are clothed with gladness.
The meadows are covered with flocks
>   and the valleys are mantled with grain;
>   they shout for joy and sing.

Praising God
Psalm 66:1-20 (NASB)

>   Shout joyfully to God, all the earth;
>   Sing the glory of His name;
>   Make His praise glorious.
>   Say to God, "How awesome are Your works!
>   Because of the greatness of Your power Your
>   enemies will give feigned obedience to You.
>   "All the earth will worship You,
>   And will sing praises to You;
>   They will sing praises to Your name."

Selah.
Come and see the works of God,
Who is awesome in His deeds toward the sons of men.
He turned the sea into dry land;
They passed through the river on foot;
There let us rejoice in Him!
He rules by His might forever;
His eyes keep watch on the nations;
Let not the rebellious exalt themselves.
Selah.

Bless our God, O peoples,
And sound His praise abroad,
Who keeps us in life
And does not allow our feet to slip.
For You have tried us, O God;
You have refined us as silver is refined.
You brought us into the net;
You laid an oppressive burden upon our loins.
You made men ride over our heads;
We went through fire and through water,
Yet You brought us out into a place of abundance.
I shall come into Your house with burnt offerings;
I shall pay You my vows,
Which my lips uttered
And my mouth spoke when I was in distress.
I shall offer to You burnt offerings of fat beasts,
With the smoke of rams;
I shall make an offering of bulls with male goats.
Selah.

Come and hear, all who fear God,
And I will tell of what He has done for my soul.
I cried to Him with my mouth,
And He was extolled with my tongue.
If I regard wickedness in my heart,
The Lord will not hear;
But certainly God has heard;
He has given heed to the voice of my prayer.
Blessed be God,
Who has not turned away my prayer
Nor His lovingkindness from me.

Praising God
Psalm 67:1-7 (NRSV)
> May God be gracious to us and bless us
> > and make his face to shine upon us,
> > Selah
> that your way may be known upon earth,
> > your saving power among all nations.
> Let the peoples praise you, O God;
> > let all the peoples praise you.
>
> Let the nations be glad and sing for joy,
> > for you judge the peoples with equity
> > and guide the nations upon earth.
> > Selah
> Let the peoples praise you, O God;
> > let all the peoples praise you.
>
> The earth has yielded its increase;
> > God, our God, has blessed us.
> May God continue to bless us;
> > let all the ends of the earth revere him.

Praising God
Psalm 68:7-10 (NAB)
> God, when you went forth before your people,
> > when you marched through the desert, Selah
> The earth quaked, the heavens shook,
> > before God, the One of Sinai,
> > before God, the God of Israel.
> You claimed a land as your own, O God;
> > your people settled there.
> There you poured abundant rains, God,
> > graciously given to the poor in their need.

Praising God/Making Requests Known
Psalm 68:18-35 (NJB)
> You have climbed the heights, taken captives,
> you have taken men as tribute, even rebels
> that Yahweh God might have a dwelling-place.
>
> Blessed be the Lord day after day,

he carries us along, God our Saviour.
    Pause

This God of ours is a God who saves;
from Lord Yahweh comes escape from death;
but God smashes the head of his enemies,
the long-haired skull of the prowling criminal.

The Lord has said, 'I will bring them back from Bashan,
I will bring them back from the depths of the sea,
so that you may bathe your feet in blood,
and the tongues of your dogs feast on your enemies.'

Your processions, God, are for all to see,
the processions of my God, of my king, to the sanctuary;
singers ahead, musicians behind,
in the middle come girls, beating their drums.

In choirs they bless God,
Yahweh, since the foundation of Israel.

Benjamin was there, the youngest in front,
the princes of Judah in bright-coloured robes,
the princes of Zebulun, the princes of Naphtali.

Take command, my God, as befits your power,
the power, God, which you have wielded for us,
from your temple high above Jerusalem.
Kings will come to you bearing tribute.

Rebuke the Beast of the Reeds,
that herd of bulls, that people of calves,
who bow down with ingots of silver.
Scatter the people who delight in war.
From Egypt nobles will come,
Ethiopia will stretch out its hands to God.

Kingdoms of the earth, sing to God,
play for the Rider of the Heavens, the primeval heavens.
    Pause
There he speaks, with a voice of power!
Acknowledge the power of God.
Over Israel his splendour, in the clouds his power.

Awesome is God in his sanctuary.
He, the God of Israel,
gives strength and power to his people.
   Blessed be God.

Making Requests Known
Psalm 69:1-36 (NLT)
Save me, O God,
   for the floodwaters are up to my neck.
Deeper and deeper I sink into the mire;
   I can't find a foothold to stand on.
I am in deep water,
   and the floods overwhelm me.
I am exhausted from crying for help;
   my throat is parched and dry.
My eyes are swollen with weeping,
   waiting for my God to help me.

Those who hate me without cause
   are more numerous than the hairs on my head.
These enemies who seek to destroy me
   are doing so without cause.
They attack me with lies,
   demanding that I give back what I didn't steal.

O God, you know how foolish I am;
   my sins cannot be hidden from you.
Don't let those who trust in you stumble because of me,
   O Sovereign Lord Almighty.
Don't let me cause them to be humiliated,
   O God of Israel.
For I am mocked and shamed for your sake;
   humiliation is written all over my face.
Even my own brothers pretend they don't know me;
   they treat me like a stranger.

Passion for your house burns within me,
   so those who insult you are also insulting me.
When I weep and fast before the Lord,
   they scoff at me.
When I dress in sackcloth to show sorrow,
   they make fun of me.

I am the favorite topic of town gossip,
   and all the drunkards sing about me.

But I keep right on praying to you, Lord,
   hoping this is the time you will show me favor.
In your unfailing love, O God,
   answer my prayer with your sure salvation.
Pull me out of the mud;
   don't let me sink any deeper!
Rescue me from those who hate me,
   and pull me from these deep waters.
Don't let the floods overwhelm me,
   or the deep waters swallow me,
   or the pit of death devour me.

Answer my prayers, O Lord,
   for your unfailing love is wonderful.
Turn and take care of me,
   for your mercy is so plentiful.
Don't hide from your servant;
   answer me quickly, for I am in deep trouble!
Come and rescue me;
   free me from all my enemies.

You know the insults I endure—
   the humiliation and disgrace.
You have seen all my enemies
   and know what they have said.
Their insults have broken my heart,
   and I am in despair.
If only one person would show some pity;
   if only one would turn and comfort me.
But instead, they give me poison for food;
   they offer me sour wine to satisfy my thirst.

Let the bountiful table set before them become a snare,
   and let their security become a trap.
Let their eyes go blind so they cannot see,
   and let their bodies grow weaker and weaker.
Pour out your fury on them;
   consume them with your burning anger.
May their homes become desolate
   and their tents be deserted.

To those you have punished, they add insult to injury;
    they scoff at the pain of those you have hurt.
Pile their sins up high,
    and don't let them go free.
Erase their names from the Book of Life;
    don't let them be counted among the righteous.

I am suffering and in pain.
    Rescue me, O God, by your saving power.

Then I will praise God's name with singing,
    and I will honor him with thanksgiving.
For this will please the Lord more than sacrificing an ox
    or presenting a bull with its horns and hooves.
The humble will see their God at work and be glad.
    Let all who seek God's help live in joy.
For the Lord hears the cries of his needy ones;
    he does not despise his people who are oppressed.

Praise him, O heaven and earth,
    the seas and all that move in them.
For God will save Jerusalem
    and rebuild the towns of Judah.
His people will live there
    and take possession of the land.
The descendants of those who obey him will inherit the land,
    and those who love him will live there in safety.

Making Requests Known
Psalm 70:1-5 (GWT)

Come quickly to rescue me, O God!
Come quickly to help me, O Lord!
Let those who seek my life
    be confused and put to shame.
Let those who want my downfall
    be turned back and disgraced.
Let those who say, "Aha! Aha!"
    be turned back because of their own shame.
Let all who seek you rejoice and be glad because of you.
Let those who love your salvation continually say,
    "God is great!"

But I am oppressed and needy.
O God, come to me quickly.
   You are my help and my savior.
      O Lord, do not delay!

Making Requests Known/Praising God
Psalm 71:1-24 (TEV)

Lord, I have come to you for protection;
   never let me be defeated!
Because you are righteous, help me and rescue me.
   Listen to me and save me!
Be my secure shelter
   and a strong fortress to protect me;
   you are my refuge and defense.

My God, rescue me from wicked people,
   from the power of cruel and evil people.
Sovereign Lord, I put my hope in you;
   I have trusted in you since I was young.
I have relied on you all my life;
   you have protected me since the day I was born.
   I will always praise you.

My life has been an example to many,
   because you have been my strong defender.
All day long I praise you
   and proclaim your glory.
Do not reject me now that I am old;
   do not abandon me now that I am feeble.
My enemies want to kill me;
   they talk and plot against me.
They say, "God has abandoned him;
   let's go after him and catch him;
   there is no one to rescue him."

Don't stay so far away, O God;
   my God, hurry to my aid!
May those who attack me
   be defeated and destroyed.
May those who try to hurt me
   be shamed and disgraced.
I will always put my hope in you;

I will praise you more and more.
I will tell of your goodness;
    all day long I will speak of your salvation,
    though it is more than I can understand.
I will go in the strength of the Lord God;
    I will proclaim your goodness, yours alone.

You have taught me ever since I was young,
    and I still tell of your wonderful acts.
Now that I am old and my hair is gray,
    do not abandon me, O God!
Be with me while I proclaim your power and might
    to all generations to come.

Your righteousness, God, reaches the skies.
    You have done great things;
    there is no one like you.
You have sent troubles and suffering on me,
    but you will restore my strength;
    you will keep me from the grave.
You will make me greater than ever;
    you will comfort me again.

I will indeed praise you with the harp;
    I will praise your faithfulness, my God.
On my harp I will play hymns to you,
    the Holy One of Israel.
I will shout for joy as I play for you;
    with my whole being I will sing
    because you have saved me.
I will speak of your righteousness all day long,
    because those who tried to harm me
    have been defeated and disgraced.

Praying for Others
Psalm 72:1-19 (CEV)
Please help the king
to be honest and fair just like you, our God.
Let him be honest and fair
with all your people, especially the poor.
Let peace and justice rule every mountain and hill.
Let the king defend the poor,

rescue the homeless, and crush everyone who hurts them.
Let the king live forever like the sun and the moon.
Let him be as helpful as rain
that refreshes the meadows and the ground.
Let the king be fair with everyone,
and let there be peace
until the moon falls from the sky.

Let his kingdom reach from sea to sea,
from the Euphrates River across all the earth.
Force the desert tribes to accept his rule,
and make his enemies crawl in the dirt.
Force the rulers of Tarshish
and of the islands to pay taxes to him.
Make the kings of Sheba and of Seba bring gifts.
Make other rulers bow down and all nations serve him.

Do this because the king
rescues the homeless when they cry out,
and he helps everyone who is poor and in need.
The king has pity
on the weak and the helpless and protects those in need.
He cares when they hurt,
and he saves them from cruel and violent deaths.

Long live the king! Give him gold from Sheba.
Always pray for the king and praise him each day.
Let cities overflow with food
and hills be covered with grain, just like Mount Lebanon.
Let the people in the cities prosper like wild flowers.
May the glory of the king
shine brightly forever like the sun in the sky.
Let him make nations prosper and learn to praise him.

Lord God of Israel,
we praise you. Only you can work miracles.
We will always praise your glorious name.
Let your glory be seen
everywhere on earth. Amen and amen.

Praising God
Psalm 73:1-28 (ESV)

Truly God is good to Israel,
 to those who are pure in heart.
But as for me, my feet had almost stumbled,
 my steps had nearly slipped.
For I was envious of the arrogant
 when I saw the prosperity of the wicked.
For they have no pangs until death;
 their bodies are fat and sleek.
They are not in trouble as others are;
 they are not stricken like the rest of mankind.
Therefore pride is their necklace;
 violence covers them as a garment.
Their eyes swell out through fatness;
 their hearts overflow with follies.
They scoff and speak with malice;
 loftily they threaten oppression.
They set their mouths against the heavens,
 and their tongue struts through the earth.
Therefore his people turn back to them,
 and find no fault in them.
And they say, "How can God know?
 Is there knowledge in the Most High?"
Behold, these are the wicked;
 always at ease, they increase in riches.
All in vain have I kept my heart clean
 and washed my hands in innocence.
For all the day long I have been stricken
 and rebuked every morning.
If I had said, "I will speak thus,"
 I would have betrayed the generation of your children.
But when I thought how to understand this,
 it seemed to me a wearisome task,
until I went into the sanctuary of God;
 then I discerned their end.
Truly you set them in slippery places;
 you make them fall to ruin.
How they are destroyed in a moment,
 swept away utterly by terrors!
Like a dream when one awakes,
 O Lord, when you rouse yourself, you despise them as phantoms.
When my soul was embittered,

when I was pricked in heart,
I was brutish and ignorant;
    I was like a beast toward you.
Nevertheless, I am continually with you;
    you hold my right hand.
You guide me with your counsel,
    and afterward you will receive me to glory.
Whom have I in heaven but you?
    And there is nothing on earth that I desire besides you.
My flesh and my heart may fail,
    but God is the strength of my heart and my portion forever.
For behold, those who are far from you shall perish;
    you put an end to everyone who is unfaithful to you.
But for me it is good to be near God;
    I have made the Lord God my refuge,
    that I may tell of all your works.

Making Requests Known
Psalm 74:1-23 (ESV)

O God, why do you cast us off forever?
    Why does your anger smoke against the sheep of your pasture?
Remember your congregation, which you have purchased of old,
    which you have redeemed to be the tribe of your heritage!
    Remember Mount Zion, where you have dwelt.
Direct your steps to the perpetual ruins;
    the enemy has destroyed everything in the sanctuary!
Your foes have roared in the midst of your meeting place;
    they set up their own signs for signs.
They were like those who swing axes
    in a forest of trees.
And all its carved wood
    they broke down with hatchets and hammers.
They set your sanctuary on fire;
    they profaned the dwelling place of your name,
    bringing it down to the ground.
They said to themselves, "We will utterly subdue them";
    they burned all the meeting places of God in the land.
We do not see our signs;
there is no longer any prophet,
    and there is none among us who knows how long.
How long, O God, is the foe to scoff?
    Is the enemy to revile your name forever?

Why do you hold back your hand, your right hand?
   Take it from the fold of your garment and destroy them!
Yet God my King is from of old,
   working salvation in the midst of the earth.
You divided the sea by your might;
   you broke the heads of the sea monsters on the waters.
You crushed the heads of Leviathan;
   you gave him as food for the creatures of the wilderness.
You split open springs and brooks;
   you dried up ever-flowing streams.
Yours is the day, yours also the night;
   you have established the heavenly lights and the sun.
You have fixed all the boundaries of the earth;
   you have made summer and winter.
Remember this, O Lord, how the enemy scoffs,
   and a foolish people reviles your name.
Do not deliver the soul of your dove to the wild beasts;
   do not forget the life of your poor forever.
Have regard for the covenant,
  for the dark places of the land are full of the habitations of violence.
Let not the downtrodden turn back in shame;
   let the poor and needy praise your name.
Arise, O God, defend your cause;
   remember how the foolish scoff at you all the day!
Do not forget the clamor of your foes,
      the uproar of those who rise against you, which goes
      up continually!

Thanksgiving & Gratitude
Psalm 75:1-10 (NASB)

We give thanks to You, O God, we give thanks,
For Your name is near;
Men declare Your wondrous works.
"When I select an appointed time,
It is I who judge with equity.
"The earth and all who dwell in it melt;
It is I who have firmly set its pillars.
Selah.
"I said to the boastful, 'Do not boast,'
And to the wicked, 'Do not lift up the horn;
Do not lift up your horn on high,
Do not speak with insolent pride.' "

> For not from the east, nor from the west,
> Nor from the desert comes exaltation;
> But God is the Judge;
> He puts down one and exalts another.
> For a cup is in the hand of the Lord, and the wine foams;
> It is well mixed, and He pours out of this;
> Surely all the wicked of the earth must drain and drink down its dregs.
> But as for me, I will declare it forever;
> I will sing praises to the God of Jacob.
> And all the horns of the wicked He will cut off,
> But the horns of the righteous will be lifted up.

Praising God
Psalm 76:6-10 (NRSV)

> At your rebuke, O God of Jacob,
>   both rider and horse lay stunned.
>
> But you indeed are awesome!
>   Who can stand before you
>   when once your anger is roused?
> From the heavens you uttered judgment;
>   the earth feared and was still
> when God rose up to establish judgment,
>   to save all the oppressed of the earth.
> Selah
>
> Human wrath serves only to praise you,
>   when you bind the last bit of your wrath around you.

Praising God
Psalm 77:1-20 (NAB)

> I cry aloud to God,
>   cry to God to hear me.
> On the day of my distress I seek the Lord;
>   by night my hands are raised unceasingly;
>   I refuse to be consoled.
> When I think of God, I groan;
>   as I ponder, my spirit grows faint. Selah

My eyes cannot close in sleep;
  I am troubled and cannot speak.
I consider the days of old;
  the years long past
I remember.
In the night I meditate in my heart;
  I ponder and my spirit broods:
"Will the Lord reject us forever,
  never again show favor?
Has God's love ceased forever?
  Has the promise failed for all ages?
Has God forgotten mercy,
  in anger withheld compassion?" Selah
I conclude: "My sorrow is this,
  the right hand of the Most High has left us."

II

I will remember the deeds of the LORD;
  yes, your wonders of old I will remember.
I will recite all your works;
  your exploits I will tell.
Your way, O God, is holy;
  what god is as great as our God?
You alone are the God who did wonders;
  among the peoples you revealed your might.
With your arm you redeemed your people,
  the descendants of Jacob and Joseph. Selah
The waters saw you, God;
  the waters saw you and lashed about,
  trembled even to their depths.
The clouds poured down their rains;
  the thunderheads rumbled;
  your arrows flashed back and forth.
The thunder of your chariot wheels resounded;
  your lightning lit up the world;
  the earth trembled and quaked.
Through the sea was your path;
  your way, through the mighty waters,
  though your footsteps were unseen.
You led your people like a flock
  under the care of Moses and Aaron.

Making Requests Known
Psalm 79:1-13 (NJB)

God, the pagans have invaded your heritage,
they have defiled your holy temple,
they have laid Jerusalem in ruins,
they have left the corpses of your servants
as food for the birds of the air,
the bodies of your faithful for the wild beasts.

Around Jerusalem they have shed blood like water,
leaving no one to bury them.
We are the scorn of our neighbours,
the butt and laughing-stock of those around us.
How long will you be angry, Yahweh? For ever?
Is your jealousy to go on smouldering like a fire?

Pour out your anger on the nations
   who do not acknowledge you,
and on the kingdoms
   that do not call on your name;
for they have devoured Jacob
   and devastated his home.

Do not count against us the guilt of former generations,
in your tenderness come quickly to meet us,
for we are utterly weakened;
help us, God our Saviour,
for the glory of your name;
Yahweh, wipe away our sins,
rescue us for the sake of your name.

Why should the nations ask,
'Where is their God?'
Let us see the nations suffer vengeance
for shedding your servants' blood.
May the groans of the captive reach you,
by your great strength save those who are condemned to death!

Repay our neighbours sevenfold
for the insults they have levelled at you, Lord.
And we, your people, the flock that you pasture,
   will thank you for ever,
   will recite your praises from age to age.

Making Requests Known
Psalm 80:1-19 (NLT)

Please listen, O Shepherd of Israel,
    you who lead Israel like a flock.
O God, enthroned above the cherubim,
    display your radiant glory
    to Ephraim, Benjamin, and Manasseh.
Show us your mighty power.
    Come to rescue us!

Turn us again to yourself, O God.
    Make your face shine down upon us.
    Only then will we be saved.

O Lord God Almighty,
    how long will you be angry and reject our prayers?
You have fed us with sorrow
    and made us drink tears by the bucketful.
You have made us the scorn of neighboring nations.
    Our enemies treat us as a joke.

Turn us again to yourself, O God Almighty.
    Make your face shine down upon us.
    Only then will we be saved.
You brought us from Egypt as though we were a tender vine;
    you drove away the pagan nations and transplanted
    us into your land.
You cleared the ground for us,
    and we took root and filled the land.
The mountains were covered with our shade;
    the mighty cedars were covered with our branches.
We spread our branches west to the Mediterranean Sea,
    our limbs east to the Euphrates River.
But now, why have you broken down our walls
    so that all who pass may steal our fruit?
The boar from the forest devours us,
    and the wild animals feed on us.

Come back, we beg you, O God Almighty.
    Look down from heaven and see our plight.
Watch over and care for this vine

that you yourself have planted,
　　　　this son you have raised for yourself.
　　For we are chopped up and burned by our enemies.
　　　May they perish at the sight of your frown.
　　Strengthen the man you love,
　　　the son of your choice.
　　Then we will never forsake you again.
　　　Revive us so we can call on your name once more.

　　Turn us again to yourself, O Lord God Almighty.
　　　Make your face shine down upon us.
　　　Only then will we be saved.

Praying for Others
Psalm 82:8 (GWT)
　　Arise, O God!
　　　Judge the earth, because all the nations belong to you.

Making Requests Known
Psalm 83:1-18 (TEV)
　　O God, do not keep silent;
　　　do not be still, do not be quiet!
　　Look! Your enemies are in revolt,
　　　and those who hate you are rebelling.
　　They are making secret plans against your people;
　　　they are plotting against those you protect.
　　"Come," they say, "let us destroy their nation,
　　　so that Israel will be forgotten forever."

　　They agree on their plan
　　　and form an alliance against you:
　　the people of Edom and the Ishmaelites;
　　　the people of Moab and the Hagrites;
　　the people of Gebal, Ammon, and Amalek,
　　　and of Philistia and Tyre.
　　Assyria has also joined them
　　　as a strong ally of the Ammonites and Moabites,
　　　the descendants of Lot.

Do to them what you did to the Midianites,
  and to Sisera and Jabin at the Kishon River.
You defeated them at Endor,
  and their bodies rotted on the ground.
Do to their leaders what you did to Oreb and Zeeb;
  defeat all their rulers as you did Zebah and Zalmunna,
who said, "We will take for our own
  the land that belongs to God."

Scatter them like dust, O God,
  like straw blown away by the wind.
As fire burns the forest,
  as flames set the hills on fire,
chase them away with your storm
  and terrify them with your fierce winds.
Cover their faces with shame, O Lord,
  and make them acknowledge your power.
May they be defeated and terrified forever;
  may they die in complete disgrace.
May they know that you alone are the Lord,
  supreme ruler over all the earth.

Blessings & Benedictions
Psalm 84:1-12 (CEV)
Lord God All-Powerful, your temple is so lovely!
Deep in my heart I long for your temple,
and with all that I am I sing joyful songs to you.

Lord God All-Powerful, my King and my God,
sparrows find a home near your altars;
swallows build nests there to raise their young.

You bless everyone
who lives in your house, and they sing your praises.
You bless all who depend on you for their strength
and all who deeply desire to visit your temple.
When they reach Dry Valley, springs start flowing,
and the autumn rain fills it with pools of water.
Your people grow stronger,
and you, the God of gods, will be seen in Zion.

Lord God All-Powerful,

the God of Jacob, please answer my prayer!
You are the shield that protects your people,
and I am your chosen one. Won't you smile on me?

One day in your temple
is better than a thousand anywhere else.
I would rather serve in your house,
than live in the homes of the wicked.

Our Lord and our God,
you are like the sun and also like a shield.
You treat us with kindness and with honor,
never denying any good thing to those who live right.

Lord God All-Powerful,
you bless everyone who trusts you.

Praising God/Making Requests Known
Psalm 85:1-13 (ESV)

>Lord, you were favorable to your land;
>>you restored the fortunes of Jacob.
>
>You forgave the iniquity of your people;
>>you covered all their sin. Selah
>
>You withdrew all your wrath;
>>you turned from your hot anger.
>
>Restore us again, O God of our salvation,
>>and put away your indignation toward us!
>
>Will you be angry with us forever?
>>Will you prolong your anger to all generations?
>
>Will you not revive us again,
>>that your people may rejoice in you?
>
>Show us your steadfast love, O Lord,
>>and grant us your salvation.
>
>Let me hear what God the Lord will speak,
>>for he will speak peace to his people, to his saints;
>>but let them not turn back to folly.
>
>Surely his salvation is near to those who fear him,
>>that glory may dwell in our land.
>
>Steadfast love and faithfulness meet;
>>righteousness and peace kiss each other.
>
>Faithfulness springs up from the ground,
>>and righteousness looks down from the sky.

Yes, the Lord will give what is good,
>   and our land will yield its increase.
Righteousness will go before him
>   and make his footsteps a way.

Making Requests Known
Psalm 86:1-17 (NIV)

Hear, O Lord, and answer me,
>   for I am poor and needy.
Guard my life, for I am devoted to you.
>   You are my God; save your servant
>   who trusts in you.
Have mercy on me, O Lord,
>   for I call to you all day long.
Bring joy to your servant,
>   for to you, O Lord,
>   I lift up my soul.
You are forgiving and good, O Lord,
>   abounding in love to all who call to you.
Hear my prayer, O Lord;
>   listen to my cry for mercy.
In the day of my trouble I will call to you,
>   for you will answer me.

Among the gods there is none like you, O Lord;
>   no deeds can compare with yours.
All the nations you have made
>   will come and worship before you, O Lord;
>   they will bring glory to your name.
For you are great and do marvelous deeds;
>   you alone are God.

Teach me your way, O Lord,
>   and I will walk in your truth;
give me an undivided heart,
>   that I may fear your name.
I will praise you, O Lord my God, with all my heart;
>   I will glorify your name forever.
For great is your love toward me;
>   you have delivered me from the depths of the grave.

The arrogant are attacking me, O God;
   a band of ruthless men seeks my life--
  men without regard for you.
But you, O Lord, are a compassionate and gracious God,
   slow to anger, abounding in love and faithfulness.
Turn to me and have mercy on me;
  grant your strength to your servant
  and save the son of your maidservant.
Give me a sign of your goodness,
    that my enemies may see it and be put to shame,
    for you, O Lord, have helped me and comforted me.

Making Requests Known
Psalm 88:1-18 (NASB)

O Lord, the God of my salvation,
I have cried out by day and in the night before You.
Let my prayer come before You;
Incline Your ear to my cry!
For my soul has had enough troubles,
And my life has drawn near to Sheol.
I am reckoned among those who go down to the pit;
I have become like a man without strength,
Forsaken among the dead,
Like the slain who lie in the grave,
Whom You remember no more,
And they are cut off from Your hand.
You have put me in the lowest pit,
In dark places, in the depths.
Your wrath has rested upon me,
And You have afflicted me with all Your waves.
Selah.
You have removed my acquaintances far from me;
You have made me an object of loathing to them;
I am shut up and cannot go out.
My eye has wasted away because of affliction;
I have called upon You every day, O Lord;
I have spread out my hands to You.

Will You perform wonders for the dead?
Will the departed spirits rise and praise You?
Selah.
Will Your lovingkindness be declared in the grave,

Your faithfulness in Abaddon?
Will Your wonders be made known in the darkness?
And Your righteousness in the land of forgetfulness?

But I, O Lord, have cried out to You for help,
And in the morning my prayer comes before You.
O Lord, why do You reject my soul?
Why do You hide Your face from me?
I was afflicted and about to die from my youth on;
I suffer Your terrors; I am overcome.
Your burning anger has passed over me;
Your terrors have destroyed me.
They have surrounded me like water all day long;
They have encompassed me altogether.
You have removed lover and friend far from me;
My acquaintances are in darkness.

Praising God
Psalm 89:1-52 (NRSV)

I will sing of your steadfast love, O Lord, forever;
   with my mouth I will proclaim your faithfulness to all generations.
I declare that your steadfast love is established forever;
   your faithfulness is as firm as the heavens.

You said, "I have made a covenant with my chosen one,
   I have sworn to my servant David:
'I will establish your descendants forever,
   and build your throne for all generations.' "
      Selah

Let the heavens praise your wonders, O Lord,
   your faithfulness in the assembly of the holy ones.
For who in the skies can be compared to the Lord?
   Who among the heavenly beings is like the Lord,
a God feared in the council of the holy ones,
   great and awesome above all that are around him?
O Lord God of hosts,
   who is as mighty as you, O Lord?
   Your faithfulness surrounds you.
You rule the raging of the sea;

when its waves rise, you still them.
You crushed Rahab like a carcass;
   you scattered your enemies with your mighty arm.
The heavens are yours, the earth also is yours;
   the world and all that is in it--you have founded them.
The north and the south--you created them;
   Tabor and Hermon joyously praise your name.
You have a mighty arm;
   strong is your hand, high your right hand.
Righteousness and justice are the foundation of your throne;
   steadfast love and faithfulness go before you.
Happy are the people who know the festal shout,
   who walk, O Lord, in the light of your countenance;
they exult in your name all day long,
   and extol your righteousness.
For you are the glory of their strength;
   by your favor our horn is exalted.
For our shield belongs to the Lord,
   our king to the Holy One of Israel.

Then you spoke in a vision to your faithful one, and said:
   "I have set the crown on one who is mighty,
   I have exalted one chosen from the people.
I have found my servant David;
   with my holy oil I have anointed him;
my hand shall always remain with him;
   my arm also shall strengthen him.
The enemy shall not outwit him,
   the wicked shall not humble him.
I will crush his foes before him
   and strike down those who hate him.
My faithfulness and steadfast love shall be with him;
   and in my name his horn shall be exalted.
I will set his hand on the sea
   and his right hand on the rivers.
He shall cry to me, 'You are my Father,
   my God, and the Rock of my salvation!'
I will make him the firstborn,
   the highest of the kings of the earth.
Forever I will keep my steadfast love for him,
   and my covenant with him will stand firm.
I will establish his line forever,
   and his throne as long as the heavens endure.

If his children forsake my law
   and do not walk according to my ordinances,
if they violate my statutes
   and do not keep my commandments,
then I will punish their transgression with the rod
   and their iniquity with scourges;
but I will not remove from him my steadfast love,
   or be false to my faithfulness.
I will not violate my covenant,
   or alter the word that went forth from my lips.
Once and for all I have sworn by my holiness;
   I will not lie to David.
His line shall continue forever,
   and his throne endure before me like the sun.
It shall be established forever like the moon,
   an enduring witness in the skies."
      Selah

But now you have spurned and rejected him;
   you are full of wrath against your anointed.
You have renounced the covenant with your servant;
   you have defiled his crown in the dust.
You have broken through all his walls;
   you have laid his strongholds in ruins.
All who pass by plunder him;
   he has become the scorn of his neighbors.
You have exalted the right hand of his foes;
   you have made all his enemies rejoice.
Moreover, you have turned back the edge of his sword,
   and you have not supported him in battle.
You have removed the scepter from his hand,
   and hurled his throne to the ground.
You have cut short the days of his youth;
   you have covered him with shame.
      Selah

How long, O Lord? Will you hide yourself forever?
   How long will your wrath burn like fire?
Remember how short my time is--
   for what vanity you have created all mortals!
Who can live and never see death?
   Who can escape the power of Sheol?
      Selah

Lord, where is your steadfast love of old,
 which by your faithfulness you swore to David?
Remember, O Lord, how your servant is taunted;
 how I bear in my bosom the insults of the peoples,
with which your enemies taunt, O Lord,
 with which they taunted the footsteps of your anointed.

Blessed be the Lord forever.
Amen and Amen.

Making Requests Known
Psalm 90:1-17 (NAB)

Lord, you have been our refuge
 through all generations.
Before the mountains were born,
 the earth and the world brought forth,
 from eternity to eternity you are God.
A thousand years in your eyes
 are merely a yesterday,
 But humans you return to dust,
 saying, "Return, you mortals!"
Before a watch passes in the night,
 you have brought them to their end;
They disappear like sleep at dawn;
 they are like grass that dies.
It sprouts green in the morning;
 by evening it is dry and withered.
Truly we are consumed by your anger,
 filled with terror by your wrath.
You have kept our faults before you,
 our hidden sins exposed to your sight.
Our life ebbs away under your wrath;
 our years end like a sigh.
Seventy is the sum of our years,
 or eighty, if we are strong;
Most of them are sorrow and toil;
 they pass quickly, we are all but gone.
Who comprehends your terrible anger?
 Your wrath matches the fear it inspires.
Teach us to count our days aright,

    that we may gain wisdom of heart.
Relent, O LORD! How long?
    Have pity on your servants!
Fill us at daybreak with your love,
    that all our days we may sing for joy.
Make us glad as many days as you humbled us,
    for as many years as we have seen trouble.
Show your deeds to your servants,
    your glory to their children.
May the favor of the Lord our God be ours.
    Prosper the work of our hands!
    Prosper the work of our hands!

Praising God
Psalm 92:1-15 (NJB)
It is good to give thanks to Yahweh,
to make music for your name, Most High,
to proclaim your faithful love at daybreak,
and your constancy all through the night,
on the lyre, the ten-stringed lyre,
to the murmur of the harp.

You have brought me joy, Yahweh, by your deeds,
at the work of your hands I cry out,
'How great are your works, Yahweh,
immensely deep your thoughts!'
Stupid people cannot realise this,
fools do not grasp it.

The wicked may sprout like weeds,
and every evil-doer flourish,
but only to be eternally destroyed;
whereas you are supreme for ever, Yahweh.

Look how your enemies perish,
how all evil-doers are scattered!
You give me the strength of the wild ox,
you anoint me with fresh oil;
I caught sight of the ambush against me,
overheard the plans of the wicked.

The upright will flourish like the palm tree,

will grow like a cedar of Lebanon.
Planted in the house of Yahweh,
they will flourish in the courts of our God.

In old age they will still bear fruit,
will remain fresh and green,
to proclaim Yahweh's integrity;
my rock, in whom no fault can be found.

Praising God
Psalm 93:1-5 (NLT)
The Lord is king! He is robed in majesty.
　Indeed, the Lord is robed in majesty and armed with strength.
The world is firmly established;
　it cannot be shaken.

Your throne, O Lord, has been established from time immemorial.
　You yourself are from the everlasting past.
The mighty oceans have roared, O Lord.
　The mighty oceans roar like thunder;
　the mighty oceans roar as they pound the shore.
But mightier than the violent raging of the seas,
　mightier than the breakers on the shore—
　the Lord above is mightier than these!
Your royal decrees cannot be changed.
　The nature of your reign, O Lord, is holiness forever.

Making Requests Known
Psalm 94:1-23 (GWT)
O Lord, God of vengeance,
　O God of vengeance, appear!
Arise, O Judge of the earth.
Give arrogant people what they deserve.
　How long, O Lord, will wicked people triumph?
　How long?

They ramble.
　They speak arrogantly.
　　All troublemakers brag about themselves.
They crush your people, O Lord.

They make those who belong to you suffer.
　　They kill widows and foreigners, and they murder orphans.
　　　They say, "The Lord doesn't see it.
　　　　The God of Jacob doesn't even pay attention to it."

Pay attention, you stupid people!
When will you become wise, you fools?
　God created ears.
　　Do you think he can't hear?
　He formed eyes.
　　Do you think he can't see?
　He disciplines nations.
　　Do you think he can't punish?
　He teaches people.
　　Do you think he doesn't know anything?
　　　The Lord knows that people's thoughts are pointless.

O Lord, blessed is the person
　whom you discipline and instruct from your teachings.
　　You give him peace and quiet from times of trouble
　　　while a pit is dug to trap wicked people.

The Lord will never desert his people
　or abandon those who belong to him.
　　The decisions of judges will again become fair,
　　　and everyone whose motives are decent will pursue justice.

Who will stand up for me against evildoers?
Who will stand by my side against troublemakers?
　If the Lord had not come to help me,
　　my soul would have quickly fallen silent {in death}.

When I said, "My feet are slipping,"
　your mercy, O Lord, continued to hold me up.
When I worried about many things,
　your assuring words soothed my soul.

Are wicked rulers who use the law to do unlawful things
　able to be your partners?
They join forces to take the lives of righteous people.
They condemn innocent people to death.
The Lord has become my stronghold.
My God has become my rock of refuge.

> He has turned their own wickedness against them.
> He will destroy them because of their sins.
> The Lord our God will destroy them.

Verses About Prayer
Psalm 96:4-9 (CEV)
The Lord is great and deserves our greatest praise!
He is the only God worthy of our worship.
Other nations worship idols,
but the Lord created the heavens.
Give honor and praise to the Lord,
whose power and beauty fill his holy temple."

Tell everyone of every nation,
"Praise the glorious power of the Lord.
He is wonderful! Praise him
and bring an offering into his temple.
Everyone on earth, now tremble
and worship the Lord, majestic and holy."

Praising God
Psalm 97:8-9 (TEV)
> The people of Zion are glad,
>   and the cities of Judah rejoice
>   because of your judgments, O Lord.
>   Lord Almighty, you are ruler of all the earth;
>   you are much greater than all the gods.

Praising God
Psalm 99:8 (CEV)
Our Lord and our God,
you answered their prayers and forgave their sins,
but when they did wrong, you punished them.

Praising God
Psalm 101:1-8 (ESV)
> I will sing of steadfast love and justice;
>   to you, O Lord, I will make music.
> I will ponder the way that is blameless.

Oh when will you come to me?
I will walk with integrity of heart
 within my house;
I will not set before my eyes
 anything that is worthless.
I hate the work of those who fall away;
 it shall not cling to me.
A perverse heart shall be far from me;
 I will know nothing of evil.
Whoever slanders his neighbor secretly
 I will destroy.
Whoever has a haughty look and an arrogant heart
 I will not endure.
I will look with favor on the faithful in the land,
 that they may dwell with me;
he who walks in the way that is blameless
 shall minister to me.
No one who practices deceit
 shall dwell in my house;
no one who utters lies
 shall continue before my eyes.
Morning by morning I will destroy
 all the wicked in the land,
cutting off all the evildoers
 from the city of the Lord.

Making Requests Known
Psalm 102:1-28 (NIV)

Hear my prayer, O Lord;
 let my cry for help come to you.
Do not hide your face from me
 when I am in distress.
Turn your ear to me;
 when I call, answer me quickly.

For my days vanish like smoke;
 my bones burn like glowing embers.
My heart is blighted and withered like grass;
 I forget to eat my food.
Because of my loud groaning
 I am reduced to skin and bones.
I am like a desert owl,

like an owl among the ruins.
I lie awake; I have become
   like a bird alone on a roof.
All day long my enemies taunt me;
   those who rail against me use my name as a curse.
For I eat ashes as my food
   and mingle my drink with tears
because of your great wrath,
   for you have taken me up and thrown me aside.
My days are like the evening shadow;
   I wither away like grass.

But you, O Lord, sit enthroned forever;
   your renown endures through all generations.
You will arise and have compassion on Zion,
   for it is time to show favor to her;
   the appointed time has come.
For her stones are dear to your servants;
   her very dust moves them to pity.
The nations will fear the name of the Lord,
   all the kings of the earth will revere your glory.
For the Lord will rebuild Zion
   and appear in his glory.
He will respond to the prayer of the destitute;
   he will not despise their plea.
Let this be written for a future generation,
   that a people not yet created may praise the Lord:
"The Lord looked down from his sanctuary on high,
   from heaven he viewed the earth,
to hear the groans of the prisoners
   and release those condemned to death."
So the name of the Lord will be declared in Zion
   and his praise in Jerusalem
when the peoples and the kingdoms
   assemble to worship the Lord.
In the course of my life he broke my strength;
   he cut short my days.
So I said:
   "Do not take me away, O my God, in the midst of my days;
   your years go on through all generations.
In the beginning you laid the foundations of the earth,
   and the heavens are the work of your hands.
They will perish, but you remain;

they will all wear out like a garment.
Like clothing you will change them
   and they will be discarded.
But you remain the same,
   and your years will never end.
The children of your servants will live in your presence;
   their descendants will be established before you."

Praising God
Psalm 103:1-22 (NASB)

Bless the Lord, O my soul,
And all that is within me, bless His holy name.
Bless the Lord, O my soul,
And forget none of His benefits;
Who pardons all your iniquities,
Who heals all your diseases;
Who redeems your life from the pit,
Who crowns you with lovingkindness and compassion;
Who satisfies your years with good things,
So that your youth is renewed like the eagle.

The Lord performs righteous deeds
And judgments for all who are oppressed.
He made known His ways to Moses,
His acts to the sons of Israel.
The Lord is compassionate and gracious,
Slow to anger and abounding in lovingkindness.
He will not always strive with us,
Nor will He keep His anger forever.
He has not dealt with us according to our sins,
Nor rewarded us according to our iniquities.
For as high as the heavens are above the earth,
So great is His lovingkindness toward those who fear Him.
As far as the east is from the west,
So far has He removed our transgressions from us.
Just as a father has compassion on his children,
So the Lord has compassion on those who fear Him.
For He Himself knows our frame;
He is mindful that we are but dust.

As for man, his days are like grass;
As a flower of the field, so he flourishes.

When the wind has passed over it, it is no more,
And its place acknowledges it no longer.
But the lovingkindness of the Lord is from everlasting
to everlasting on those who fear Him,
And His righteousness to children's children,
To those who keep His covenant
And remember His precepts to do them.

The Lord has established His throne in the heavens,
And His sovereignty rules over all.
Bless the Lord, you His angels,
Mighty in strength, who perform His word,
Obeying the voice of His word!
Bless the Lord, all you His hosts,
You who serve Him, doing His will.
Bless the Lord, all you works of His,
In all places of His dominion;
Bless the Lord, O my soul!

Praising God
Psalm 104:1-35 (NRSV)

Bless the Lord, O my soul.
   O Lord my God, you are very great.
You are clothed with honor and majesty,
   wrapped in light as with a garment.
You stretch out the heavens like a tent,
   you set the beams of your chambers on the waters,
you make the clouds your chariot,
   you ride on the wings of the wind,
you make the winds your messengers,
   fire and flame your ministers.

You set the earth on its foundations,
   so that it shall never be shaken.
You cover it with the deep as with a garment;
   the waters stood above the mountains.
At your rebuke they flee;
   at the sound of your thunder they take to flight.
They rose up to the mountains, ran down to the valleys
   to the place that you appointed for them.
You set a boundary that they may not pass,
   so that they might not again cover the earth.

You make springs gush forth in the valleys;
  they flow between the hills,
giving drink to every wild animal;
  the wild asses quench their thirst.
By the streams the birds of the air have their habitation;
  they sing among the branches.
From your lofty abode you water the mountains;
  the earth is satisfied with the fruit of your work.

You cause the grass to grow for the cattle,
  and plants for people to use,
to bring forth food from the earth,
  and wine to gladden the human heart,
oil to make the face shine,
  and bread to strengthen the human heart.
The trees of the Lord are watered abundantly,
  the cedars of Lebanon that he planted.
In them the birds build their nests;
  the stork has its home in the fir trees.
The high mountains are for the wild goats;
  the rocks are a refuge for the coneys.
You have made the moon to mark the seasons;
  the sun knows its time for setting.
You make darkness, and it is night,
  when all the animals of the forest come creeping out.
The young lions roar for their prey,
  seeking their food from God.
When the sun rises, they withdraw
  and lie down in their dens.
People go out to their work
  and to their labor until the evening.

O Lord, how manifold are your works!
  In wisdom you have made them all;
  the earth is full of your creatures.
Yonder is the sea, great and wide,
  creeping things innumerable are there,
  living things both small and great.
There go the ships,
  and Leviathan that you formed to sport in it.

These all look to you

to give them their food in due season;
when you give to them, they gather it up;
   when you open your hand, they are filled with good things.
When you hide your face, they are dismayed;
   when you take away their breath, they die
   and return to their dust.
When you send forth your spirit, they are created;
   and you renew the face of the ground.

May the glory of the Lord endure forever;
   may the Lord rejoice in his works--
who looks on the earth and it trembles,
   who touches the mountains and they smoke.
I will sing to the Lord as long as I live;
   I will sing praise to my God while I have being.
May my meditation be pleasing to him,
   for I rejoice in the Lord.
Let sinners be consumed from the earth,
   and let the wicked be no more.
Bless the Lord, O my soul.
Praise the Lord!

Thanksgiving & Gratitude
Psalm 106:1-48 (NAB)

Hallelujah!
Give thanks to the LORD, who is good,
   whose love endures forever.
Who can tell the mighty deeds of the LORD,
   proclaim in full God's praise?
Happy those who do what is right,
   whose deeds are always just.
Remember me, LORD, as you favor your people;
   come to me with your saving help,
That I may see the prosperity of your chosen,
   rejoice in the joy of your people,
   and glory with your heritage.
We have sinned like our ancestors;
   we have done wrong and are guilty.

        I

Our ancestors in Egypt
   did not attend to your wonders.

They did not remember your great love;
   they defied the Most High at the Red Sea.
Yet he saved them for his name's sake
   to make his power known.
He roared at the Red Sea and it dried up.
   He led them through the deep as through a desert.
He rescued them from hostile hands,
   freed them from the power of the enemy.
The waters covered their oppressors;
   not one of them survived.
Then they believed his words
   and sang songs of praise.

II

But they soon forgot all he had done;
   they had no patience for his plan.
In the desert they gave way to their cravings,
   tempted God in the wasteland.
So he gave them what they asked
   and sent among them a wasting disease.

III

In the camp they challenged Moses
   and Aaron, the holy one of the LORD.
The earth opened and swallowed Dathan,
   it closed on the followers of Abiram.
Against that company the fire blazed;
   flames consumed the wicked.

IV

At Horeb they fashioned a calf,
   worshiped a metal statue.
They exchanged their glorious God
   for the image of a grass-eating bull.
They forgot the God who saved them,
   who did great deeds in Egypt,
Amazing deeds in the land of Ham,
   fearsome deeds at the Red Sea.
He would have decreed their destruction,
   had not Moses, the chosen leader,
Withstood him in the breach
   to turn back his destroying anger.

V

Next they despised the beautiful land;

they did not believe the promise.
In their tents they complained;
    they did not obey the LORD.
So with raised hand he swore
    to destroy them in the desert,
To scatter their descendants among the nations,
    disperse them in foreign lands.

VI

They joined in the rites of Baal of Peor,
    ate food sacrificed to dead gods.
They provoked him by their actions,
    and a plague broke out among them.
Then Phinehas rose to intervene,
    and the plague was brought to a halt.
This was counted for him as a righteous deed
    for all generations to come.

VII

At the waters of Meribah they angered God,
    and Moses suffered because of them.
They so embittered his spirit
    that rash words crossed his lips.

VIII

They did not destroy the peoples
    as the LORD had commanded them,
But mingled with the nations
    and imitated their ways.
They worshiped their idols
    and were ensnared by them.
They sacrificed to the gods
    their own sons and daughters,
Shedding innocent blood,
    the blood of their own sons and daughters,
Whom they sacrificed to the idols of Canaan,
    desecrating the land with bloodshed.
They defiled themselves by their actions,
    became adulterers by their conduct.
So the LORD grew angry with his people,
    abhorred his own heritage.
He handed them over to the nations,
    and their adversaries ruled them.

Their enemies oppressed them,
 kept them under subjection.
Many times did he rescue them,
 but they kept rebelling and scheming
 and were brought low by their own guilt.
Still God had regard for their affliction
 when he heard their wailing.
For their sake he remembered his covenant
 and relented in his abundant love,
Winning for them compassion
 from all who held them captive.
Save us, LORD, our God;
 gather us from among the nations
That we may give thanks to your holy name
 and glory in praising you.
Blessed be the LORD, the God of Israel,
 from everlasting to everlasting!
 Let all the people say, Amen!
Hallelujah!

Thanksgiving & Gratitude / Making Requests Known
Psalm 107:1-43 (ASV)
O give thanks unto Jehovah;
For he is good;
For his lovingkindness endureth for ever.
Let the redeemed of Jehovah say so,
Whom he hath redeemed from the hand of the adversary,
And gathered out of the lands,
From the east and from the west,
From the north and from the south.
They wandered in the wilderness in a desert way;
They found no city of habitation.
Hungry and thirsty,
Their soul fainted in them.
Then they cried unto Jehovah in their trouble,
And he delivered them out of their distresses,
He led them also by a straight way,
That they might go to a city of habitation.
Oh that men would praise Jehovah for his lovingkindness,
And for his wonderful works to the children of men!
For he satisfieth the longing soul,
And the hungry soul he filleth with good.

Such as sat in darkness and in the shadow of death,
Being bound in affliction and iron,
Because they rebelled against the words of God,
And contemned the counsel of the Most High:
Therefore he brought down their heart with labor;
They fell down, and there was none to help.
Then they cried unto Jehovah in their trouble,
And he saved them out of their distresses.
He brought them out of darkness and the shadow of death,
And brake their bonds in sunder.
Oh that men would praise Jehovah for his lovingkindness,
And for his wonderful works to the children of men!
For he hath broken the gates of brass,
And cut the bars of iron in sunder.

Fools because of their transgression,
And because of their iniquities, are afflicted.
Their soul abhorreth all manner of food;
And they draw near unto the gates of death.
Then they cry unto Jehovah in their trouble,
And he saveth them out of their distresses.
He sendeth his word, and healeth them,
And delivereth them from their destructions.
Oh that men would praise Jehovah for his lovingkindness,
And for his wonderful works to the children of men!
And let them offer the sacrifices of thanksgiving,
And declare his works with singing.

They that go down to the sea in ships,
That do business in great waters;
These see the works of Jehovah,
And his wonders in the deep.
For he commandeth, and raiseth the stormy wind,
Which lifteth up the waves thereof.
They mount up to the heavens, they go down again to the depths:
Their soul melteth away because of trouble.
They reel to and fro, and stagger like a drunken man,
And are at their wits' end.
Then they cry unto Jehovah in their trouble,
And he bringeth them out of their distresses.
He maketh the storm a calm,
So that the waves thereof are still.

Then are they glad because they are quiet;
So he bringeth them unto their desired haven.
Oh that men would praise Jehovah for his lovingkindness,
And for his wonderful works to the children of men!
Let them exalt him also in the assembly of the people,
And praise him in the seat of the elders.

He turneth rivers into a wilderness,
And watersprings into a thirsty ground;
A fruitful land into a salt desert,
For the wickedness of them that dwell therein.
He turneth a wilderness into a pool of water,
And a dry land into watersprings.
And there he maketh the hungry to dwell,
That they may prepare a city of habitation,
And sow fields, and plant vineyards,
And get them fruits of increase.
He blesseth them also, so that they are multiplied greatly;
And he suffereth not their cattle to decrease.
Again, they are diminished and bowed down
Through oppression, trouble, and sorrow.
He poureth contempt upon princes,
And causeth them to wander in the waste, where there is no way.
Yet setteth he the needy on high from affliction,
And maketh him families like a flock.
The upright shall see it, and be glad;
And all iniquity shall stop her mouth.
Whoso is wise will give heed to these things;
And they will consider the lovingkindnesses of Jehovah.

Praising God/Making Requests Known
Psalm 108:1-13 (NJB)

My heart is ready, God,
   I will sing and make music;
      come, my glory!
Awake, lyre and harp,
   I will awake the Dawn!

I will praise you among the peoples, Yahweh,
I will play to you among nations,
for your faithful love towers to heaven,
and your constancy to the clouds.

Be exalted above the heavens, God.
Your glory over the whole earth!

To rescue those you love,
save with your right hand and answer us.

God has spoken from his sanctuary,
'In triumph I will divide up Shechem,
and share out the Valley of Succoth.

'Mine is Gilead, mine Manasseh,
Ephraim the helmet on my head,
Judah my commander's baton,

'Moab a bowl for me to wash in,
on Edom I plant my sandal,
over Philistia I cry victory.'

Who will lead me against a fortified city,
who will guide me into Edom,
if not you, the God who has rejected us?
God, you no longer march with our armies.

Bring us help in our time of crisis,
any human assistance is worthless.
With God we shall do deeds of valour,
he will trample down our enemies.

Making Requests Known
Psalm 109:1-31 (NLT)

O God, whom I praise,
    don't stand silent and aloof
while the wicked slander me
    and tell lies about me.
They are all around me with their hateful words,
    and they fight against me for no reason.
I love them, but they try to destroy me—
    even as I am praying for them!
They return evil for good,
    and hatred for my love.

Arrange for an evil person to turn on him.

Send an accuser to bring him to trial.
When his case is called for judgment,
   let him be pronounced guilty.
   Count his prayers as sins.
Let his years be few;
   let his position be given to someone else.
May his children become fatherless,
   and may his wife become a widow.
May his children wander as beggars;
   may they be evicted from their ruined homes.
May creditors seize his entire estate,
   and strangers take all he has earned.
Let no one be kind to him;
   let no one pity his fatherless children.
May all his offspring die.
   May his family name be blotted out in a single generation.
May the Lord never forget the sins of his ancestors;
   may his mother's sins never be erased from the record.
May these sins always remain before the Lord,
   but may his name be cut off from human memory.
For he refused all kindness to others;
   he persecuted the poor and needy,
   and he hounded the brokenhearted to death.
He loved to curse others;
   now you curse him.
He never blessed others;
   now don't you bless him.
Cursing is as much a part of him as his clothing,
   or as the water he drinks,
   or the rich food he eats.
Now may his curses return and cling to him like clothing;
   may they be tied around him like a belt.

May those curses become the Lord's punishment for my accusers
   who are plotting against my life.
But deal well with me, O Sovereign Lord,
   for the sake of your own reputation!
Rescue me because you are so faithful and good.
   For I am poor and needy,
   and my heart is full of pain.
I am fading like a shadow at dusk;
   I am falling like a grasshopper that is brushed aside.
My knees are weak from fasting,

and I am skin and bones.
I am an object of mockery to people everywhere;
> when they see me, they shake their heads.

Help me, O Lord my God!
> Save me because of your unfailing love.
Let them see that this is your doing,
> that you yourself have done it, Lord.
Then let them curse me if they like,
> but you will bless me!
When they attack me, they will be disgraced!
> But I, your servant, will go right on rejoicing!
Make their humiliation obvious to all;
> clothe my accusers with disgrace.
But I will give repeated thanks to the Lord,
> praising him to everyone.
For he stands beside the needy,
> ready to save them from those who condemn them.

Blessings & Benedictions/Praising God
Psalm 115:1 (GWT)

Don't give glory to us, O Lord.
Don't give glory to us.
> Instead, give glory to your name
> > because of your mercy and faithfulness.

Praising God
Psalm 116:1-19 (TEV)

I love the Lord, because he hears me;
> he listens to my prayers.
He listens to me
> every time I call to him.
The danger of death was all around me;
> the horrors of the grave closed in on me;
> I was filled with fear and anxiety.
Then I called to the Lord,
> "I beg you, Lord, save me!"

The Lord is merciful and good;
> our God is compassionate.
The Lord protects the helpless;

when I was in danger, he saved me.
Be confident, my heart,
    because the Lord has been good to me.

The Lord saved me from death;
    he stopped my tears
    and kept me from defeat.
And so I walk in the presence of the Lord
    in the world of the living.
I kept on believing, even when I said,
    "I am completely crushed,"
even when I was afraid and said,
    "No one can be trusted."

What can I offer the Lord
    for all his goodness to me?
I will bring a wine offering to the Lord,
    to thank him for saving me.
In the assembly of all his people
    I will give him what I have promised.

How painful it is to the Lord
    when one of his people dies!
I am your servant, Lord;
    I serve you just as my mother did.
You have saved me from death.
I will give you a sacrifice of thanksgiving
    and offer my prayer to you.
  In the assembly of all your people,
    in the sanctuary of your Temple in Jerusalem,
    I will give you what I have promised.
Praise the Lord!

Thanksgiving & Gratitude
Psalm 118:25-29 (CEV)
We'll ask the Lord to save us!
We'll sincerely ask the Lord to let us win.

God bless the one who comes in the name of the Lord!
We praise you from here in the house of the Lord.

The Lord is our God, and he has given us light!

Start the celebration!
March with palm branches all the way to the altar.

The Lord is my God!
I will praise him and tell him how thankful I am.

Tell the Lord how thankful you are,
because he is kind and always merciful.

Making Requests Known/Praising God
Psalm 119:1-176 (ESV)

    Aleph
Blessed are those whose way is blameless,
    who walk in the law of the Lord!
Blessed are those who keep his testimonies,
    who seek him with their whole heart,
who also do no wrong,
    but walk in his ways!
You have commanded your precepts
    to be kept diligently.
Oh that my ways may be steadfast
    in keeping your statutes!
Then I shall not be put to shame,
    having my eyes fixed on all your commandments.
I will praise you with an upright heart,
    when I learn your righteous rules.
I will keep your statutes;
    do not utterly forsake me!

    Beth
How can a young man keep his way pure?
    By guarding it according to your word.
With my whole heart I seek you;
    let me not wander from your commandments!
I have stored up your word in my heart,
    that I might not sin against you.
Blessed are you, O Lord;
    teach me your statutes!
With my lips I declare
    all the rules of your mouth.
In the way of your testimonies I delight
    as much as in all riches.

I will meditate on your precepts
    and fix my eyes on your ways.
I will delight in your statutes;
    I will not forget your word.

       Gimel

Deal bountifully with your servant,
    that I may live and keep your word.
Open my eyes, that I may behold
    wondrous things out of your law.
I am a sojourner on the earth;
    hide not your commandments from me!
My soul is consumed with longing
    for your rules at all times.
You rebuke the insolent, accursed ones,
    who wander from your commandments.
Take away from me scorn and contempt,
    for I have kept your testimonies.
Even though princes sit plotting against me,
    your servant will meditate on your statutes.
Your testimonies are my delight;
    they are my counselors.

       Daleth

My soul clings to the dust;
    give me life according to your word!
When I told of my ways, you answered me;
    teach me your statutes!
Make me understand the way of your precepts,
    and I will meditate on your wondrous works.
My soul melts away for sorrow;
    strengthen me according to your word!
Put false ways far from me
    and graciously teach me your law!
I have chosen the way of faithfulness;
    I set your rules before me.
I cling to your testimonies, O Lord;
    let me not be put to shame!
I will run in the way of your commandments
    when you enlarge my heart!

       He

Teach me, O Lord, the way of your statutes;

and I will keep it to the end.
Give me understanding, that I may keep your law
    and observe it with my whole heart.
Lead me in the path of your commandments,
    for I delight in it.
Incline my heart to your testimonies,
    and not to selfish gain!
Turn my eyes from looking at worthless things;
    and give me life in your ways.
Confirm to your servant your promise,
    that you may be feared.
Turn away the reproach that I dread,
    for your rules are good.
Behold, I long for your precepts;
    in your righteousness give me life!

    Waw

Let your steadfast love come to me, O Lord,
    your salvation according to your promise;
then shall I have an answer for him who taunts me,
    for I trust in your word.
And take not the word of truth utterly out of my mouth,
    for my hope is in your rules.
I will keep your law continually,
    forever and ever,
and I shall walk in a wide place,
    for I have sought your precepts.
I will also speak of your testimonies before kings
    and shall not be put to shame,
for I find my delight in your commandments,
    which I love.
I will lift up my hands toward your commandments, which I love,
    and I will meditate on your statutes.

    Zayin

Remember your word to your servant,
    in which you have made me hope.
This is my comfort in my affliction,
    that your promise gives me life.
The insolent utterly deride me,
    but I do not turn away from your law.
When I think of your rules from of old,
    I take comfort, O Lord.

Hot indignation seizes me because of the wicked,
>   who forsake your law.
Your statutes have been my songs
>   in the house of my sojourning.
I remember your name in the night, O Lord,
>   and keep your law.
This blessing has fallen to me,
>   that I have kept your precepts.

Heth

The Lord is my portion;
>   I promise to keep your words.
I entreat your favor with all my heart;
>   be gracious to me according to your promise.
When I think on my ways,
>   I turn my feet to your testimonies;
I hasten and do not delay
>   to keep your commandments.
Though the cords of the wicked ensnare me,
>   I do not forget your law.
At midnight I rise to praise you,
>   because of your righteous rules.
I am a companion of all who fear you,
>   of those who keep your precepts.
The earth, O Lord, is full of your steadfast love;
>   teach me your statutes!

Teth

You have dealt well with your servant,
>   O Lord, according to your word.
Teach me good judgment and knowledge,
>   for I believe in your commandments.
Before I was afflicted I went astray,
>   but now I keep your word.
You are good and do good;
>   teach me your statutes.
The insolent smear me with lies,
>   but with my whole heart I keep your precepts;
their heart is unfeeling like fat,
>   but I delight in your law.
It is good for me that I was afflicted,
>   that I might learn your statutes.

The law of your mouth is better to me
    than thousands of gold and silver pieces.
        Yodh
Your hands have made and fashioned me;
    give me understanding that I may learn your commandments.
Those who fear you shall see me and rejoice,
    because I have hoped in your word.
I know, O Lord, that your rules are righteous,
    and that in faithfulness you have afflicted me.
Let your steadfast love comfort me
    according to your promise to your servant.
Let your mercy come to me, that I may live;
    for your law is my delight.
Let the insolent be put to shame,
    because they have wronged me with falsehood;
    as for me, I will meditate on your precepts.
Let those who fear you turn to me,
    that they may know your testimonies.
May my heart be blameless in your statutes,
    that I may not be put to shame!

        Kaph
My soul longs for your salvation;
    I hope in your word.
My eyes long for your promise;
    I ask, "When will you comfort me?"
For I have become like a wineskin in the smoke,
    yet I have not forgotten your statutes.
How long must your servant endure?
    When will you judge those who persecute me?
The insolent have dug pitfalls for me;
    they do not live according to your law.
All your commandments are sure;
    they persecute me with falsehood; help me!
They have almost made an end of me on earth,
    but I have not forsaken your precepts.
In your steadfast love give me life,
    that I may keep the testimonies of your mouth.

        Lamedh
Forever, O Lord, your word
    is firmly fixed in the heavens.
Your faithfulness endures to all generations;

you have established the earth, and it stands fast.
By your appointment they stand this day,
    for all things are your servants.
If your law had not been my delight,
    I would have perished in my affliction.
I will never forget your precepts,
    for by them you have given me life.
I am yours; save me,
    for I have sought your precepts.
The wicked lie in wait to destroy me,
    but I consider your testimonies.
I have seen a limit to all perfection,
    but your commandment is exceedingly broad.

    Mem
Oh how I love your law!
    It is my meditation all the day.
Your commandment makes me wiser than my enemies,
    for it is ever with me.
I have more understanding than all my teachers,
    for your testimonies are my meditation.
I understand more than the aged,
    for I keep your precepts.
I hold back my feet from every evil way,
    in order to keep your word.
I do not turn aside from your rules,
    for you have taught me.
How sweet are your words to my taste,
    sweeter than honey to my mouth!
Through your precepts I get understanding;
    therefore I hate every false way.

    Nun
Your word is a lamp to my feet
    and a light to my path.
I have sworn an oath and confirmed it,
    to keep your righteous rules.
I am severely afflicted;
    give me life, O Lord, according to your word!
Accept my freewill offerings of praise, O Lord,
    and teach me your rules.
I hold my life in my hand continually,
    but I do not forget your law.

The wicked have laid a snare for me,
 but I do not stray from your precepts.
Your testimonies are my heritage forever,
 for they are the joy of my heart.
I incline my heart to perform your statutes
 forever, to the end.

Samekh
I hate the double-minded,
 but I love your law.
You are my hiding place and my shield;
 I hope in your word.
Depart from me, you evildoers,
 that I may keep the commandments of my God.
Uphold me according to your promise, that I may live,
 and let me not be put to shame in my hope!
Hold me up, that I may be safe
 and have regard for your statutes continually!
You spurn all who go astray from your statutes,
 for their cunning is in vain.
All the wicked of the earth you discard like dross,
 therefore I love your testimonies.
My flesh trembles for fear of you,
 and I am afraid of your judgments.

Ayin
I have done what is just and right;
 do not leave me to my oppressors.
Give your servant a pledge of good;
 let not the insolent oppress me.
My eyes long for your salvation
 and for the fulfillment of your righteous promise.
Deal with your servant according to your steadfast love,
 and teach me your statutes.
I am your servant; give me understanding,
 that I may know your testimonies!
It is time for the Lord to act,
 for your law has been broken.
Therefore I love your commandments
 above gold, above fine gold.
Therefore I consider all your precepts to be right;
 I hate every false way.

Pe

Your testimonies are wonderful;
  therefore my soul keeps them.
The unfolding of your words gives light;
  it imparts understanding to the simple.
I open my mouth and pant,
  because I long for your commandments.
Turn to me and be gracious to me,
  as is your way with those who love your name.
Keep steady my steps according to your promise,
  and let no iniquity get dominion over me.
Redeem me from man's oppression,
  that I may keep your precepts.
Make your face shine upon your servant,
  and teach me your statutes.
My eyes shed streams of tears,
  because people do not keep your law.

Tsadhe

Righteous are you, O Lord,
  and right are your rules.
You have appointed your testimonies in righteousness
  and in all faithfulness.
My zeal consumes me,
  because my foes forget your words.
Your promise is well tried,
  and your servant loves it.
I am small and despised,
  yet I do not forget your precepts.
Your righteousness is righteous forever,
  and your law is true.
Trouble and anguish have found me out,
  but your commandments are my delight.
Your testimonies are righteous forever;
  give me understanding that I may live.

Qoph

With my whole heart I cry; answer me, O Lord!
  I will keep your statutes.
I call to you; save me,
  that I may observe your testimonies.
I rise before dawn and cry for help;
  I hope in your words.

My eyes are awake before the watches of the night,
    that I may meditate on your promise.
Hear my voice according to your steadfast love;
    O Lord, according to your justice give me life.
They draw near who persecute me with evil purpose;
    they are far from your law.
But you are near, O Lord,
    and all your commandments are true.
Long have I known from your testimonies
    that you have founded them forever.

Resh

Look on my affliction and deliver me,
    for I do not forget your law.
Plead my cause and redeem me;
    give me life according to your promise!
Salvation is far from the wicked,
    for they do not seek your statutes.
Great is your mercy, O Lord;
    give me life according to your rules.
Many are my persecutors and my adversaries,
    but I do not swerve from your testimonies.
I look at the faithless with disgust,
    because they do not keep your commands.
Consider how I love your precepts!
    Give me life according to your steadfast love.
The sum of your word is truth,
    and every one of your righteous rules endures forever.

Sin and Shin

Princes persecute me without cause,
    but my heart stands in awe of your words.
I rejoice at your word
    like one who finds great spoil.
I hate and abhor falsehood,
    but I love your law.
Seven times a day I praise you
    for your righteous rules.
Great peace have those who love your law;
    nothing can make them stumble.
I hope for your salvation, O Lord,
    and I do your commandments.
My soul keeps your testimonies;

    I love them exceedingly.
I keep your precepts and testimonies,
    for all my ways are before you.

        Taw
Let my cry come before you, O Lord;
    give me understanding according to your word!
Let my plea come before you;
    deliver me according to your word.
My lips will pour forth praise,
    for you teach me your statutes.
My tongue will sing of your word,
    for all your commandments are right.
Let your hand be ready to help me,
    for I have chosen your precepts.
I long for your salvation, O Lord,
    and your law is my delight.
Let my soul live and praise you,
    and let your rules help me.
I have gone astray like a lost sheep; seek your servant,
    for I do not forget your commandments.

English Standard Version.

Making Requests Known
Psalm 120:2 (NIV)

Save me, O Lord, from lying lips
    and from deceitful tongues.

Making Requests Known
Psalm 123:1-4 (NASB)

    To You I lift up my eyes,
O You who are enthroned in the heavens!
Behold, as the eyes of servants look to the hand of their master,
As the eyes of a maid to the hand of her mistress,
So our eyes look to the Lord our God,
Until He is gracious to us.

Be gracious to us, O Lord, be gracious to us,
For we are greatly filled with contempt.
Our soul is greatly filled
With the scoffing of those who are at ease,

And with the contempt of the proud.

Praying for Others
Psalm 125:4 (NRSV)
Do good, O Lord, to those who are good,
and to those who are upright in their hearts.

Making Requests Known
Psalm 126:4 (NAB)
Restore again our fortunes, LORD,
like the dry stream beds of the Negeb.

Making Requests Known
Psalm 130:1-8 (NJB)
From the depths I call to you, Yahweh:
Lord, hear my cry.
Listen attentively
to the sound of my pleading!

If you kept a record of our sins,
Lord, who could stand their ground?
But with you is forgiveness,
that you may be revered.

I rely, my whole being relies,
Yahweh, on your promise.
My whole being hopes in the Lord,
more than watchmen for daybreak;
more than watchmen for daybreak
let Israel hope in Yahweh.
For with Yahweh is faithful love,
with him generous ransom;
and he will ransom Israel
from all its sins.

Responding to God
Psalm 131:1-3 (NLT)
Lord, my heart is not proud;
my eyes are not haughty.
I don't concern myself with matters too great
or awesome for me.

But I have stilled and quieted myself,
>   just as a small child is quiet with its mother.
>   Yes, like a small child is my soul within me.
> O Israel, put your hope in the Lord—
>   now and always.

Praying for Others
Psalm 132:1-10 (GWT)

> O Lord, remember David and all the hardships he endured.
> Remember how he swore an oath to the Lord
>   and made this vow to the Mighty One of Jacob:
>   "I will not step inside my house,
>   get into my bed, shut my eyes, or close my eyelids
>   until I find a place for the Lord,
>   a dwelling place for the Mighty One of Jacob."
>
> Now, we have heard about the ark {of the promise}
>   being in Ephrathah.
>   We have found it in Jaar.
> Let's go to his dwelling place.
> Let's worship at his footstool.
> O Lord, arise, and come to your resting place
>   with the ark of your power.
> Clothe your priests with righteousness.
> Let your godly ones sing with joy.
> For the sake of your servant David,
>   do not reject your anointed one.

Praising God
Psalm 135:13 (TEV)

> Lord, you will always be proclaimed as God;
>   all generations will remember you.

Making Requests Known
Psalm 137:7 (CEV)

Our Lord, punish the Edomites!
Because the day Jerusalem fell, they shouted,
"Completely destroy the city! Tear down every building!"

Praising God
Psalm 138:1-8 (ESV)

I give you thanks, O Lord, with my whole heart;
   before the gods I sing your praise;
I bow down toward your holy temple
   and give thanks to your name for your steadfast
   love and your faithfulness,
   for you have exalted above all things
   your name and your word.
On the day I called, you answered me;
   my strength of soul you increased.
All the kings of the earth shall give you thanks, O Lord,
   for they have heard the words of your mouth,
and they shall sing of the ways of the Lord,
   for great is the glory of the Lord.
For though the Lord is high, he regards the lowly,
   but the haughty he knows from afar.
Though I walk in the midst of trouble,
   you preserve my life;
you stretch out your hand against the wrath of my enemies,
   and your right hand delivers me.
The Lord will fulfill his purpose for me;
   your steadfast love, O Lord, endures forever.
   Do not forsake the work of your hands.

Making Requests Known/Praising God
Psalm 139:1-24 (NIV)

O Lord, you have searched me
   and you know me.
You know when I sit and when I rise;
   you perceive my thoughts from afar.
You discern my going out and my lying down;
   you are familiar with all my ways.
Before a word is on my tongue
   you know it completely, O Lord.

You hem me in--behind and before;
   you have laid your hand upon me.
Such knowledge is too wonderful for me,
   too lofty for me to attain.

Where can I go from your Spirit?
  Where can I flee from your presence?
If I go up to the heavens, you are there;
  if I make my bed in the depths, you are there.
If I rise on the wings of the dawn,
  if I settle on the far side of the sea,
even there your hand will guide me,
  your right hand will hold me fast.

If I say, "Surely the darkness will hide me
  and the light become night around me,"
even the darkness will not be dark to you;
  the night will shine like the day,
  for darkness is as light to you.

For you created my inmost being;
  you knit me together in my mother's womb.
I praise you because I am fearfully and wonderfully made;
  your works are wonderful,
  I know that full well.
My frame was not hidden from you
  when I was made in the secret place.
When I was woven together in the depths of the earth,
  your eyes saw my unformed body.
All the days ordained for me
  were written in your book
  before one of them came to be.

How precious to me are your thoughts, O God!
  How vast is the sum of them!
Were I to count them,
  they would outnumber the grains of sand.
When I awake,
  I am still with you.

If only you would slay the wicked, O God!
  Away from me, you bloodthirsty men!
They speak of you with evil intent;
  your adversaries misuse your name.
Do I not hate those who hate you, O Lord,
  and abhor those who rise up against you?
I have nothing but hatred for them;
  I count them my enemies.

Search me, O God, and know my heart;
   test me and know my anxious thoughts.
See if there is any offensive way in me,
    and lead me in the way everlasting.

Making Requests Known
Psalm 140:1-13 (NASB)

Rescue me, O Lord, from evil men;
Preserve me from violent men
Who devise evil things in their hearts;
They continually stir up wars.
They sharpen their tongues as a serpent;
Poison of a viper is under their lips.
Selah.

Keep me, O Lord, from the hands of the wicked;
Preserve me from violent men
Who have purposed to trip up my feet.
The proud have hidden a trap for me, and cords;
They have spread a net by the wayside;
They have set snares for me.
Selah.

I said to the Lord, "You are my God;
Give ear, O Lord, to the voice of my supplications.
"O God the Lord, the strength of my salvation,
You have covered my head in the day of battle.
"Do not grant, O Lord, the desires of the wicked;
Do not promote his evil device, that they not be exalted.
Selah.

"As for the head of those who surround me,
May the mischief of their lips cover them.
"May burning coals fall upon them;
May they be cast into the fire,
Into deep pits from which they cannot rise.
"May a slanderer not be established in the earth;
May evil hunt the violent man speedily."

I know that the Lord will maintain the cause of the afflicted
And justice for the poor.

Surely the righteous will give thanks to Your name;
The upright will dwell in Your presence.

Making Requests Known
Psalm 141:1-10 (NRSV)

I call upon you, O Lord; come quickly to me;
    give ear to my voice when I call to you.
Let my prayer be counted as incense before you,
    and the lifting up of my hands as an evening sacrifice.
Set a guard over my mouth, O Lord;
    keep watch over the door of my lips.
Do not turn my heart to any evil,
    to busy myself with wicked deeds
in company with those who work iniquity;
    do not let me eat of their delicacies.

Let the righteous strike me;
    let the faithful correct me.
Never let the oil of the wicked anoint my head,
    for my prayer is continually against their wicked deeds.
When they are given over to those who shall condemn them,
    then they shall learn that my words were pleasant.
Like a rock that one breaks apart and shatters on the land,
    so shall their bones be strewn at the mouth of Sheol.

But my eyes are turned toward you, O God, my Lord;
    in you I seek refuge; do not leave me defenseless.
Keep me from the trap that they have laid for me,
    and from the snares of evildoers.
Let the wicked fall into their own nets,
    while I alone escape.

Making Requests Known
Psalm 142:1-7 (NAB)

With full voice I cry to the LORD;
    with full voice I beseech the LORD.
Before God I pour out my complaint,
    lay bare my distress.
My spirit is faint within me,
    but you know my path.

Along the way I walk
   they have hidden a trap for me.
I look to my right hand,
   but no friend is there.
There is no escape for me;
   no one cares for me.
I cry out to you, LORD,
I say, You are my refuge,
   my portion in the land of the living.
Listen to my cry for help,
   for I am brought very low.
Rescue me from my pursuers,
   for they are too strong for me.
Lead me out of my prison,
   that I may give thanks to your name.
Then the just shall gather around me
   because you have been good to me.

Making Requests Known
Psalm 143:1-12 (NJB)

Yahweh, hear my prayer,
listen to my pleading;
in your constancy answer me,
in your saving justice;
do not put your servant on trial,
for no one living can be found guiltless at your tribunal.

An enemy is in deadly pursuit,
crushing me into the ground,
forcing me to live in darkness,
like those long dead.
My spirit is faint,
and within me my heart is numb with fear.

I recall the days of old,
reflecting on all your deeds,
I ponder the works of your hands.
I stretch out my hands to you,
my heart like a land thirsty for you.
    Pause

Answer me quickly, Yahweh,

my spirit is worn out;
do not turn away your face from me,
or I shall be like those who sink into oblivion.

Let dawn bring news of your faithful love,
for I place my trust in you;
show me the road I must travel
for you to relieve my heart.

Rescue me from my enemies, Yahweh,
since in you I find protection.
Teach me to do your will,
for you are my God.
May your generous spirit lead me
on even ground.

Yahweh, for the sake of your name,
in your saving justice give me life,
rescue me from distress.
In your faithful love annihilate my enemies,
destroy all those who oppress me,
for I am your servant.

Praising God/Making Requests Known
Psalm 144:1-15 (NLT)

Bless the Lord, who is my rock.
> He gives me strength for war
> and skill for battle.

He is my loving ally and my fortress,
> my tower of safety, my deliverer.

He stands before me as a shield, and I take refuge in him.
> He subdues the nations under me.

O Lord, what are mortals that you should notice us,
> mere humans that you should care for us?

For we are like a breath of air;
> our days are like a passing shadow.

Bend down the heavens, Lord, and come down.
> Touch the mountains so they billow smoke.

Release your lightning bolts and scatter your enemies!
> Release your arrows and confuse them!

>   Reach down from heaven and rescue me;
>   deliver me from deep waters,
>   from the power of my enemies.
>   Their mouths are full of lies;
>   they swear to tell the truth, but they lie.
>
>   I will sing a new song to you, O God!
>   I will sing your praises with a ten-stringed harp.
>   For you grant victory to kings!
>   You are the one who rescued your servant David.
>   Save me from the fatal sword!
>   Rescue me from the power of my enemies.
>   Their mouths are full of lies;
>   they swear to tell the truth, but they lie.
>
>   May our sons flourish in their youth
>   like well-nurtured plants.
>   May our daughters be like graceful pillars,
>   carved to beautify a palace.
>   May our farms be filled
>   with crops of every kind.
>   May the flocks in our fields multiply by the thousands,
>   even tens of thousands,
>   and may our oxen be loaded down with produce.
>   May there be no breached walls, no forced exile,
>   no cries of distress in our squares.
>   Yes, happy are those who have it like this!
>   Happy indeed are those whose God is the Lord.

Praising God
Psalm 145:1-21 (GWT)

>   I will highly praise you, my God, the king.
>   I will bless your name forever and ever.
>   I will bless you every day.
>   I will praise your name forever and ever.
>
>   The Lord is great, and he should be highly praised.
>   His greatness is unsearchable.
>   One generation will praise your deeds to the next.
>   Each generation will talk about your mighty acts.
>   I will think about the glorious honor of your majesty
>   and the miraculous things you have done.

People will talk about the power of your terrifying deeds,
    and I will tell about your greatness.
They will announce what they remember of your great goodness,
    and they will joyfully sing about your righteousness.
The Lord is merciful, compassionate, patient,
    and always ready to forgive.
The Lord is good to everyone
    and has compassion for everything that he has made.
Everything that you have made will give thanks to you, O Lord,
    and your faithful ones will praise you.
Everyone will talk about the glory of your kingdom
    and will tell the descendants of Adam about your might
        in order to make known your mighty deeds
            and the glorious honor of your kingdom.
Your kingdom is an everlasting kingdom.
Your empire endures throughout every generation.

The Lord supports everyone who falls.
He straightens {the backs} of those who are bent over.
    The eyes of all creatures look to you,
        and you give them their food at the proper time.
    You open your hand,
        and you satisfy the desire of every living thing.
The Lord is fair in all his ways
    and faithful in everything he does.
The Lord is near to everyone who prays to him,
    to every faithful person who prays to him.
He fills the needs of those who fear him.
He hears their cries for help and saves them.
The Lord protects everyone who loves him,
    but he will destroy all wicked people.

My mouth will speak the praise of the Lord,
    and all living creatures will praise his holy name
        forever and ever.

Praising God
Psalm 146:1 (TEV)

Praise the Lord!
    Praise the Lord, my soul!

Verses about Prayer
Proverbs 3:5-6 (ESV)

Trust in the Lord with all your heart,
  and do not lean on your own understanding.
In all your ways acknowledge him,
  and he will make straight your paths.

Verses about Prayer
Proverbs 15:8 (GWT)

A sacrifice brought by wicked people is disgusting to the Lord,
  but the prayers of decent people please him.

Verses about Prayer
Proverbs 15:29 (CEV)

The Lord never even hears the prayers of the wicked,
but he answers the prayers of all who obey him.

Verses about Prayer
Proverbs 21:13 (ASV)

Whoso stoppeth his ears at the cry of the poor,
He also shall cry, but shall not be heard.

Verses about Prayer
Eccles. 5:2 (ESV)

Be not rash with your mouth, nor let your heart be hasty to utter a word before God, for God is in heaven and you are on earth. Therefore let your words be few.

Verses about Prayer
Isaiah 1:15 (TLB)

From now on, when you pray with your hands stretched out to heaven, I won't look or listen. Even though you make many prayers, I will not hear, for your hands are those of murderers; they are covered with the blood of your innocent victims.

Praising God
Isaiah 6:3 (NIV)

And they were calling to one another:
"Holy, holy, holy is the Lord Almighty;
  the whole earth is full of his glory."

Confessing Sin
Isaiah 6:5 (NASB)
Then I said,
"Woe is me, for I am ruined!
Because I am a man of unclean lips,
And I live among a people of unclean lips;
For my eyes have seen the King, the Lord of hosts."

Responding to God
Isaiah 6:8 (NRSV)
Then I heard the voice of the Lord saying, "Whom shall I send, and who will go for us?" And I said, "Here am I; send me!"

Seeking God's Will
Isaiah 6:11 (NAB)
"How long, O Lord?" I asked. And he replied:
Until the cities are desolate,
    without inhabitants,
Houses, without a man,
    and the earth is a desolate waste.

Praising God
Isaiah 12:1-6 (NJB)
And, that day, you will say:
'I praise you, Yahweh,
    you have been angry with me
but your anger is now appeased
    and you have comforted me.
Look, he is the God of my salvation:
I shall have faith and not be afraid,
for Yahweh is my strength and my song,
he has been my salvation.'

Joyfully you will draw water
from the springs of salvation
and, that day, you will say,
'Praise Yahweh, invoke his name.
Proclaim his deeds to the people,
declare his name sublime.
Sing of Yahweh,

for his works are majestic,
make them known throughout the world.
Cry and shout for joy,
you who live in Zion,
For the Holy One of Israel
is among you in his greatness.'

Praising God
Isaiah 25:1-5 (TLB)

O Lord, I will honor and praise your name, for you are my God; you do such wonderful things! You planned them long ago, and now you have accomplished them, just as you said! You turn mighty cities into heaps of ruins. The strongest forts are turned to rubble. Beautiful palaces in distant lands disappear and will never be rebuilt. Therefore strong nations will shake with fear before you; ruthless nations will obey and glorify your name.

But to the poor, O Lord, you are a refuge from the storm, a shadow from the heat, a shelter from merciless men who are like a driving rain that melts down an earthen wall. As a hot, dry land is cooled by clouds, you will cool the pride of ruthless nations.

Praising God
Isaiah 25:9 (GWT)

On that day {his people} will say,
"This is our God; we have waited for him, and now he will save us.
This is the Lord; we have waited for him.
Let us rejoice and be glad because he will save us."

Praising God
Isaiah 26:1-21 (TEV)

A day is coming when the people will sing this song in the land of Judah:
Our city is strong!
God himself defends its walls!
Open the city gates
and let the faithful nation enter,
the nation whose people do what is right.
You, Lord, give perfect peace
to those who keep their purpose firm
and put their trust in you.
Trust in the Lord forever;

he will always protect us.
He has humbled those who were proud;
> he destroyed the strong city they lived in,
> and sent its walls crashing into the dust.
Those who were oppressed walk over it now
> and trample it under their feet.

Lord, you make the path smooth for good people;
> the road they travel is level.
We follow your will and put our hope in you;
> you are all that we desire.
At night I long for you with all my heart;
> when you judge the earth and its people,
> they will all learn what justice is.
Even though you are kind to the wicked,
> they never learn to do what is right.
Even here in a land of righteous people
> they still do wrong;
> they refuse to recognize your greatness.
Your enemies do not know that you will punish them.
Lord, put them to shame and let them suffer;
> let them suffer the punishment you have prepared.
Show them how much you love your people.

You will give us prosperity, Lord;
> everything that we achieve
> is the result of what you do.
Lord our God, we have been ruled by others,
> but you alone are our Lord.
Now they are dead and will not live again;
> their ghosts will not rise,
> for you have punished them and destroyed them.
No one remembers them any more.
Lord, you have made our nation grow,
> enlarging its territory on every side;
> and this has brought you honor.
You punished your people, Lord,
> and in anguish they prayed to you.
You, Lord, have made us cry out,
> as a woman in labor cries out in pain.
We were in pain and agony,
> but we gave birth to nothing.
We have won no victory for our land;

we have accomplished nothing.

> Those of our people who have died will live again!
> Their bodies will come back to life.
> All those sleeping in their graves
> > will wake up and sing for joy.
> As the sparkling dew refreshes the earth,
> > so the Lord will revive those who have long been dead.

Go into your houses, my people, and shut the door behind you. Hide yourselves for a little while until God's anger is over. The Lord is coming from his heavenly dwelling place to punish the people of the earth for their sins. The murders that were secretly committed on the earth will be revealed, and the ground will no longer hide those who have been killed.

Making Requests Known
Isaiah 30:19 (TLB)

O my people in Jerusalem, you shall weep no more, for he will surely be gracious to you at the sound of your cry. He will answer you.

Making Requests Known
Isaiah 33:2-4 (CEV)

Please, Lord, be kind to us! We depend on you.
Make us strong each morning,
and come to save us when we are in trouble.
Nations scatter when you roar and show your greatness.
We attack our enemies like swarms of locusts;
we take everything that belongs to them.

Making Requests Known
Isaiah 37:14-20 (CEV)

After Hezekiah had read the note from the king of Assyria, he took it to the temple and spread it out for the Lord to see. Then he prayed:

Lord God All-Powerful of Israel, your throne is above the winged creatures. You created the heavens and the earth, and you alone rule the kingdoms of this world. Just look and see how Sennacherib has insulted you, the living God.

It is true, our Lord, that Assyrian kings have turned nations into deserts. They destroyed the idols of wood and stone that the people of those nations had made and worshiped. But you are our Lord and our

God! We ask you to keep us safe from the Assyrian king. Then everyone in every kingdom on earth will know that you are the only Lord.

Making Requests Known
Isaiah 38:2-3 (ASV)
Then Hezekiah turned his face to the wall, and prayed unto Jehovah, and said, Remember now, O Jehovah, I beseech thee, how I have walked before thee in truth and with a perfect heart, and have done that which is good in thy sight. And Hezekiah wept sore.

Making Requests Known
Isaiah 38:14 (ESV)
Like a swallow or a crane I chirp;
   I moan like a dove.
My eyes are weary with looking upward.
   O Lord, I am oppressed; be my pledge of safety!

Confessing Sin
Isaiah 55:6-7 (NIV)
Seek the Lord while he may be found;
   call on him while he is near.
Let the wicked forsake his way
   and the evil man his thoughts.
Let him turn to the Lord, and he will have mercy on him,
   and to our God, for he will freely pardon.

Making Requests Known
Isaiah 58:9 (GWT)
Then you will call, and the Lord will answer.
You will cry for help, and he will say, "Here I am!"
Get rid of that yoke.
   Don't point your finger and say wicked things.

Confessing Sin
Isaiah 59:9-15 (NASB)
Therefore justice is far from us,
And righteousness does not overtake us;
We hope for light, but behold, darkness,
For brightness, but we walk in gloom.
We grope along the wall like blind men,

We grope like those who have no eyes;
We stumble at midday as in the twilight,
Among those who are vigorous we are like dead men.
All of us growl like bears,
And moan sadly like doves;
We hope for justice, but there is none,
For salvation, but it is far from us.
For our transgressions are multiplied before You,
And our sins testify against us;
For our transgressions are with us,
And we know our iniquities:
Transgressing and denying the Lord,
And turning away from our God,
Speaking oppression and revolt,
Conceiving in and uttering from the heart lying words.
Justice is turned back,
And righteousness stands far away;
For truth has stumbled in the street,
And uprightness cannot enter.
Yes, truth is lacking;
And he who turns aside from evil makes himself a prey.
Now the Lord saw,
And it was displeasing in His sight that there was no justice.

Praising God
Isaiah 63:7-19 (NRSV)

I will recount the gracious deeds of the Lord,
    the praiseworthy acts of the Lord,
because of all that the Lord has done for us,
    and the great favor to the house of Israel
that he has shown them according to his mercy,
    according to the abundance of his steadfast love.
For he said, "Surely they are my people,
    children who will not deal falsely";
and he became their savior
    in all their distress.
It was no messenger or angel
    but his presence that saved them;
in his love and in his pity he redeemed them;
    he lifted them up and carried them all the days of old.

But they rebelled
    and grieved his holy spirit;

therefore he became their enemy;
    he himself fought against them.
Then they remembered the days of old,
    of Moses his servant.
Where is the one who brought them up out of the sea
    with the shepherds of his flock?
Where is the one who put within them
    his holy spirit,
who caused his glorious arm
    to march at the right hand of Moses,
who divided the waters before them
    to make for himself an everlasting name,
    who led them through the depths?
Like a horse in the desert,
    they did not stumble.
Like cattle that go down into the valley,
    the spirit of the Lord gave them rest.
Thus you led your people,
    to make for yourself a glorious name.

Look down from heaven and see,
    from your holy and glorious habitation.
Where are your zeal and your might?
    The yearning of your heart and your compassion?
    They are withheld from me.
For you are our father,
    though Abraham does not know us
    and Israel does not acknowledge us;
you, O Lord, are our father;
    our Redeemer from of old is your name.
Why, O Lord, do you make us stray from your ways
    and harden our heart, so that we do not fear you?
Turn back for the sake of your servants,
    for the sake of the tribes that are your heritage.
Your holy people took possession for a little while;
    but now our adversaries have trampled down your sanctuary.
We have long been like those whom you do not rule,
    like those not called by your name.

Confessing Sin/Making Requests Known
Isaiah 64:1-12 (NAB)
Oh, that you would rend the heavens and come down,

with the mountains quaking before you,
  As when brushwood is set ablaze,
    or fire makes the water boil!
Thus your name would be made known to your enemies
  and the nations would tremble before you,
While you wrought awesome deeds we could
    not hope for,
      such as they had not heard of from of old.
No ear has ever heard, no eye ever seen,
    any God but you
      doing such deeds for those who wait for him.
  Would that you might meet us doing right,
    that we were mindful of you in our ways!
Behold, you are angry, and we are sinful;
    all of us have become like unclean men,
    all our good deeds are like polluted rags;
We have all withered like leaves,
    and our guilt carries us away like the wind.
  There is none who calls upon your name,
    who rouses himself to cling to you;
For you have hidden your face from us
    and have delivered us up to our guilt.
  Yet, O LORD, you are our father;
    we are the clay and you the potter:
    we are all the work of your hands.
  Be not so very angry, LORD,
    keep not our guilt forever in mind;
    look upon us, who are all your people.
  Your holy cities have become a desert,
    Zion is a desert, Jerusalem a waste.
  Our holy and glorious temple
    in which our fathers praised you
Has been burned with fire;
    all that was dear to us is laid waste.
  Can you hold back, O LORD, after all this?
    Can you remain silent, and afflict us so severely?

Responding to God
Jeremiah 1:6 (NJB)
I then said, 'Ah, ah, ah, Lord Yahweh; you see, I do not know how to speak: I am only a child!'

Making Requests Known
Jeremiah 4:10-31 (TLB)

(Then I said, "But Lord, the people have been deceived by what you said, for you promised great blessings on Jerusalem. Yet the sword is even now poised to strike them dead!")

At that time he will send a burning wind from the desert upon them--not in little gusts but in a roaring blast--and he will pronounce their doom.

The enemy shall roll down upon us like a storm wind; his chariots are like a whirlwind; his steeds are swifter than eagles. Woe, woe upon us, for we are doomed.

O Jerusalem, cleanse your hearts while there is time. You can yet be saved by casting out your evil thoughts. From Dan and from Mount Ephraim your doom has been announced. Warn the other nations that the enemy is coming from a distant land, and they shout against Jerusalem and the cities of Judah. They surround Jerusalem like shepherds moving in on some wild animal! For my people have rebelled against me, says the Lord. Your ways have brought this down upon you; it is a bitter dose of your own medicine, striking deep within your hearts.

My heart, my heart--I writhe in pain; my heart pounds within me. I cannot be still because I have heard, O my soul, the blast of the enemies' trumpets and the enemies' battle cries. Wave upon wave of destruction rolls over the land, until it lies in utter ruin; suddenly, in a moment, every house is crushed. How long must this go on? How long must I see war and death surrounding me?

"Until my people leave their foolishness, for they refuse to listen to me; they are dull, retarded children who have no understanding. They are smart enough at doing wrong, but for doing right they have no talent, none at all."

I looked down upon their land, and as far as I could see in all directions everything was ruins. And all the heavens were dark. I looked at the mountains and saw that they trembled and shook. I looked, and mankind was gone, and the birds of the heavens had fled.

The fertile valleys were wilderness, and all the cities were broken down before the presence of the Lord, crushed by his fierce anger. The Lord's decree of desolation covers all the land.

"Yet," he says, "there will be a little remnant of my people left. The earth shall mourn, the heavens shall be draped with black, because of my decree against my people; I have made up my mind and will not change it."

All the cities flee in terror at the noise of marching armies coming near. The people hide in the bushes and flee to the mountains. All the cities are abandoned--all have fled in terror. Why do you put on your most beautiful clothing and jewelry and brighten your eyes with mascara? It will do you no good! Your allies despise you and will kill you.

I have heard great crying like that of a woman giving birth to her first child; it is the cry of my people gasping for breath, pleading for help, prostrate before their murderers.

Seeking God's Will
Jeremiah 5:3 (GWT)
>Lord, your eyes look for the truth.
>>You strike these people, but they don't feel it.
>>You crush them, but they refuse to be corrected.
>>>They are more stubborn than rocks.
>>>They refuse to turn back.

Making Requests Known
Jeremiah 8:18 (CEV)
I'm burdened with sorrow and feel like giving up.

Praising God
Jeremiah 10:6-10 (ASV)
There is none like unto thee, O Jehovah; thou art great, and thy name is great in might. Who should not fear thee, O King of the nations? for to thee doth it appertain; forasmuch as among all the wise men of the nations, and in all their royal estate, there is none like unto thee. But they are together brutish and foolish: the instruction of idols! it is but a stock. There is silver beaten into plates, which is brought from Tarshish, and gold from Uphaz, the work of the artificer and of the hands of the goldsmith; blue and purple for their clothing; they are all the work of skilful men. But Jehovah is the true God; he is the living God, and an everlasting King: at his wrath the earth trembleth, and the nations are not able to abide his indignation.

Making Requests Known
Jeremiah 10:23-25 (ESV)
>I know, O Lord, that the way of man is not in himself,
>>that it is not in man who walks to direct his steps.
>Correct me, O Lord, but in justice;
>>not in your anger, lest you bring me to nothing.
>Pour out your wrath on the nations that know you not,
>>and on the peoples that call not on your name,
>for they have devoured Jacob;
>>they have devoured him and consumed him,

and have laid waste his habitation.

Praising God
Jeremiah 11:5 (NIV)
Then I will fulfill the oath I swore to your forefathers, to give them a land flowing with milk and honey'--the land you possess today."
I answered, "Amen, Lord."

Making Requests Known
Jeremiah 11:20 (NASB)
But, O Lord of hosts, who judges righteously,
Who tries the feelings and the heart,
Let me see Your vengeance on them,
For to You have I committed my cause.

Seeking God's Will/Making Requests Known
Jeremiah 12:1-4 (NRSV)
You will be in the right, O Lord,
    when I lay charges against you;
    but let me put my case to you.
Why does the way of the guilty prosper?
    Why do all who are treacherous thrive?
You plant them, and they take root;
    they grow and bring forth fruit;
you are near in their mouths
    yet far from their hearts.
But you, O Lord, know me;
    You see me and test me--my heart is with you.
Pull them out like sheep for the slaughter,
    and set them apart for the day of slaughter.
How long will the land mourn,
    and the grass of every field wither?
For the wickedness of those who live in it
    the animals and the birds are swept away,
    and because people said, "He is blind to our ways."

Confessing Sin/Making Requests Known
Jeremiah 14:7-9 (NAB)
Even though our crimes bear witness against us,
    take action, O LORD, for the honor of your name--
Even though our rebellions are many,

though we have sinned against you.
O Hope of Israel, O LORD,
  our savior in time of need!
Why should you be a stranger in this land,
  like a traveler who has stopped but for a night?
Why are you like a man dumbfounded,
  a champion who cannot save?
You are in our midst, O LORD,
  your name we bear:
  do not forsake us!

Responding to God
Jeremiah 14:13 (NJB)
'Ah, Lord Yahweh,' I answered, 'here are the prophets telling them, "You will not see the sword, famine will not touch you; I promise you true peace in this place." '

Seeking God's Will/Making Requests Known
Jeremiah 14:19-22 (TLB)
"O Lord," the people will cry, "have you completely rejected Judah? Do you abhor Jerusalem? Even after punishment, will there be no peace? We thought, 'Now at last he will heal us and bind our wounds.' But no peace has come, and there is only trouble and terror everywhere. O Lord, we confess our wickedness, and that of our fathers too. Do not hate us, Lord, for the sake of your own name. Do not disgrace yourself and the throne of your glory by forsaking your promise to bless us! What heathen god can give us rain? Who but you alone, O Lord our God, can do such things as this? Therefore we will wait for you to help us."

Making Requests Known
Jeremiah 15:15-21 (GWT)
O Lord, you understand.
Remember me, take care of me,
  and take revenge on those who persecute me.
Be patient, and don't take me away.
You should know that I've been insulted because of you.

Your words were found, and I devoured them.
Your words are my joy and my heart's delight,
  because I am called by your name, O Lord God of Armies.
I didn't keep company with those who laugh and have fun.
I sat alone because your hand was on me.

You filled me with outrage.
Why is my pain unending
    and my wound incurable, refusing to heal?
Will you disappoint me like a stream
    that dries up in summertime?

This is what the Lord says:
    If you will return, I will take you back.
    If you will speak what is worthwhile and not what is worthless,
        you will stand in my presence.
    The people will return to you, but you will not return to them.
    I will make you like a solid bronze wall in front of these people.
    They will fight you, but they will not defeat you.
        I am with you, and I will save you and rescue you,
            declares the Lord.
    I will rescue you from the power of wicked people
        and free you from the power of tyrants.

Praising God
Jeremiah 16:19-21 (CEV)
I prayed to the Lord:
Our Lord, you are the one who gives me strength
and protects me like a fortress when I am in trouble.
People will come to you from distant nations and say,
"Our ancestors worshiped false and useless gods,
worthless idols made by human hands."

Then the Lord replied,
"That's why I will teach them about my power,
and they will know that I am the true God."

Praising God/Making Requests Known
Jeremiah 17:12-18 (ASV)
    A glorious throne, set on high from the beginning, is the place of our sanctuary. O Jehovah, the hope of Israel, all that forsake thee shall be put to shame. They that depart from me shall be written in the earth, because they have forsaken Jehovah, the fountain of living waters. Heal me, O Jehovah, and I shall be healed; save me, and I shall be saved: for thou art my praise. Behold, they say unto me, Where is the word of Jehovah? let it come now. As for me, I have not hastened from being a shepherd after

thee; neither have I desired the woeful day; thou knowest: that which came out of my lips was before thy face. Be not a terror unto me: thou art my refuge in the day of evil. Let them be put to shame that persecute me, but let not me be put to shame; let them be dismayed, but let not me be dismayed; bring upon them the day of evil, and destroy them with double destruction.

Making Requests Known
Jeremiah 18:19-23 (ESV)

>Hear me, O Lord,
>>and listen to the voice of my adversaries.
>
>Should good be repaid with evil?
>>Yet they have dug a pit for my life.
>
>Remember how I stood before you
>>to speak good for them,
>>to turn away your wrath from them.
>
>Therefore deliver up their children to famine;
>>give them over to the power of the sword;
>
>let their wives become childless and widowed.
>>May their men meet death by pestilence,
>>their youths be struck down by the sword in battle.
>
>May a cry be heard from their houses,
>>when you bring the plunderer suddenly upon them!
>
>For they have dug a pit to take me
>>and laid snares for my feet.
>
>Yet you, O Lord, know
>>all their plotting to kill me.
>
>Forgive not their iniquity,
>>nor blot out their sin from your sight.
>
>Let them be overthrown before you;
>>deal with them in the time of your anger.

Making Requests Known/Praising God
Jeremiah 20:7-13 (NIV)

>O Lord, you deceived me, and I was deceived;
>>you overpowered me and prevailed.
>
>I am ridiculed all day long;
>>everyone mocks me.
>
>Whenever I speak, I cry out
>>proclaiming violence and destruction.
>
>So the word of the Lord has brought me

insult and reproach all day long.
But if I say, "I will not mention him
    or speak any more in his name,"
his word is in my heart like a fire,
    a fire shut up in my bones.
I am weary of holding it in;
    indeed, I cannot.
I hear many whispering,
    "Terror on every side!
    Report him! Let's report him!"
All my friends
    are waiting for me to slip, saying,
"Perhaps he will be deceived;
    then we will prevail over him
    and take our revenge on him."

But the Lord is with me like a mighty warrior;
    so my persecutors will stumble and not prevail.
They will fail and be thoroughly disgraced;
    their dishonor will never be forgotten.
O Lord Almighty, you who examine the righteous
    and probe the heart and mind,
let me see your vengeance upon them,
    for to you I have committed my cause.

Sing to the Lord!
    Give praise to the Lord!
He rescues the life of the needy
    from the hands of the wicked.

Praying for Others
Jeremiah 28:6 (NASB)

And the prophet Jeremiah said, "Amen! May the Lord do so; may the Lord confirm your words which you have prophesied to bring back the vessels of the Lord's house and all the exiles, from Babylon to this place.

Making Requests Known
Jeremiah 29:7 (NRSV)

But seek the welfare of the city where I have sent you into exile, and pray to the Lord on its behalf, for in its welfare you will find your welfare.

Making Requests Known
Jeremiah 29:12 (NAB)
When you call me, when you go to pray to me, I will listen to you.

Praising God/Making Requests Known
Jeremiah 32:16-25 (NJB)
'After I had entrusted the deed of purchase to Baruch son of Neriah, I prayed to Yahweh as follows, "Ah, Lord Yahweh, you made the heavens and the earth by your great power and outstretched arm. To you nothing is impossible. You show faithful love to thousands but repay the fathers' guilt in full to their children after them. Great and mighty God, whose name is Yahweh Sabaoth, great in purpose, mighty in deed, whose eyes are open on all human ways, rewarding every individual as that person's ways and actions deserve! You performed signs and wonders in Egypt, as you still do in Israel and among humanity today. You have won the name for yourself which is yours today. You brought your people Israel out of Egypt with signs and wonders, with mighty hand and outstretched arm and fearsome terror. Then you gave them this country which you had promised on oath to their ancestors, a country flowing with milk and honey. They then entered it, taking possession of it, but they would not listen to your voice nor follow your Law: they would do nothing you ordered them to do; and so you made this total disaster befall them. Look! The earthworks are already in place to take the city and, by means of sword, famine and plague, the city is now within the clutches of the Chaldaeans attacking it. What you said has now come true, as you see. Yet you yourself, Lord Yahweh, told me: Buy the field, pay for it, have it witnessed although the city is already in the Chaldaeans' clutches."

Praying for Others
Jeremiah 42:2-4 (TLB)
And said, "Please pray for us to the Lord your God, for as you know so well, we are only a tiny remnant of what we were before. Beg the Lord your God to show us what to do and where to go."

"All right," Jeremiah replied. "I will ask him and I will tell you what he says. I will hide nothing from you."

Making Requests Known
Lament. 1:9 (GWT)
Jerusalem's own filth {covers} its clothes.
  It gave no thought to its future.
  Its downfall was shocking.
    No one offers it comfort.

'O Lord, look at my suffering,
>   because my enemies have triumphed.'

Making Requests Known
Lament. 1:11 (CEV)
Everyone in the city groans while searching for food;
they trade their valuables
for barely enough scraps to stay alive.
Jerusalem Speaks:
Jerusalem shouts to the Lord,
"Please look and see how miserable I am!"

Making Requests Known
Lament. 1:20-22 (ASV)
Behold, O Jehovah; for I am in distress; my heart is troubled;
My heart is turned within me; for I have grievously rebelled:
Abroad the sword bereaveth, at home there is as death.
They have heard that I sigh; there is none to comfort me;
All mine enemies have heard of my trouble; they are glad that thou hast done it:
Thou wilt bring the day that thou hast proclaimed, and they shall be like unto me.
Let all their wickedness come before thee;
And do unto them, as thou hast done unto me for all my transgressions:
For my sighs are many, and my heart is faint.

Seeking God's Will
Lament. 2:20-22 (ESV)
>   Look, O Lord, and see!
>   With whom have you dealt thus?
>   Should women eat the fruit of their womb,
>   the children of their tender care?
>   Should priest and prophet be killed
>   in the sanctuary of the Lord?
>   In the dust of the streets
>   lie the young and the old;
>   my young women and my young men
>   have fallen by the sword;
>   you have killed them in the day of your anger,
>   slaughtering without pity.
>   You summoned as if to a festival day

>   my terrors on every side,
> and on the day of the anger of the Lord
>   no one escaped or survived;
>   those whom I held and raised
>   my enemy destroyed.

Verses about Prayer
Lament. 3:25-26 (CEV)
The Lord is kind to everyone who trusts and obeys him.
It is good to wait patiently for the Lord to save us.

Making Requests Known
Lament. 3:37-66 (NIV)
>   Who can speak and have it happen
>   if the Lord has not decreed it?
>   Is it not from the mouth of the Most High
>   that both calamities and good things come?
>   Why should any living man complain
>   when punished for his sins?
>
>   Let us examine our ways and test them,
>   and let us return to the Lord.
>   Let us lift up our hearts and our hands
>   to God in heaven, and say:
>   "We have sinned and rebelled
>   and you have not forgiven.
>
>   "You have covered yourself with anger and pursued us;
>   you have slain without pity.
>   You have covered yourself with a cloud
>   so that no prayer can get through.
>   You have made us scum and refuse
>   among the nations.
>
>   "All our enemies have opened their mouths
>   wide against us.
>   We have suffered terror and pitfalls,
>   ruin and destruction."
>   Streams of tears flow from my eyes
>   because my people are destroyed.
>
>   My eyes will flow unceasingly,

without relief,
until the Lord looks down
   from heaven and sees.
What I see brings grief to my soul
   because of all the women of my city.

Those who were my enemies without cause
   hunted me like a bird.
They tried to end my life in a pit
   and threw stones at me;
the waters closed over my head,
   and I thought I was about to be cut off.

I called on your name, O Lord,
   from the depths of the pit.
You heard my plea: "Do not close your ears
   to my cry for relief."
You came near when I called you,
   and you said, "Do not fear."

O Lord, you took up my case;
   you redeemed my life.
You have seen, O Lord, the wrong done to me.
   Uphold my cause!
You have seen the depth of their vengeance,
   all their plots against me.

O Lord, you have heard their insults,
   all their plots against me--
what my enemies whisper and mutter
   against me all day long.
Look at them! Sitting or standing,
   they mock me in their songs.

Pay them back what they deserve, O Lord,
   for what their hands have done.
Put a veil over their hearts,
   and may your curse be on them!
Pursue them in anger and destroy them
   from under the heavens of the Lord.

Making Requests Known
Lament. 5:1-3 (NASB)
>Remember, O Lord, what has befallen us;
>Look, and see our reproach!
>Our inheritance has been turned over to strangers,
>Our houses to aliens.
>We have become orphans without a father,
>Our mothers are like widows.

Praising God/Making Requests Known
Lament. 5:19-22 (NRSV)
>But you, O Lord, reign forever;
>   your throne endures to all generations.
>Why have you forgotten us completely?
>   Why have you forsaken us these many days?
>Restore us to yourself, O Lord, that we may be restored;
>   renew our days as of old--
>unless you have utterly rejected us,
>   and are angry with us beyond measure.

Responding to God
Ezekiel 4:14 (NAB)
"Oh no, Lord GOD!" I protested. "Never have I been made unclean, and from my youth till now, never have I eaten carrion flesh or that torn by wild beasts; never has any unclean meat entered my mouth."

Seeking God's Will
Ezekiel 9:8 (NJB)
While they were hacking them down, I was left alone; I fell on my face, crying out, 'Ah, Lord Yahweh, are you going to annihilate all that is left of Israel by venting your fury on Jerusalem?'

Praying for Others
Ezekiel 11:13 (TLB)
While I was still speaking and telling them this, Pelatiah (son of Benaiah) suddenly died. Then I fell to the ground on my face and cried out: "O Lord God, are you going to kill everyone in all Israel?"

Making Requests Known
Daniel 2:18 (GWT)
He told them to ask the God of heaven to be merciful and to explain this secret to them so that they would not be destroyed with the rest of the wise advisers in Babylon.

Praising God/Thanksgiving & Gratitude
Daniel 2:20-23 (CEV)
"Our God, your name
will be praised forever and forever.
You are all-powerful, and you know everything.
You control human events—
you give rulers their power and take it away,
and you are the source of wisdom and knowledge.

"You explain deep mysteries,
because even the dark is light to you.
You are the God
who was worshiped by my ancestors.
Now I thank you and praise you for making me wise
and telling me the king's dream, together with its meaning."

Thanksgiving & Gratitude/Making Requests Known
Daniel 6:10-11 (ASV)
And when Daniel knew that the writing was signed, he went into his house (now his windows were open in his chamber toward Jerusalem) and he kneeled upon his knees three times a day, and prayed, and gave thanks before his God, as he did aforetime. Then these men assembled together, and found Daniel making petition and supplication before his God.

Confessing Sin/Making Requests Known
Daniel 9:4-19 (ESV)
I prayed to the Lord my God and made confession, saying, "O Lord, the great and awesome God, who keeps covenant and steadfast love with those who love him and keep his commandments, we have sinned and done wrong and acted wickedly and rebelled, turning aside from your commandments and rules. We have not listened to your servants the prophets, who spoke in your name to our kings, our princes, and our fathers, and to all the people of the land. To you, O Lord, belongs righteousness, but to us open shame, as at this day, to the men of Judah,

to the inhabitants of Jerusalem, and to all Israel, those who are near and those who are far away, in all the lands to which you have driven them, because of the treachery that they have committed against you. To us, O Lord, belongs open shame, to our kings, to our princes, and to our fathers, because we have sinned against you. To the Lord our God belong mercy and forgiveness, for we have rebelled against him and have not obeyed the voice of the Lord our God by walking in his laws, which he set before us by his servants the prophets. All Israel has transgressed your law and turned aside, refusing to obey your voice. And the curse and oath that are written in the Law of Moses the servant of God have been poured out upon us, because we have sinned against him. He has confirmed his words, which he spoke against us and against our rulers who ruled us, by bringing upon us a great calamity. For under the whole heaven there has not been done anything like what has been done against Jerusalem. As it is written in the Law of Moses, all this calamity has come upon us; yet we have not entreated the favor of the Lord our God, turning from our iniquities and gaining insight by your truth. Therefore the Lord has kept ready the calamity and has brought it upon us, for the Lord our God is righteous in all the works that he has done, and we have not obeyed his voice. And now, O Lord our God, who brought your people out of the land of Egypt with a mighty hand, and have made a name for yourself, as at this day, we have sinned, we have done wickedly. "O Lord, according to all your righteous acts, let your anger and your wrath turn away from your city Jerusalem, your holy hill, because for our sins, and for the iniquities of our fathers, Jerusalem and your people have become a byword among all who are around us. Now therefore, O our God, listen to the prayer of your servant and to his pleas for mercy, and for your own sake, O Lord, make your face to shine upon your sanctuary, which is desolate. O my God, incline your ear and hear. Open your eyes and see our desolations, and the city that is called by your name. For we do not present our pleas before you because of our righteousness, but because of your great mercy. O Lord, hear; O Lord, forgive. O Lord, pay attention and act. Delay not, for your own sake, O my God, because your city and your people are called by your name."

Making Requests Known
Hosea 9:14 (NIV)
Give them, O Lord--
   what will you give them?
Give them wombs that miscarry
   and breasts that are dry.

Making Requests Known
Joel 1:19-20 (NASB)
To You, O Lord, I cry;
For fire has devoured the pastures of the wilderness
And the flame has burned up all the trees of the field.
Even the beasts of the field pant for You;
For the water brooks are dried up
And fire has devoured the pastures of the wilderness.

Making Requests Known
Joel 2:17 (NRSV)
Between the vestibule and the altar
   let the priests, the ministers of the Lord, weep.
Let them say, "Spare your people, O Lord,
   and do not make your heritage a mockery,
   a byword among the nations.
Why should it be said among the peoples,
   'Where is their God?' "

Praying for Others
Amos 7:2 (NAB)
While they were eating all the grass in the land, I said:
Forgive, O Lord GOD!
   How can Jacob stand?
   He is so small!

Praying for Others
Amos 7:5 (NJB)
when I said, 'Lord Yahweh, stop,
   I beg you.
How can Jacob survive, being so small?'

Responding to God
Amos 7:8 (TLB)
And the Lord said to me, "Amos, what do you see?"
I answered, "A plumbline."
And he replied, "I will test my people with a plumbline. I will no longer turn away from punishing.

Making Requests Known
Jonah 1:14 (GWT)

So they cried to the Lord for help: "Please, Lord, don't let us die for taking this man's life. Don't hold us responsible for the death of an innocent man, because you, Lord, do whatever you want."

Pledge & Commitment
Jonah 1:16 (CEV)

The sailors were so terrified that they offered a sacrifice to the Lord and made all kinds of promises.

Thanksgiving & Gratitude
Jonah 2:1-9 (ASV)

Then Jonah prayed unto Jehovah his God out of the fish's belly. And he said, I called by reason of mine affliction unto Jehovah, And he answered me; Out of the belly of Sheol cried I, And thou heardest my voice. For thou didst cast me into the depth, in the heart of the seas, And the flood was round about me; All thy waves and thy billows passed over me. And I said, I am cast out from before thine eyes; Yet I will look again toward thy holy temple. The waters compassed me about, even to the soul; The deep was round about me; The weeds were wrapped about my head. I went down to the bottoms of the mountains; The earth with its bars closed upon me for ever: Yet hast thou brought up my life from the pit, O Jehovah my God. When my soul fainted within me, I remembered Jehovah; And my prayer came in unto thee, into thy holy temple. They that regard lying vanities Forsake their own mercy. But I will sacrifice unto thee with the voice of thanksgiving; I will pay that which I have vowed. Salvation is of Jehovah.

Confessing Sin
Jonah 3:5-9 (ESV)

And the people of Nineveh believed God. They called for a fast and put on sackcloth, from the greatest of them to the least of them.

The word reached the king of Nineveh, and he arose from his throne, removed his robe, covered himself with sackcloth, and sat in ashes. And he issued a proclamation and published through Nineveh, "By the decree of the king and his nobles: Let neither man nor beast, herd nor flock, taste anything. Let them not feed or drink water, but let man and beast be covered with sackcloth, and let them call out mightily to God. Let everyone turn from his evil way and from the violence that is in his hands. Who knows? God may turn and relent and turn from his fierce anger, so that we may not perish."

Making Requests Known
Jonah 4:2-3 (NIV)
He prayed to the Lord, "O Lord, is this not what I said when I was still at home? That is why I was so quick to flee to Tarshish. I knew that you are a gracious and compassionate God, slow to anger and abounding in love, a God who relents from sending calamity. Now, O Lord, take away my life, for it is better for me to die than to live."

Praising God
Micah 6:6 (NASB)
>With what shall I come to the Lord
>And bow myself before the God on high?
>Shall I come to Him with burnt offerings,
>With yearling calves?

Seeking God's Will
Habakkuk 1:2-4 (NRSV)
>O Lord, how long shall I cry for help,
>>and you will not listen?
>
>Or cry to you "Violence!"
>>and you will not save?
>
>Why do you make me see wrongdoing
>>and look at trouble?
>
>Destruction and violence are before me;
>>strife and contention arise.
>
>So the law becomes slack
>>and justice never prevails.
>
>The wicked surround the righteous--
>>therefore judgment comes forth perverted.

Seeking God's Will
Habakkuk 1:12-17 (NAB)
>Are you not from eternity, O LORD,
>>my holy God, immortal?
>
>O LORD you have marked him for judgment,
>>O Rock, you have readied him for punishment!
>
>Too pure are your eyes to look upon evil,
>>and the sight of misery you cannot endure.
>
>Why, then, do you gaze on the faithless in silence

while the wicked man devours
one more just than himself?
You have made man like the fish of the sea,
    like creeping things without a ruler.
He brings them all up with his hook,
    he hauls them away with his net,
He gathers them in his seine;
    and so he rejoices and exults.
Therefore he sacrifices to his net,
    and burns incense to his seine;
For thanks to them his portion is generous,
    and his repast sumptuous.
Shall he, then, keep on brandishing his sword
    to slay peoples without mercy?

Praising God
Habakkuk 3:2-19 (NJB)

Yahweh, I have heard of your renown;
your work, Yahweh,
    inspires me with dread.
Make it live again in our time,
make it known in our time;
in wrath remember mercy.

Eloah comes from Teman,
and the Holy One
    from Mount Paran.
        Pause
His majesty covers the heavens,
and his glory fills the earth.

His brightness is like the day,
rays flash from his hands,
that is where his power lies hidden.

Pestilence goes before him
and Plague follows close behind.

When he stands up,
    he makes the earth tremble,
with his glance
    he makes the nations quake.
And the eternal mountains are dislodged,

the everlasting hills sink down,
his pathway from of old.

I saw the tents of Cushan in trouble,
the tent-curtains of Midian shuddering.

Yahweh, are you enraged with the rivers,
are you angry with the sea,
that you should mount your chargers,
your rescuing chariots?

You uncover your bow,
and give the string its fill of arrows.
    Pause
You drench the soil with torrents;
the mountains see you and tremble,
great floods sweep by,
the abyss roars aloud,
lifting high its waves.

Sun and moon stay inside their dwellings,
they flee at the light of your arrows,
at the flash of your lightning-spear.

In rage you stride across the land,
in anger you trample the nations.

You marched to save your people,
to save your anointed one;
you wounded
    the head of the house of the wicked,
laid bare the foundation to the rock.
    Pause

With your shafts
    you pierced the leader of his warriors
who stormed out with shouts of joy
    to scatter us,
as if they meant to devour
    some poor wretch in their lair.

With your horses
    you trampled through the sea,

through the surging abyss!

When I heard, I trembled to the core,
my lips quivered at the sound;
my bones became disjointed
and my legs gave way beneath me.
Calmly I await the day of anguish
which is dawning
   on the people now attacking us.

(For the fig tree is not to blossom,
nor will the vines bear fruit,
the olive crop will disappoint
and the fields will yield no food;
the sheep will vanish from the fold;
no cattle in the stalls.)

But I shall rejoice in Yahweh,
I shall exult in God my Saviour.

Yahweh my Lord is my strength,
he will make my feet as light as a doe's,
and set my steps on the heights.
For the choirmaster; on stringed instruments.

Seeking God's Will
Malachi 1:2 (TLB)

"I have loved you very deeply," says the Lord.
But you retort, "Really? When was this?"
And the Lord replies, "I showed my love for you by loving your father, Jacob. I didn't need to.

Seeking God's Will
Malachi 1:7 (GWT)

"You offer contaminated food on my altar.
"But you ask, 'Then how have we contaminated you?'
"When you say that the Lord's table may be despised.

Responding to God
Malachi 1:13 (CEV)
You get so disgusted that you even make vulgar signs at me. And for an offering, you bring stolen animals or those that are crippled or sick. Should I accept these?

Seeking God's Will
Malachi 2:17 (ASV)
Ye have wearied Jehovah with your words. Yet ye say, Wherein have we wearied him? In that ye say, Every one that doeth evil is good in the sight of Jehovah, and he delighteth in them; or where is the God of justice?

Seeking God's Will
Malachi 3:7-8 (ESV)
From the days of your fathers you have turned aside from my statutes and have not kept them. Return to me, and I will return to you, says the Lord of hosts. But you say, 'How shall we return?' Will man rob God? Yet you are robbing me. But you say, 'How have we robbed you?' In your tithes and contributions.

The
New Testament

Verses About Prayer
Matthew 5:43-45 (ASV)
Ye have heard that it was said, Thou shalt love thy neighbor, and hate thine enemy: but I say unto you, love your enemies, and pray for them that persecute you; that ye may be sons of your Father who is in heaven: for he maketh his sun to rise on the evil and the good, and sendeth rain on the just and the unjust.

Verses about Prayer
Matthew 6:9-13 (NIV)
"This, then, is how you should pray:
"'Our Father in heaven,
hallowed be your name,
your kingdom come,
your will be done
    on earth as it is in heaven.
Give us today our daily bread.
Forgive us our debts,
    as we also have forgiven our debtors.
And lead us not into temptation,
but deliver us from the evil one.'

Making Requests Known
Matthew 8:31 (NASB)
The demons began to entreat Him, saying, "If You are going to cast us out, send us into the herd of swine."

Making Requests Known
Matthew 9:37-38 (NRSV)
Then he said to his disciples, "The harvest is plentiful, but the laborers are few; therefore ask the Lord of the harvest to send out laborers into his harvest."

Praising God
Matthew 11:25-26 (NAB)
At that time Jesus said in reply, "I give praise to you, Father, Lord of heaven and earth, for although you have hidden these things from the wise and the learned you have revealed them to the childlike. Yes, Father, such has been your gracious will.

Thanksgiving & Gratitude
Matthew 14:19 (NJB)

He gave orders that the people were to sit down on the grass; then he took the five loaves and the two fish, raised his eyes to heaven and said the blessing. And breaking the loaves he handed them to his disciples, who gave them to the crowds.

Making Requests Known
Matthew 14:23 (TLB)

Then afterwards he went up into the hills to pray. Night fell,

Praising God
Matthew 14:33 (GWT)

The men in the boat bowed down in front of Jesus and said, "You are truly the Son of God."

Praying for Others
Matthew 19:13 (CEV)

Some people brought their children to Jesus, so that he could place his hands on them and pray for them. His disciples told the people to stop bothering him.

Praising God
Matthew 21:9-10 (ASV)

And the multitudes that went before him, and that followed, cried, saying, Hosanna to the son of David: Blessed is he that cometh in the name of the Lord; Hosanna in the highest. And when he was come into Jerusalem, all the city was stirred, saying, Who is this?

Making Requests Known
Matthew 21:22 (ESV)

And whatever you ask in prayer, you will receive, if you have faith."

Thanksgiving & Gratitude
Matthew 26:26 (ESV)

Now as they were eating, Jesus took bread, and after blessing it broke it and gave it to the disciples, and said, "Take, eat; this is my body."

Making Requests Known
Matthew 26:36-44 (NIV)
Then Jesus went with his disciples to a place called Gethsemane, and he said to them, "Sit here while I go over there and pray." He took Peter and the two sons of Zebedee along with him, and he began to be sorrowful and troubled. Then he said to them, "My soul is overwhelmed with sorrow to the point of death. Stay here and keep watch with me."

Going a little farther, he fell with his face to the ground and prayed, "My Father, if it is possible, may this cup be taken from me. Yet not as I will, but as you will."

Then he returned to his disciples and found them sleeping. "Could you men not keep watch with me for one hour?" he asked Peter. "Watch and pray so that you will not fall into temptation. The spirit is willing, but the body is weak."

He went away a second time and prayed, "My Father, if it is not possible for this cup to be taken away unless I drink it, may your will be done."

When he came back, he again found them sleeping, because their eyes were heavy. So he left them and went away once more and prayed the third time, saying the same thing.

Making Requests Known
Matthew 27:46 (NASB)
About the ninth hour Jesus cried out with a loud voice, saying, "Eli, Eli, lama sabachthani?" that is, "My God, My God, why have You forsaken Me?"

Making Requests Known
Matthew 27:50 (NRSV)
Then Jesus cried again with a loud voice and breathed his last.

Praising God
Matthew 28:9 (NAB)
And behold, Jesus met them on their way and greeted them. They approached, embraced his feet, and did him homage.

Praising God
Matthew 28:17 (NJB)
When they saw him they fell down before him, though some hesitated.

Seeking God's Will
Mark 1:23-24 (TLB)
A man possessed by a demon was present and began shouting, "Why are you bothering us, Jesus of Nazareth--have you come to destroy us demons? I know who you are--the holy Son of God!"

Making Requests Known
Mark 1:35 (GWT)
In the morning, long before sunrise, Jesus went to a place where he could be alone to pray.

Verses about Prayer
Mark 2:18 (CEV)
The followers of John the Baptist and the Pharisees often went without eating. Some people came and asked Jesus, "Why do the followers of John and those of the Pharisees often go without eating, while your disciples never do?"

Making Requests Known
Mark 5:10 (ASV)
And he besought him much that he would not send them away out of the country.

Thanksgiving & Gratitude
Mark 6:41 (ESV)
And taking the five loaves and the two fish he looked up to heaven and said a blessing and broke the loaves and gave them to the disciples to set before the people. And he divided the two fish among them all.

Praying for Others
Mark 6:46 (NIV)
After leaving them, he went up on a mountainside to pray.

Thanksgiving & Gratitude
Mark 8:7 (NASB)
They also had a few small fish; and after He had blessed them, He ordered these to be served as well.

Making Requests Known
Mark 9:24 (NRSV)
Immediately the father of the child cried out, "I believe; help my unbelief!"

Verses about Prayer
Mark 9:28-29 (TLB)
Afterwards, when Jesus was alone in the house with his disciples, they asked him, "Why couldn't we cast that demon out?"

Jesus replied, "Cases like this require prayer."

Praising God
Mark 11:9-10 (NAB)
Those preceding him as well as those following kept crying out: "Hosanna!

Blessed is he who comes in the name of the Lord!

Blessed is the kingdom of our father David that is to come!

Hosanna in the highest!"

Making Requests Known
Mark 11:22-26 (GWT)
Jesus said to them, "Have faith in God! I can guarantee this truth: This is what will be done for someone who doesn't doubt but believes what he says will happen: He can say to this mountain, 'Be uprooted and thrown into the sea,' and it will be done for him. That's why I tell you to have faith that you have already received whatever you pray for, and it will be yours. Whenever you pray, forgive anything you have against anyone. Then your Father in heaven will forgive your failures."

Verses about Prayer
Mark 12:40 (CEV)
But they cheat widows out of their homes and pray long prayers just to show off. They will be punished most of all.

Thanksgiving & Gratitude
Mark 14:22 (NJB)
And as they were eating he took bread, and when he had said the blessing he broke it and gave it to them. 'Take it,' he said, 'this is my body.'

Making Requests Known
Mark 14:32-39 (TLB)
And now they came to an olive grove called the Garden of Gethsemane, and he instructed his disciples, "Sit here, while I go and pray."

He took Peter, James, and John with him and began to be filled with horror and deepest distress. And he said to them, "My soul is crushed by sorrow to the point of death; stay here and watch with me."

He went on a little further and fell to the ground and prayed that if it were possible the awful hour awaiting him might never come.

"Father, Father," he said, "everything is possible for you. Take away this cup from me. Yet I want your will, not mine."

Then he returned to the three disciples and found them asleep.

"Simon!" he said. "Asleep? Couldn't you watch with me even one hour? Watch with me and pray lest the Tempter overpower you. For though the spirit is willing enough, the body is weak."

And he went away again and prayed, repeating his pleadings.

Making Requests Known
Mark 15:34 (GWT)
At three o'clock Jesus cried out in a loud voice, "Eloi, Eloi, lema sabachthani?" which means, "My God, my God, why have you abandoned me?"

Praising God
Luke 1:8-10 (CEV)
One day Zechariah's group of priests were on duty, and he was serving God as a priest. According to the custom of the priests, he had been chosen to go into the Lord's temple that day and to burn incense, while the people stood outside praying.

Making Requests Known
Luke 1:13 (ASV)
But the angel said unto him, Fear not, Zacharias: because thy supplication is heard, and thy wife Elisabeth shall bear thee a son, and thou shalt call his name John.

Praising God
Luke 2:14 (ESV)
"Glory to God in the highest,
and on earth peace among those with whom he is pleased!"

Praising God
Luke 2:20 (NIV)
The shepherds returned, glorifying and praising God for all the things they had heard and seen, which were just as they had been told.

Praising God
Luke 2:28-32 (NASB)
Then he took Him into his arms, and blessed God, and said,
"Now Lord, You are releasing Your bond-servant to depart in peace,
According to Your word;
For my eyes have seen Your salvation,
Which You have prepared in the presence of all peoples,
A Light of revelation to the Gentiles,
And the glory of Your people Israel."

Thanksgiving & Gratitude
Luke 2:38 (NRSV)
At that moment she came, and began to praise God and to speak about the child to all who were looking for the redemption of Jerusalem.

Praying for Others
Luke 3:21 (NAB)
After all the people had been baptized and Jesus also had been baptized and was praying, heaven was opened

Confessing Sin
Luke 5:8 (NJB)
When Simon Peter saw this he fell at the knees of Jesus saying, 'Leave me, Lord; I am a sinful man.'

Verses about Prayer
Luke 5:16 (TLB)
But he often withdrew to the wilderness for prayer.

Praying for Others
Luke 6:12 (GWT)
At that time Jesus went to a mountain to pray. He spent the whole night in prayer to God.

Praying for Others
Luke 6:27-28 (ASV)
But I say unto you that hear, Love your enemies, do good to them that hate you, bless them that curse you, pray for them that despitefully use you.

Making Requests Known
Luke 8:31 (CEV)
They begged Jesus not to send them to the deep pit, where they would be punished.

Thanksgiving & Gratitude
Luke 9:16 (ASV)
And he took the five loaves and the two fishes, and looking up to heaven, he blessed them, and brake; and gave to the disciples to set before the multitude.

Verses about Prayer
Luke 9:18 (ESV)
Now it happened that as he was praying alone, the disciples were with him. And he asked them, "Who do the crowds say that I am?"

Verses about Prayer
Luke 9:28-29 (NIV)
About eight days after Jesus said this, he took Peter, John and James with him and went up onto a mountain to pray. As he was praying, the appearance of his face changed, and his clothes became as bright as a flash of lightning.

Verses about Prayer
Luke 11:1-4 (NASB)
It happened that while Jesus was praying in a certain place, after He had finished, one of His disciples said to Him, "Lord, teach us to pray just as John also taught his disciples." And He said to them, "When you pray, say:
> 'Father, hallowed be Your name.
> Your kingdom come.
> 'Give us each day our daily bread.
> 'And forgive us our sins,
> For we ourselves also forgive everyone who is indebted to us.
> And lead us not into temptation.' "

Verses about Prayer
Luke 12:22-31 (ESV)
And he said to his disciples, "Therefore I tell you, do not be anxious about your life, what you will eat, nor about your body, what you will put on. For life is more than food, and the body more than clothing. Consider the ravens: they neither sow nor reap, they have neither storehouse nor barn, and yet God feeds them. Of how much more value are you than the birds! And which of you by being anxious can add a single hour to his span of life? If then you are not able to do as small a thing as that, why are you anxious about the rest? Consider the lilies, how they grow: they neither toil nor spin, yet I tell you, even Solomon in all his glory was not arrayed like one of these. But if God so clothes the grass, which is alive in the field today, and tomorrow is thrown into the oven, how much more will he clothe you, O you of little faith! And do not seek what you are to eat and what you are to drink, nor be worried. For all the nations of the world seek after these things, and your Father knows that you need them. Instead, seek his kingdom, and these things will be added to you.

Making Requests Known/Verses about Prayer
Luke 18:1-8 (TLB)
One day Jesus told his disciples a story to illustrate their need for constant prayer and to show them that they must keep praying until the answer comes.

"There was a city judge," he said, "a very godless man who had great contempt for everyone. A widow of that city came to him frequently to appeal for justice against a man who had harmed her. The judge ignored her for a while, but eventually she got on his nerves.

" 'I fear neither God nor man,' he said to himself, 'but this woman bothers me. I'm going to see that she gets justice, for she is wearing me out with her constant coming!' "

Then the Lord said, "If even an evil judge can be worn down like that, don't you think that God will surely give justice to his people who plead with him day and night? Yes! He will answer them quickly! But the question is: When I, the Messiah, return, how many will I find who have faith [and are praying]?"

Verses about Prayer
Luke 18:9-14 (NRSV)
He also told this parable to some who trusted in themselves that they were righteous and regarded others with contempt: "Two men went up to the temple to pray, one a Pharisee and the other a tax collector. The Pharisee, standing by himself, was praying thus, 'God, I thank you that

I am not like other people: thieves, rogues, adulterers, or even like this tax collector. I fast twice a week; I give a tenth of all my income.' But the tax collector, standing far off, would not even look up to heaven, but was beating his breast and saying, 'God, be merciful to me, a sinner!' I tell you, this man went down to his home justified rather than the other; for all who exalt themselves will be humbled, but all who humble themselves will be exalted."

Praising God
Luke 19:38 (NAB)
They proclaimed:
"Blessed is the king who comes in the name of the Lord.
Peace in heaven and glory in the highest."

Verses about Prayer
Luke 20:47 (GWT)
They rob widows by taking their houses and then say long prayers to make themselves look good. The scribes will receive the most severe punishment."

Verses about Prayer
Luke 21:36 (CEV)
Watch out and keep praying that you can escape all that is going to happen and that the Son of Man will be pleased with you.

Thanksgiving & Gratitude
Luke 22:17 (NJB)
Then, taking a cup, he gave thanks and said, 'Take this and share it among you,

Thanksgiving & Gratitude
Luke 22:19 (TLB)
Then he took a loaf of bread; and when he had thanked God for it, he broke it apart and gave it to them, saying, "This is my body, given for you. Eat it in remembrance of me."

Praying for Others
Luke 22:31-32 (GWT)
{Then the Lord said,} "Simon, Simon, listen! Satan has demanded to

have you apostles for himself. He wants to separate you from me as a farmer separates wheat from husks. But I have prayed for you, Simon, that your faith will not fail. So when you recover, strengthen the other disciples."

Making Requests Known
Luke 22:39-46 (CEV)

Jesus went out to the Mount of Olives, as he often did, and his disciples went with him. When they got there, he told them, "Pray that you won't be tested."

Jesus walked on a little way before he knelt down and prayed, "Father, if you will, please don't make me suffer by having me drink from this cup. But do what you want, and not what I want."

Then an angel from heaven came to help him. Jesus was in great pain and prayed so sincerely that his sweat fell to the ground like drops of blood.

Jesus got up from praying and went over to his disciples. They were asleep and worn out from being so sad. He said to them, "Why are you asleep? Wake up and pray that you won't be tested."

Praying for Others
Luke 23:34 (ASV)

And Jesus said, Father, forgive them; for they know not what they do. And parting his garments among them, they cast lots.

Making Requests Known
Luke 23:42 (ESV)

And he said, "Jesus, remember me when you come into your kingdom."

Making Requests Known
Luke 23:46 (NIV)

Jesus called out with a loud voice, "Father, into your hands I commit my spirit." When he had said this, he breathed his last.

Thanksgiving & Gratitude
Luke 24:30 (NASB)

When He had reclined at the table with them, He took the bread and blessed it, and breaking it, He began giving it to them.

Blessings & Benedictions
Luke 24:50-53 (NRSV)
Then he led them out as far as Bethany, and, lifting up his hands, he blessed them. While he was blessing them, he withdrew from them and was carried up into heaven. And they worshiped him, and returned to Jerusalem with great joy; and they were continually in the temple blessing God.

Thanksgiving & Gratitude
John 6:11 (NAB)
Then Jesus took the loaves, gave thanks, and distributed them to those who were reclining, and also as much of the fish as they wanted.

Praising God
John 9:38 (NJB)
The man said, 'Lord, I believe,' and worshipped him.

Thanksgiving & Gratitude
John 11:41-42 (TLB)
So they rolled the stone aside. Then Jesus looked up to heaven and said, "Father, thank you for hearing me. (You always hear me, of course, but I said it because of all these people standing here, so that they will believe you sent me.)"

Praising God
John 12:13 (GWT)
So they took palm branches and went to meet him. They were shouting,
"Hosanna!
Blessed is the one who comes in the name of the Lord,
the king of Israel!"

Making Requests Known
John 12:27-28 (CEV)
Now I am deeply troubled, and I don't know what to say. But I must not ask my Father to keep me from this time of suffering. In fact, I came into the world to suffer. So Father, bring glory to yourself.

A voice from heaven then said, "I have already brought glory to myself, and I will do it again!"

Verses about Prayer
John 14:13-14 (ASV)
And whatsoever ye shall ask in my name, that will I do, that the Father may be glorified in the Son. If ye shall ask anything in my name, that will I do.

Praying for Others
John 14:16 (ASV)
And I will pray the Father, and he shall give you another Comforter, that he may be with you for ever,

Verses about Prayer
John 15:7 (ESV)
If you abide in me, and my words abide in you, ask whatever you wish, and it will be done for you.

Making Requests Known
John 15:16 (ESV)
You did not choose me, but I chose you and appointed you that you should go and bear fruit and that your fruit should abide, so that whatever you ask the Father in my name, he may give it to you.

Making Requests Known/Praying for Others
John 17:1-26 (CEV)
After Jesus had finished speaking to his disciples, he looked up toward heaven and prayed:

Father, the time has come for you to bring glory to your Son, in order that he may bring glory to you. And you gave him power over all people, so that he would give eternal life to everyone you give him. Eternal life is to know you, the only true God, and to know Jesus Christ, the one you sent. I have brought glory to you here on earth by doing everything you gave me to do. Now, Father, give me back the glory that I had with you before the world was created.

You have given me some followers from this world, and I have shown them what you are like. They were yours, but you gave them to me, and they have obeyed you. They know that you gave me everything I have. I told my followers what you told me, and they accepted it. They know that I came from you, and they believe that you are the one who sent me. I am praying for them, but not for those who belong to this world. My followers belong to you, and I am praying for them. All that I have is yours, and all that you have is mine, and they will bring glory to me.

Holy Father, I am no longer in the world. I am coming to you, but my followers are still in the world. So keep them safe by the power of the name that you have given me. Then they will be one with each other, just as you and I are one. While I was with them, I kept them safe by the power you have given me. I guarded them, and not one of them was lost, except the one who had to be lost. This happened so that what the Scriptures say would come true.

I am on my way to you. But I say these things while I am still in the world, so that my followers will have the same complete joy that I do. I have told them your message. But the people of this world hate them, because they don't belong to this world, just as I don't.

Father, I don't ask you to take my followers out of the world, but keep them safe from the evil one. They don't belong to this world, and neither do I. Your word is the truth. So let this truth make them completely yours. I am sending them into the world, just as you sent me. I have given myself completely for their sake, so that they may belong completely to the truth.

I am not praying just for these followers. I am also praying for everyone else who will have faith because of what my followers will say about me. I want all of them to be one with each other, just as I am one with you and you are one with me. I also want them to be one with us. Then the people of this world will believe that you sent me.

I have honored my followers in the same way that you honored me, in order that they may be one with each other, just as we are one. I am one with them, and you are one with me, so that they may become completely one. Then this world's people will know that you sent me. They will know that you love my followers as much as you love me.

Father, I want everyone you have given me to be with me, wherever I am. Then they will see the glory that you have given me, because you loved me before the world was created. Good Father, the people of this world don't know you. But I know you, and my followers know that you sent me. I told them what you are like, and I will tell them even more. Then the love that you have for me will become part of them, and I will be one with them.

Making Requests Known
Acts 1:13-14 (NIV)

When they arrived, they went upstairs to the room where they were staying. Those present were Peter, John, James and Andrew; Philip and Thomas, Bartholomew and Matthew; James son of Alphaeus and Simon the Zealot, and Judas son of James. They all joined together constantly in prayer, along with the women and Mary the mother of Jesus, and with his brothers.

Making Requests Known
Acts 1:24-26 (NASB)

And they prayed and said, "You, Lord, who know the hearts of all men, show which one of these two You have chosen to occupy this ministry and apostleship from which Judas turned aside to go to his own place." And they drew lots for them, and the lot fell to Matthias; and he was added to the eleven apostles.

Verses about Prayer
Acts 2:42-3:1 (NRSV)

They devoted themselves to the apostles' teaching and fellowship, to the breaking of bread and the prayers.

Awe came upon everyone, because many wonders and signs were being done by the apostles. All who believed were together and had all things in common; they would sell their possessions and goods and distribute the proceeds to all, as any had need. Day by day, as they spent much time together in the temple, they broke bread at home and ate their food with glad and generous hearts, praising God and having the goodwill of all the people. And day by day the Lord added to their number those who were being saved.

One day Peter and John were going up to the temple at the hour of prayer, at three o'clock in the afternoon.

Praising God/Making Requests Known
Acts 4:23-31 (NAB)

After their release they went back to their own people and reported what the chief priests and elders had told them. And when they heard it, they raised their voices to God with one accord and said, "Sovereign Lord, maker of heaven and earth and the sea and all that is in them, you said by the holy Spirit through the mouth of our father David, your servant:
'Why did the Gentiles rage
  and the peoples entertain folly?
The kings of the earth took their stand
  and the princes gathered together
  against the Lord and against his anointed.'
Indeed they gathered in this city against your holy servant Jesus whom you anointed, Herod and Pontius Pilate, together with the Gentiles and the peoples of Israel, to do what your hand and (your) will had long ago planned to take place. And now, Lord, take note of their threats, and enable your servants to speak your word with all boldness, as you stretch forth (your) hand to heal, and signs and wonders are done through the

name of your holy servant Jesus." As they prayed, the place where they were gathered shook, and they were all filled with the holy Spirit and continued to speak the word of God with boldness.

Praying for Others
Acts 6:4-6 (NJB)

We ourselves will continue to devote ourselves to prayer and to the service of the word.' The whole assembly approved of this proposal and elected Stephen, a man full of faith and of the Holy Spirit, together with Philip, Prochorus, Nicanor, Timon, Parmenas, and Nicolaus of Antioch, a convert to Judaism. They presented these to the apostles, and after prayer they laid their hands on them.

Making Requests Known
Acts 7:55-60 (TLB)

But Stephen, full of the Holy Spirit, gazed steadily upward into heaven and saw the glory of God and Jesus standing at God's right hand. And he told them, "Look, I see the heavens opened and Jesus the Messiah standing beside God, at his right hand!"

Then they mobbed him, putting their hands over their ears, and drowning out his voice with their shouts, and dragged him out of the city to stone him. The official witnesses--the executioners--took off their coats and laid them at the feet of a young man named Paul.

And as the murderous stones came hurtling at him, Stephen prayed, "Lord Jesus, receive my spirit." And he fell to his knees, shouting, "Lord, don't charge them with this sin!" and with that, he died.

Praying for Others
Acts 8:15-17 (GWT)

Peter and John went to Samaria and prayed that the Samaritans would receive the Holy Spirit. (Before this the Holy Spirit had not come to any of the Samaritans. They had only been baptized in the name of the Lord Jesus.) Then Peter and John placed their hands on them, and the Samaritans received the Holy Spirit.

Seeking God's Will
Acts 9:5-6 (CEV)

"Who are you?" Saul asked.

"I am Jesus," the Lord answered. "I am the one you are so cruel to. Now get up and go into the city, where you will be told what to do."

Making Requests Known
Acts 9:11 (CEV)
The Lord said to him, "Get up and go to the house of Judas on Straight Street. When you get there, you will find a man named Saul from the city of Tarsus. Saul is praying,

Praying for Others
Acts 9:40-41 (ASV)
But Peter put them all forth, and kneeled down and prayed; and turning to the body, he said, Tabitha, arise. And she opened her eyes; and when she saw Peter, she sat up. And he gave her his hand, and raised her up; and calling the saints and widows, he presented her alive.

Verses about Prayer
Acts 10:2-4 (ESV)
A devout man who feared God with all his household, gave alms generously to the people, and prayed continually to God. About the ninth hour of the day he saw clearly in a vision an angel of God come in and say to him, "Cornelius." And he stared at him in terror and said, "What is it, Lord?" And he said to him, "Your prayers and your alms have ascended as a memorial before God.

Verses about Prayer
Acts 10:9 (NIV)
About noon the following day as they were on their journey and approaching the city, Peter went up on the roof to pray.

Seeking God's Will
Acts 10:14 (NASB)
But Peter said, "By no means, Lord, for I have never eaten anything unholy and unclean."

Making Requests Known
Acts 10:31 (NRSV)
He said, 'Cornelius, your prayer has been heard and your alms have been remembered before God.

Praying for Others
Acts 12:5 (NAB)
Peter thus was being kept in prison, but prayer by the church was fervently being made to God on his behalf.

Praying for Others
Acts 12:12 (NJB)
As soon as he realised this he went straight to the house of Mary the mother of John Mark, where a number of people had assembled and were praying.

Praising God
Acts 13:2-3 (TLB)
One day as these men were worshiping and fasting the Holy Spirit said, "Dedicate Barnabas and Paul for a special job I have for them." So after more fasting and prayer, the men laid their hands on them--and sent them on their way.

Praying for Others
Acts 14:23 (GWT)
They had the disciples in each church choose spiritual leaders, and with prayer and fasting they entrusted the leaders to the Lord in whom they believed.

Praying for Others
Acts 14:26 (CEV)
And sailed to Antioch in Syria. It was there that they had been placed in God's care for the work they had now completed.

Verses about Prayer
Acts 16:13 (ASV)
And on the sabbath day we went forth without the gate by a river side, where we supposed there was a place of prayer; and we sat down, and spake unto the women that were come together.

Verses about Prayer
Acts 16:16 (ESV)
As we were going to the place of prayer, we were met by a slave girl who had a spirit of divination and brought her owners much gain by fortune-telling.

Praising God
Acts 16:25 (NIV)
About midnight Paul and Silas were praying and singing hymns to God, and the other prisoners were listening to them.

Verses about Prayer
Acts 17:24-27 (TLB)
"He made the world and everything in it, and since he is Lord of heaven and earth, he doesn't live in man-made temples; and human hands can't minister to his needs--for he has no needs! He himself gives life and breath to everything, and satisfies every need there is. He created all the people of the world from one man, Adam, and scattered the nations across the face of the earth. He decided beforehand which should rise and fall, and when. He determined their boundaries.

"His purpose in all of this is that they should seek after God, and perhaps feel their way toward him and find him--though he is not far from any one of us.

Verses about Prayer
Acts 20:36 (NASB)
When he had said these things, he knelt down and prayed with them all.

Verses about Prayer
Acts 21:5 (NRSV)
When our days there were ended, we left and proceeded on our journey; and all of them, with wives and children, escorted us outside the city. There we knelt down on the beach and prayed

Verses about Prayer
Acts 22:17 (NAB)
"After I had returned to Jerusalem and while I was praying in the temple, I fell into a trance

Praying for Others
Acts 26:29 (NJB)
Paul replied, 'Little or much, I wish before God that not only you but all who are listening to me today would come to be as I am—except for these chains.'

Making Requests Known
Acts 27:29 (TLB)
At this rate they knew they would soon be driven ashore; and fearing rocks along the coast, they threw out four anchors from the stern and prayed for daylight.

Thanksgiving & Gratitude
Acts 27:35 (GWT)
After Paul said this, he took some bread, thanked God in front of everyone, broke it, and began to eat.

Praying for Others
Acts 28:8 (CEV)
His father was in bed, sick with fever and stomach trouble, and Paul went to visit him. Paul healed the man by praying and placing his hands on him.

Thanksgiving & Gratitude
Acts 28:15 (ASV)
And from thence the brethren, when they heard of us, came to meet us as far as The Market of Appius and The Three Taverns; whom when Paul saw, he thanked God, and took courage.

Thanksgiving & Gratitude/Making Requests Known
Romans 1:8-15 (CEV)
First, I thank God in the name of Jesus Christ for all of you. I do this because people everywhere in the world are talking about your faith. God has seen how I never stop praying for you, while I serve him with all my heart and tell the good news about his Son.

In all my prayers, I ask God to make it possible for me to visit you. I want to see you and share with you the same blessings that God's Spirit has given me. Then you will grow stronger in your faith. What I am saying is that we can encourage each other by the faith that is ours.

My friends, I want you to know that I have often planned to come for a visit. But something has always kept me from doing it. I want to win followers to Christ in Rome, as I have done in many other places. It doesn't matter if people are civilized and educated, or if they are uncivilized and uneducated. I must tell the good news to everyone. That's why I am eager to visit all of you in Rome.

Praising God
Romans 8:15 (ESV)
For you did not receive the spirit of slavery to fall back into fear, but you have received the Spirit of adoption as sons, by whom we cry, "Abba! Father!"

Making Requests Known
Romans 8:23 (NIV)
Not only so, but we ourselves, who have the firstfruits of the Spirit, groan inwardly as we wait eagerly for our adoption as sons, the redemption of our bodies.

Verses about Prayer
Romans 8:26-27 (GWT)
At the same time the Spirit also helps us in our weakness, because we don't know how to pray for what we need. But the Spirit intercedes along with our groans that cannot be expressed in words. The one who searches our hearts knows what the Spirit has in mind. The Spirit intercedes for God's people the way God wants him to.

Praying for Others
Romans 10:1 (NASB)
Brethren, my heart's desire and my prayer to God for them is for their salvation.

Praising God
Romans 11:36 (NRSV)
For from him and through him and to him are all things. To him be the glory forever. Amen.

Verses about Prayer
Romans 12:12 (CEV)
Let your hope make you glad. Be patient in time of trouble and never stop praying.

Praying for Others
Romans 15:5-6 (NAB)
May the God of endurance and encouragement grant you to think in harmony with one another, in keeping with Christ Jesus, that with one accord you may with one voice glorify the God and Father of our Lord Jesus Christ.

Making Requests Known
Romans 15:30-33 (NJB)
Meanwhile I urge you, brothers, by our Lord Jesus Christ and by the love of the Spirit, that in your prayers to God for me you exert yourselves to help me; praying that I may escape the unbelievers in Judaea, and that

the aid I am carrying to Jerusalem will be acceptable to God's holy people. Then I shall come to you, if God wills, for a happy time of relaxation in your company. The God of peace be with you all. Amen.

Blessings & Benedictions
Romans 16:20 (TLB)
The God of peace will soon crush Satan under your feet. The blessings from our Lord Jesus Christ be upon you.

Praising God
Romans 16:25-27 (GWT)
God can strengthen you by the Good News and the message I tell about Jesus Christ. He can strengthen you by revealing the mystery that was kept in silence for a very long time but now is publicly known. The everlasting God ordered that what the prophets wrote must be shown to the people of every nation to bring them to the obedience that is associated with faith. God alone is wise. Glory belongs to him through Jesus Christ forever! Amen.

Thanksgiving & Gratitude
1 Cor. 1:2-9 (CEV)
To God's church in Corinth. Christ Jesus chose you to be his very own people, and you worship in his name, as we and all others do who call him Lord.

My prayer is that God our Father and the Lord Jesus Christ will be kind to you and will bless you with peace!

I never stop thanking my God for being kind enough to give you Christ Jesus, who helps you speak and understand so well. Now you are certain that everything we told you about our Lord Christ Jesus is true. You are not missing out on any blessings, as you wait for him to return. And until the day Christ does return, he will keep you completely innocent. God can be trusted, and he chose you to be partners with his Son, our Lord Jesus Christ.

Verses about Prayer
1 Cor. 11:4-5 (ESV)
Every man who prays or prophesies with his head covered dishonors

his head, but every wife who prays or prophesies with her head uncovered dishonors her head—it is the same as if her head were shaven.

Verses about Prayer
1 Cor. 11:13 (NIV)

Judge for yourselves: Is it proper for a woman to pray to God with her head uncovered?

Verses about Prayer
1 Cor. 14:13-17 (ASV)

Wherefore let him that speaketh in a tongue pray that he may interpret. For if I pray in a tongue, my spirit prayeth, but my understanding is unfruitful. What is it then? I will pray with the spirit, and I will pray with the understanding also: I will sing with the spirit, and I will sing with the understanding also. Else if thou bless with the spirit, how shall he that filleth the place of the unlearned say the Amen at thy giving of thanks, seeing he knoweth not what thou sayest? For thou verily givest thanks well, but the other is not edified.

Blessings & Benedictions
1 Cor. 16:22-24 (ASV)

If any man loveth not the Lord, let him be anathema. Maranatha. The grace of the Lord Jesus Christ be with you. My love be with you all in Christ Jesus. Amen.

Blessings & Benedictions
2 Cor. 1:2-4 (ESV)

Grace to you and peace from God our Father and the Lord Jesus Christ.

Blessed be the God and Father of our Lord Jesus Christ, the Father of mercies and God of all comfort, who comforts us in all our affliction, so that we may be able to comfort those who are in any affliction, with the comfort with which we ourselves are comforted by God.

Making Requests Known
2 Cor. 12:7-10 (NIV)

To keep me from becoming conceited because of these surpassingly great revelations, there was given me a thorn in my flesh, a messenger of Satan, to torment me. Three times I pleaded with the Lord to take it away from me. But he said to me, "My grace is sufficient for you, for my power is made perfect in weakness." Therefore I will boast all the more gladly about my weaknesses, so that Christ's power may rest on me. That is why, for Christ's sake, I delight in weaknesses, in insults, in hardships, in persecutions, in difficulties. For when I am weak, then I am strong.

Praying for Others
2 Cor. 13:7-9 (NASB)
Now we pray to God that you do no wrong; not that we ourselves may appear approved, but that you may do what is right, even though we may appear unapproved. For we can do nothing against the truth, but only for the truth. For we rejoice when we ourselves are weak but you are strong; this we also pray for, that you be made complete.

Blessings & Benedictions
2 Cor. 13:14 (NRSV)
The grace of the Lord Jesus Christ, the love of God, and the communion of the Holy Spirit be with all of you.

Blessings & Benedictions
Galatians 1:3-5 (NAB)
Grace to you and peace from God our Father and the Lord Jesus Christ, who gave himself for our sins that he might rescue us from the present evil age in accord with the will of our God and Father, to whom be glory forever and ever. Amen.

Blessings & Benedictions
Galatians 6:18 (NJB)
The grace of our Lord Jesus Christ be with your spirit, my brothers. Amen.

Blessings & Benedictions
Ephes. 1:2-10 (TLB)
May his blessings and peace be yours, sent to you from God our Father and Jesus Christ our Lord.

How we praise God, the Father of our Lord Jesus Christ, who has blessed us with every blessing in heaven because we belong to Christ.

Long ago, even before he made the world, God chose us to be his very own through what Christ would do for us; he decided then to make us holy in his eyes, without a single fault--we who stand before him covered with his love. His unchanging plan has always been to adopt us into his own family by sending Jesus Christ to die for us. And he did this because he wanted to!

Now all praise to God for his wonderful kindness to us and his favor that he has poured out upon us because we belong to his dearly loved Son. So overflowing is his kindness toward us that he took away all our sins through the blood of his Son, by whom we are saved; and he has showered down upon us the richness of his grace--for how well he understands us and knows what is best for us at all times.

God has told us his secret reason for sending Christ, a plan he decided on in mercy long ago; and this was his purpose: that when the time is ripe he will gather us all together from wherever we are--in heaven or on earth--to be with him in Christ forever.

Thanksgiving & Gratitude/Praying for Others
Ephes. 1:15-23 (GWT)

I, too, have heard about your faith in the Lord Jesus and your love for all of God's people. For this reason I never stop thanking God for you. I always remember you in my prayers. I pray that the glorious Father, the God of our Lord Jesus Christ, would give you a spirit of wisdom and revelation as you come to know Christ better. Then you will have deeper insight. You will know the confidence that he calls you to have and the glorious wealth that God's people will inherit. You will also know the unlimited greatness of his power as it works with might and strength for us, the believers. He worked with that same power in Christ when he brought him back to life and gave him the highest position in heaven. He is far above all rulers, authorities, powers, lords, and all other names that can be named, not only in this present world but also in the world to come. God has put everything under the control of Christ. He has made Christ the head of everything for the good of the church. The church is Christ's body and completes him as he fills everything in every way.

Verses about Prayer
Ephes. 2:18 (CEV)

And because of Christ, all of us can come to the Father by the same Spirit.

Verses about Prayer
Ephes. 3:12 (NRSV)

In whom we have access to God in boldness and confidence through faith in him.

Praying for Others
Ephes. 3:14-21 (ASV)
For this cause I bow my knees unto the Father, from whom every family in heaven and on earth is named, that he would grant you, according to the riches of his glory, that ye may be strengthened with power through his Spirit in the inward man; that Christ may dwell in your hearts through faith; to the end that ye, being rooted and grounded in love, may be strong to apprehend with all the saints what is the breadth and length and height and depth, and to know the love of Christ which passeth knowledge, that ye may be filled unto all the fulness of God. Now unto him that is able to do exceeding abundantly above all that we ask or think, according to the power that worketh in us, unto him be the glory in the church and in Christ Jesus unto all generations for ever and ever. Amen.

Thanksgiving & Gratitude
Ephes. 5:19-20 (ESV)
Addressing one another in psalms and hymns and spiritual songs, singing and making melody to the Lord with all your heart, giving thanks always and for everything to God the Father in the name of our Lord Jesus Christ.

Praying for Others
Ephes. 6:19-20 (NIV)
Pray also for me, that whenever I open my mouth, words may be given me so that I will fearlessly make known the mystery of the gospel, for which I am an ambassador in chains. Pray that I may declare it fearlessly, as I should.

Blessings & Benedictions
Ephes. 6:23-24 (NASB)
Peace be to the brethren, and love with faith, from God the Father and the Lord Jesus Christ. Grace be with all those who love our Lord Jesus Christ with incorruptible love.

Thanksgiving & Gratitude/Praying for Others
Philip. 1:2-6 (NRSV)
Grace to you and peace from God our Father and the Lord Jesus Christ.
I thank my God every time I remember you, constantly praying with joy in every one of my prayers for all of you, because of your sharing in

the gospel from the first day until now. I am confident of this, that the one who began a good work among you will bring it to completion by the day of Jesus Christ.

Praying for Others
Philip. 1:9-11 (NAB)
And this is my prayer: that your love may increase ever more and more in knowledge and every kind of perception, to discern what is of value, so that you may be pure and blameless for the day of Christ, filled with the fruit of righteousness that comes through Jesus Christ for the glory and praise of God.

Praying for Others
Philip. 1:19 (NJB)
Because I know that this is what will save me, with your prayers and with the support of the Spirit of Jesus Christ.

Making Requests Known
Philip. 4:6-7 (NAB)
Have no anxiety at all, but in everything, by prayer and petition, with thanksgiving, make your requests known to God. Then the peace of God that surpasses all understanding will guard your hearts and minds in Christ Jesus.

Praising God/Blessings & Benedictions
Philip. 4:19-20 (TLB)
And it is he who will supply all your needs from his riches in glory because of what Christ Jesus has done for us. Now unto God our Father be glory forever and ever. Amen.
Sincerely,
Paul

Blessings & Benedictions
Philip. 4:23 (GWT)
May the good will of our Lord Jesus Christ be with you.

Thanksgiving & Gratitude/Praying for Others
Col. 1:2-14 (CEV)
To God's people who live in Colossae and are faithful followers of Christ.

I pray that God our Father will be kind to you and will bless you with peace!

Each time we pray for you, we thank God, the Father of our Lord Jesus Christ. We have heard of your faith in Christ and of your love for all of God's people, because what you hope for is kept safe for you in heaven. You first heard about this hope when you believed the true message, which is the good news.

The good news is spreading all over the world with great success. It has spread in that same way among you, ever since the first day you learned the truth about God's wonderful kindness from our good friend Epaphras. He works together with us for Christ and is a faithful worker for you. He is also the one who told us about the love that God's Spirit has given you.

We have not stopped praying for you since the first day we heard about you. In fact, we always pray that God will show you everything he wants you to do and that you may have all the wisdom and understanding that his Spirit gives. Then you will live a life that honors the Lord, and you will always please him by doing good deeds. You will come to know God even better. His glorious power will make you patient and strong enough to endure anything, and you will be truly happy.

I pray that you will be grateful to God for letting you have part in what he has promised his people in the kingdom of light. God rescued us from the dark power of Satan and brought us into the kingdom of his dear Son, who forgives our sins and sets us free.

Verses About Prayer
Col. 3:16-17 (NJB)

Let the Word of Christ, in all its richness, find a home with you. Teach each other, and advise each other, in all wisdom. With gratitude in your hearts sing psalms and hymns and inspired songs to God; and whatever you say or do, let it be in the name of the Lord Jesus, in thanksgiving to God the Father through him.

Verses about Prayer/Praying for Others
Col. 4:2-4 (ASV)

Continue stedfastly in prayer, watching therein with thanksgiving; withal praying for us also, that God may open unto us a door for the word, to speak the mystery of Christ, for which I am also in bonds; that I may make it manifest, as I ought to speak.

Praying for Others
Col. 4:12 (ESV)
Epaphras, who is one of you, a servant of Christ Jesus, greets you, always struggling on your behalf in his prayers, that you may stand mature and fully assured in all the will of God.

Verses about Prayer
Col. 4:17 (NIV)
Tell Archippus: "See to it that you complete the work you have received in the Lord."

Thanksgiving & Gratitude
1 Thes. 1:1-3 (NASB)
Paul and Silvanus and Timothy,

To the church of the Thessalonians in God the Father and the Lord Jesus Christ: Grace to you and peace.

We give thanks to God always for all of you, making mention of you in our prayers; constantly bearing in mind your work of faith and labor of love and steadfastness of hope in our Lord Jesus Christ in the presence of our God and Father.

Verses about Prayer
1 Thes. 5:16-18 (TLB)
Always be joyful. Always keep on praying. No matter what happens, always be thankful, for this is God's will for you who belong to Christ Jesus.

Thanksgiving & Gratitude/Making Requests Known/Praying for Others
1 Thes. 3:9-13 (NRSV)
How can we thank God enough for you in return for all the joy that we feel before our God because of you? Night and day we pray most earnestly that we may see you face to face and restore whatever is lacking in your faith.

Now may our God and Father himself and our Lord Jesus direct our way to you. And may the Lord make you increase and abound in love for one another and for all, just as we abound in love for you. And may he so strengthen your hearts in holiness that you may be blameless before our God and Father at the coming of our Lord Jesus with all his saints.

Praying for Others
1 Thes. 5:23-24 (NAB)
May the God of peace himself make you perfectly holy and may you entirely, spirit, soul, and body, be preserved blameless for the coming of our Lord Jesus Christ. The one who calls you is faithful, and he will also accomplish it.

Blessings & Benedictions
1 Thes. 5:28 (NAB)
The grace of our Lord Jesus Christ be with you.

Thanksgiving & Gratitude
2 Thes. 1:3 (NAB)
We ought to thank God always for you, brothers, as is fitting, because your faith flourishes ever more, and the love of every one of you for one another grows ever greater.

Praying for Others
2 Thes. 1:11-12 (NJB)
In view of this we also pray continually that our God will make you worthy of his call, and by his power fulfil all your desires for goodness, and complete all that you have been doing through faith; so that the name of our Lord Jesus Christ may be glorified in you and you in him, by the grace of our God and the Lord Jesus Christ.

Thanksgiving & Gratitude
2 Thes. 2:13 (TLB)
But we must forever give thanks to God for you, our brothers loved by the Lord, because God chose from the very first to give you salvation, cleansing you by the work of the Holy Spirit and by your trusting in the Truth.

Praying for Others
2 Thes. 2:16-3:5 (TLB)
May our Lord Jesus Christ himself and God our Father, who has loved us and given us everlasting comfort and hope, which we don't deserve, comfort your hearts with all comfort, and help you in every good thing you say and do.

Finally, dear brothers, as I come to the end of this letter, I ask you to pray for us. Pray first that the Lord's message will spread rapidly and triumph wherever it goes, winning converts everywhere as it did when it came to you. Pray, too, that we will be saved out of the clutches of evil men, for not everyone loves the Lord. But the Lord is faithful; he will make you strong and guard you from satanic attacks of every kind. And we trust the Lord that you are putting into practice the things we taught you, and that you always will. May the Lord bring you into an ever deeper understanding of the love of God and of the patience that comes from Christ.

Praying for Others
2 Thes. 3:1-2 (GWT)

Finally, brothers and sisters, pray that we spread the Lord's word rapidly and that it will be honored the way it was among you. Also pray that we may be rescued from worthless and evil people, since not everyone shares our faith.

Praying for Others
2 Thes. 3:16 (TLB)

May the Lord of peace himself give you his peace no matter what happens. The Lord be with you all.

Blessings & Benedictions
2 Thes. 3:18 (GWT)

The good will of our Lord Jesus Christ be with all of you.

Blessings & Benedictions
1 Tim. 1:2 (CEV)

Timothy, because of our faith, you are like a son to me. I pray that God our Father and our Lord Jesus Christ will be kind and merciful to you. May they bless you with peace!

Thanksgiving & Gratitude
1 Tim. 1:12-14 (ASV)

I thank him that enabled me, even Christ Jesus our Lord, for that he counted me faithful, appointing me to his service; though I was before a blasphemer, and a persecutor, and injurious: howbeit I obtained mercy, because I did it ignorantly in unbelief; and the grace of our Lord abounded exceedingly with faith and love which is in Christ Jesus.

Praising God
1 Tim. 1:17 (ESV)

To the King of ages, immortal, invisible, the only God, be honor and glory forever and ever. Amen.

Praying for Others
1 Tim. 2:1-4 (NIV)

I urge, then, first of all, that requests, prayers, intercession and thanksgiving be made for everyone-- for kings and all those in authority, that we may live peaceful and quiet lives in all godliness and holiness. This is good, and pleases God our Savior, who wants all men to be saved and to come to a knowledge of the truth.

Verses about Prayer
1 Tim. 2:8 (CEV)

I want everyone everywhere to lift innocent hands toward heaven and pray, without being angry or arguing with each other.

Thanksgiving & Gratitude
1 Tim. 4:4-5 (NASB)

For everything created by God is good, and nothing is to be rejected if it is received with gratitude; for it is sanctified by means of the word of God and prayer.

Making Requests Known
1 Tim. 5:5 (NRSV)

The real widow, left alone, has set her hope on God and continues in supplications and prayers night and day.

Praising God
1 Tim. 6:16 (NAB)

Who alone has immortality, who dwells in unapproachable light, and whom no human being has seen or can see. To him be honor and eternal power. Amen.

Blessings & Benedictions
1 Tim. 6:21 (NJB)

By adopting this, some have missed the goal of faith. Grace be with you.

Thanksgiving & Gratitude/Praying for Others
2 Tim. 1:2-7 (TLB)

To: Timothy, my dear son. May God the Father and Christ Jesus our Lord shower you with his kindness, mercy, and peace.

How I thank God for you, Timothy. I pray for you every day, and many times during the long nights I beg my God to bless you richly. He is my fathers' God and mine, and my only purpose in life is to please him.

How I long to see you again. How happy I would be, for I remember your tears as we left each other.

I know how much you trust the Lord, just as your mother Eunice and your grandmother Lois do; and I feel sure you are still trusting him as much as ever.

This being so, I want to remind you to stir into flame the strength and boldness that is in you, that entered into you when I laid my hands upon your head and blessed you. For the Holy Spirit, God's gift, does not want you to be afraid of people, but to be wise and strong, and to love them and enjoy being with them.

Praying for Others
2 Tim. 1:16-18 (GWT)

May the Lord be merciful to the family of Onesiphorus. He often took care of my needs and wasn't ashamed that I was a prisoner. When he arrived in Rome, he searched hard for me and found me. May the Lord grant that Onesiphorus finds mercy when that day comes. You know very well that he did everything possible to help me in Ephesus.

Praising God
2 Tim. 4:18 (CEV)

The Lord will always keep me from being harmed by evil, and he will bring me safely into his heavenly kingdom. Praise him forever and ever! Amen.

Blessings & Benedictions
2 Tim. 4:22 (ASV)

The Lord be with thy spirit. Grace be with you.

Blessings & Benedictions
Titus 1:4 (ESV)
To Titus, my true child in a common faith:
Grace and peace from God the Father and Christ Jesus our Savior.

Blessings & Benedictions
Titus 3:15 (NIV)
Everyone with me sends you greetings. Greet those who love us in the faith.
Grace be with you all.

Blessings & Benedictions
Philemon 1:3 (NASB)
Grace to you and peace from God our Father and the Lord Jesus Christ.

Thanksgiving & Gratitude
Philemon 1:4 (ESV)
I thank my God always when I remember you in my prayers.

Blessings & Benedictions
Philemon 1:25 (NRSV)
The grace of the Lord Jesus Christ be with your spirit.

Praising God
Hebrews 1:10-12 (NAB)
And:
"At the beginning, O Lord, you established the earth,
 and the heavens are the works of your hands.
They will perish, but you remain;
 and they will all grow old like a garment.
You will roll them up like a cloak,
 and like a garment they will be changed.
But you are the same, and your years will have no end."

Making Requests Known
Hebrews 4:16 (NJB)
Let us, then, have no fear in approaching the throne of grace to receive mercy and to find grace when we are in need of help.

Making Requests Known
Hebrews 5:7-8 (TLB)

Yet while Christ was here on earth he pleaded with God, praying with tears and agony of soul to the only one who would save him from [premature] death. And God heard his prayers because of his strong desire to obey God at all times.

And even though Jesus was God's Son, he had to learn from experience what it was like to obey when obeying meant suffering.

Confessing Sin/Making Requests Known/Verses about Prayer
Hebrews 10:19-22 (NIV)

Therefore, brothers, since we have confidence to enter the Most Holy Place by the blood of Jesus, by a new and living way opened for us through the curtain, that is, his body, and since we have a great priest over the house of God, let us draw near to God with a sincere heart in full assurance of faith, having our hearts sprinkled to cleanse us from a guilty conscience and having our bodies washed with pure water.

Praising God/Thanksgiving & Gratitude
Hebrews 12:28-29 (NASB)

Therefore, since we receive a kingdom which cannot be shaken, let us show gratitude, by which we may offer to God an acceptable service with reverence and awe; for our God is a consuming fire.

Praising God
Hebrews 13:15 (NRSV)

Through him, then, let us continually offer a sacrifice of praise to God, that is, the fruit of lips that confess his name.

Praying for Others
Hebrews 13:18-19 (NAB)

Pray for us, for we are confident that we have a clear conscience, wishing to act rightly in every respect. I especially ask for your prayers that I may be restored to you very soon.

Blessings & Benedictions/Praying for Others/Making Requests Known
Hebrews 13:20-21 (GWT)
The God of peace brought the great shepherd of the sheep, our Lord Jesus, back to life through the blood of an eternal promise. May this God of peace prepare you to do every good thing he wants. May he work in us through Jesus Christ to do what is pleasing to him. Glory belongs to Jesus Christ forever. Amen.

Verses About Prayer
James 1:5-8 (NJB)
Any of you who lacks wisdom must ask God, who gives to all generously and without scolding; it will be given. But the prayer must be made with faith, and no trace of doubt, because a person who has doubts is like the waves thrown up in the sea by the buffeting of the wind. That sort of person, in two minds, inconsistent in every activity, must not expect to receive anything from the Lord.

Verses about Prayer
James 4:2-3 (TLB)
You want what you don't have, so you kill to get it. You long for what others have, and can't afford it, so you start a fight to take it away from them. And yet the reason you don't have what you want is that you don't ask God for it. And even when you do ask you don't get it because your whole aim is wrong--you want only what will give you pleasure.

Making Requests Known/Verses about Prayer
James 4:7-10 (GWT)
So place yourselves under God's authority. Resist the devil, and he will run away from you. Come close to God, and he will come close to you. Clean up your lives, you sinners, and clear your minds, you doubters. Be miserable, mourn, and cry. Turn your laughter into mourning and your joy into gloom. Humble yourselves in the Lord's presence. Then he will give you a high position.

Verses about Prayer
James 5:13-18 (CEV)
If you are having trouble, you should pray. And if you are feeling good, you should sing praises. If you are sick, ask the church leaders to come and pray for you. Ask them to put olive oil on you in the name of the Lord. If you have faith when you pray for sick people, they will get well. The Lord will heal them, and if they have sinned, he will forgive them.

If you have sinned, you should tell each other what you have done. Then you can pray for one another and be healed. The prayer of an innocent person is powerful, and it can help a lot. Elijah was just as human as we are, and for three and a half years his prayers kept the rain from falling. But when he did pray for rain, it fell from the skies and made the crops grow.

Praising God
1 Peter 1:3 (CEV)
Praise God, the Father of our Lord Jesus Christ. God is so good, and by raising Jesus from death, he has given us new life and a hope that lives on.

Verses about Prayer
1 Peter 3:7 (ASV)
Ye husbands, in like manner, dwell with your wives according to knowledge, giving honor unto the woman, as unto the weaker vessel, as being also joint-heirs of the grace of life; to the end that your prayers be not hindered.

Verses about Prayer
1 Peter 3:12 (ESV)
For the eyes of the Lord are on the righteous,
   and his ears are open to their prayer.
But the face of the Lord is against those who do evil."

Verses about Prayer
1 Peter 4:7 (NIV)
The end of all things is near. Therefore be clear minded and self-controlled so that you can pray.

Verses about Prayer
1 Peter 4:11 (ASV)

If any man speaketh, speaking as it were oracles of God; is any man ministereth, ministering as of the strength which God supplieth: that in all things God may be glorified through Jesus Christ, whose is the glory and the dominion for ever and ever. Amen.

Making Requests Known
1 Peter 5:6-7 (NASB)

Therefore humble yourselves under the mighty hand of God, that He may exalt you at the proper time, casting all your anxiety on Him, because He cares for you.

Praising God
1 Peter 5:10-11 (ESV)

And after you have suffered a little while, the God of all grace, who has called you to his eternal glory in Christ, will himself restore, confirm, strengthen, and establish you. To him be the dominion forever and ever. Amen.

Blessings & Benedictions
1 Peter 5:14 (NIV)

Greet one another with a kiss of love.
Peace to all of you who are in Christ.

Blessings & Benedictions
2 Peter 1:2 (NASB)

Grace and peace be multiplied to you in the knowledge of God and of Jesus our Lord;

Praising God
2 Peter 3:18 (NRSV)

But grow in the grace and knowledge of our Lord and Savior Jesus Christ. To him be the glory both now and to the day of eternity. Amen.

Confessing Sin
1 John 1:9 (NRSV)

If we confess our sins, he who is faithful and just will forgive us our sins and cleanse us from all unrighteousness.

Making Requests Known
1 John 3:21-22 (NAB)
Beloved, if (our) hearts do not condemn us, we have confidence in God and receive from him whatever we ask, because we keep his commandments and do what pleases him.

Making Requests Known/Verses about Prayer
1 John 5:14-16 (NJB)
Our fearlessness towards him
> consists in this,

that if we ask anything
> in accordance with his will

he hears us.
And if we know
> that he listens to whatever we ask him,

we know that we already possess
> whatever we have asked of him.

If anyone sees his brother commit a sin
that is not a deadly sin,
he has only to pray,
> and God will give life to this brother

—provided that it is not a deadly sin.
There is sin that leads to death
and I am not saying
> you must pray about that.

Blessings & Benedictions
2 John 1:3 (NAB)
Grace, mercy, and peace will be with us from God the Father and from Jesus Christ the Father's Son in truth and love.

Praying for Others
3 John 1:2-4 (NJB)
My dear friend, I hope everything is going happily with you and that you are as well physically as you are spiritually. It was a great joy to me when some brothers came and told of your faithfulness to the truth, and of your life in the truth. It is always my greatest joy to hear that my children are living according to the truth.

Blessings & Benedictions
Jude 1:2 (TLB)
May you be given more and more of God's kindness, peace, and love.

Verses about Prayer
Jude 1:20 (TLB)
But you, dear friends, must build up your lives ever more strongly upon the foundation of our holy faith, learning to pray in the power and strength of the Holy Spirit.

Praising God
Jude 1:24 (GWT)
God can guard you so that you don't fall and so that you can be full of joy as you stand in his glorious presence without fault.

Praising God
Rev. 1:6 (CEV)
He lets us rule as kings
and serve God his Father as priests.
To him be glory and power forever and ever! Amen.

Praising God
Rev. 4:8 (ASV)
And the four living creatures, having each one of them six wings, are full of eyes round about and within: and they have no rest day and night, saying,

Holy, holy, holy, is the Lord God, the Almighty, who was and who is and who is to come.

Praising God
Rev. 4:10-11 (ESV)
The twenty-four elders fall down before him who is seated on the throne and worship him who lives forever and ever. They cast their crowns before the throne, saying,

"Worthy are you, our Lord and God,
   to receive glory and honor and power,
for you created all things,
   and by your will they existed and were created."

Praising God
Rev. 5:8-10 (NASB)
When He had taken the book, the four living creatures and the twenty-four elders fell down before the Lamb, each one holding a harp and golden bowls full of incense, which are the prayers of the saints. And they sang a new song, saying,

"Worthy are You to take the book and to break its seals; for You were slain, and purchased for God with Your blood men from every tribe and tongue and people and nation. "You have made them to be a kingdom and priests to our God; and they will reign upon the earth."

Praising God
Rev. 5:12-14 (NRSV)
Singing with full voice,
"Worthy is the Lamb that was slaughtered
to receive power and wealth and wisdom and might
and honor and glory and blessing!"
Then I heard every creature in heaven and on earth and under the earth and in the sea, and all that is in them, singing,
"To the one seated on the throne and to the Lamb
be blessing and honor and glory and might
forever and ever!"
And the four living creatures said, "Amen!" And the elders fell down and worshiped.

Seeking God's Will
Rev. 6:10 (NAB)
They cried out in a loud voice, "How long will it be, holy and true master, before you sit in judgment and avenge our blood on the inhabitants of the earth?"

Praising God
Rev. 7:10-12 (NJB)
They shouted in a loud voice, 'Salvation to our God, who sits on the throne, and to the Lamb!' And all the angels who were standing in a circle round the throne, surrounding the elders and the four living creatures, prostrated themselves before the throne, and touched the ground with their foreheads, worshipping God with these words:
Amen. Praise and glory and wisdom,
thanksgiving and honour
and power and strength
to our God for ever and ever. Amen.

Verses about Prayer
Rev. 8:3-4 (TLB)

Then another angel with a golden censer came and stood at the altar; and a great quantity of incense was given to him to mix with the prayers of God's people, to offer upon the golden altar before the throne. And the perfume of the incense mixed with prayers ascended up to God from the altar where the angel had poured them out.

Thanksgiving & Gratitude
Rev. 11:15-18 (GWT)

When the seventh angel blew his trumpet, there were loud voices in heaven, saying,
"The kingdom of the world has become
the kingdom of our Lord and of his Messiah,
and he will rule as king forever and ever."
Then the 24 leaders, who were sitting on their thrones in God's presence, immediately bowed, worshiped God,
and said,
"We give thanks to you, Lord God Almighty,
who is and who was,
because you have taken your great power
and have begun ruling as king.
The nations were angry, but your anger has come.
The time has come for the dead to be judged:
to reward your servants, the prophets,
your holy people,
and those who fear your name,
no matter if they are important or unimportant,
and to destroy those who destroy the earth."

Praising God
Rev. 15:3-4 (CEV)

And they were singing the song that his servant Moses and the Lamb had sung. They were singing,
"Lord God All-Powerful,
you have done great and marvelous things.
You are the ruler of all nations,
and you do what is right and fair.
Lord, who doesn't honor and praise your name?
You alone are holy,
and all nations will come and worship you,
because you have shown

that you judge with fairness."

Praising God
Rev. 19:1-10 (ASV)
After these things I heard as it were a great voice of a great multitude in heaven, saying,

Hallelujah; Salvation, and glory, and power, belong to our God: for true and righteous are his judgments; for he hath judged the great harlot, her that corrupted the earth with her fornication, and he hath avenged the blood of his servants at her hand.

And a second time they say, Hallelujah. And her smoke goeth up for ever and ever. And the four and twenty elders and the four living creatures fell down and worshipped God that sitteth on the throne, saying, Amen; Hallelujah. And a voice came forth from the throne, saying,

Give praise to our God, all ye his servants, ye that fear him, the small and the great.

And I heard as it were the voice of a great multitude, and as the voice of many waters, and as the voice of mighty thunders, saying,

Hallelujah: for the Lord our God, the Almighty, reigneth. Let us rejoice and be exceeding glad, and let us give the glory unto him: for the marriage of the Lamb is come, and his wife hath made herself ready. And it was given unto her that she should array herself in fine linen, bright and pure: for the fine linen is the righteous acts of the saints.

And he saith unto me, Write, Blessed are they that are bidden to the marriage supper of the Lamb. And he saith unto me, These are true words of God. And I fell down before his feet to worship him. And he saith unto me, See thou do it not: I am a fellow-servant with thee and with thy brethren that hold the testimony of Jesus: worship God; for the testimony of Jesus is the spirit of prophecy.

Praising God
Rev. 22:17 (ESV)
The Spirit and the Bride say, "Come." And let the one who hears say, "Come." And let the one who is thirsty come; let the one who desires take the water of life without price.

Making Requests Known/Blessings & Benedictions
Rev. 22:20-21 (NIV)
He who testifies to these things says, "Yes, I am coming soon."
Amen. Come, Lord Jesus.
The grace of the Lord Jesus be with God's people. Amen.

Prayer Index

Blessing and Benediction

Reference	Page
Genesis 28:3-4	10
Numbers 6:24-27	18
Deut. 1:11	21
Judges 17:2	33
Ruth 1:8-9	34
Ruth 2:4	34
Ruth 2:12	34
Ruth 3:10	35
Ruth 4:11	35
2 Samuel 2:5-6	41
1 Kings 1:36-37	47
1 Kings 1:47-48	47
Psalm 84:1-12	145
Psalm 115:1	170
Luke 24:50-53	235
Romans 16:20	245
1 Cor. 16:22-24	246
2 Cor. 1:2-4	246
2 Cor. 13:14	247
Galatians 1:3-5	247
Galatians 6:18	247
Ephes. 1:2-10	247
Ephes. 6:23-24	249
Philip. 4:19-20	250
Philip. 4:23	250
1 Thes. 5:28	253
2 Thes. 3:18	254
1 Tim. 1:2	254
1 Tim. 6:21	255
2 Tim. 4:22	256
Titus 1:4	257
Titus 3:15	257
Philemon 1:3	257
Philemon 1:25	257
Hebrews 13:20-21	259
1 Peter 5:14	261
2 Peter 1:2	261
2 John 1:3	262
Jude 1:2	262
Rev. 22:20-21	266

Confessing Sin

Reference	Page
Judges 10:10	32
Judges 10:15	32
1 Samuel 7:6	37
Samuel 12:10	38
2 Samuel 24:10	46
2 Samuel 24:17	46
2 Kings 5:18	52
1 Chron. 21:8	56
1 Chron. 21:17	56
2 Chron. 7:14	60
Ezra 9:5-10:1	65
Neh. 1:4-11	65
Neh. 9:2-3	67
Psalm 25:1-22	96
Isaiah 6:5	193
Isaiah 55:6-7	197
Isaiah 59:9-15	197
Isaiah 64:1-12	199
Jeremiah 14:7-9	203
Daniel 9:4-19	213
Jonah 3:5-9	216
Luke 5:8	230
Hebrews 10:19	258
1 John 1:9	261

Making Requests Known

Reference	Page
Genesis 4:26	6
Genesis 15:2-3	6
Genesis 24:12-15	8
Genesis 24:42-45	9
Genesis 32:9-12	10
Genesis 49:18	11
Exodus 2:23	11
Exodus 4:13	12
Exodus 14:10-12	14
Exodus 15:25	15
Exodus 17:4	15
Exodus 22:22-24	16
Exodus 33:9-13	17
Exodus 33:15-16	17
Exodus 33:18	17
Exodus 34:8-9	18
Numbers 10:35-36	18
Numbers 11:10-15	19

Every Prayer in the Bible — Index

Numbers 16:15 20	Job 7:7 71
Numbers 22:10-11 20	Job 7:17-21 71
Numbers 23:3-4 20	Job 10:1-22 72
Deut. 26:5-15 22	Job 12:4 73
Joshua 10:12-13 28	Job 13:20-14:22 73
Judges 3:9 28	Job 17:3-5 75
Judges 3:15 28	Job 22:17 75
Judges 4:3 28	Job 22:27 76
Judges 6:6-7 31	Job 23:3-5 76
Judges 6:17-18 32	Job 30:20 76
Judges 6:36-37 32	Psalm 3:1-8 77
Judges 6:39 32	Psalm 4:1-8 78
Judges 13:8 33	Psalm 5:1-12 78
Judges 15:18 33	Psalm 6:1-10 79
Judges 16:28-30 33	Psalm 7:1-17 80
1 Samuel 12:10 38	Psalm 12:1-8 84
1 Samuel 14:41 39	Psalm 13:1-6 85
2 Samuel 15:31 43	Psalm 16:1-11 86
2 Samuel 21:1 43	Psalm 17:1-15 86
2 Samuel 21:14 43	Psalm 19:1-14 90
1 Kings 3:6-9 47	Psalm 22:1-31 93
1 Kings 8:14-61 48	Psalm 25:1-22 96
1 Kings 18:36-37 51	Psalm 26:1-12 97
1 Kings 18:42 51	Psalm 27:1-14 98
1 Kings 19:4 51	Psalm 28:1-9 99
2 Kings 1:12 52	Psalm 31:1-24 101
2 Kings 19:15-19 53	Psalm 34:1-22 104
2 Kings 20:1-3 53	Psalm 35:1-28 104
2 Kings 20:11 53	Psalm 36:5-12 106
1 Chron. 4:10 53	Psalm 37:4-7 107
1 Chron. 5:20 54	Psalm 38:1-22 107
2 Chron. 1:8-10 58	Psalm 39:1-13 108
2 Chron. 6:12-42 58	Psalm 40:1-17 109
2 Chron. 13:14 61	Psalm 41:1-13 111
2 Chron. 14:11 61	Psalm 42:1-11 112
2 Chron. 20:4-12 61	Psalm 43:1-5 113
2 Chron. 24:22 62	Psalm 44:1-26 113
2 Chron. 32:20 63	Psalm 51:1-19 117
2 Chron. 32:24 63	Psalm 54:1-7 118
2 Chron. 33:12-13 63	Psalm 55:1-23 119
2 Chron. 33:18 63	Psalm 56:1-13 120
Ezra 6:12 64	Psalm 57:1-11 121
Ezra 8:21-23 64	Psalm 58:6 122
Neh. 1:4-11 65	Psalm 59:1-17 122
Neh. 2:4 66	Psalm 60:1-12 123
Neh. 4:4-5 66	Psalm 61:1-8 124
Neh. 4:9 66	Psalm 64:1-10 126
Neh. 5:19 67	Psalm 68:18-35 129
Neh. 6:9 67	Psalm 69:1-36 131
Neh. 6:14 67	Psalm 70:1-5 133
Neh. 13:14 70	Psalm 71:1-24 134
Neh. 13:29 71	Psalm 74:1-23 138
Neh. 13:31 71	Psalm 79:1-13 142

Index — Every Prayer in the Bible

Reference	Page
Psalm 80:1-19	143
Psalm 83:1-18	144
Psalm 85:1-13	146
Psalm 86:1-17	147
Psalm 88:1-18	148
Psalm 90:1-17	152
Psalm 94:1-23	154
Psalm 102:1-28	157
Psalm 107:1-43	165
Psalm 108:1-13	167
Psalm 109:1-31	168
Psalm 119:1-176	172
Psalm 120:2	181
Psalm 123:1-4	181
Psalm 126:4	182
Psalm 130:1-8	182
Psalm 137:7	183
Psalm 139:1-24	184
Psalm 140:1-13	186
Psalm 141:1-10	187
Psalm 142:1-7	187
Psalm 143:1-12	188
Psalm 144:1-15	189
Isaiah 30:19	196
Isaiah 33:2-4	196
Isaiah 37:14-20	196
Isaiah 38:2-3	197
Isaiah 38:14	197
Isaiah 58:9	197
Isaiah 64:1-12	199
Jeremiah 4:10-31	201
Jeremiah 8:18	202
Jeremiah 10:23-25	202
Jeremiah 11:20	203
Jeremiah 12:1-4	203
Jeremiah 14:7-9	203
Jeremiah 14:19-22	204
Jeremiah 15:15-21	204
Jeremiah 17:12-18	205
Jeremiah 18:19-23	206
Jeremiah 20:7-13	206
Jeremiah 29:7	207
Jeremiah 29:12	208
Jeremiah 32:16-25	208
Lament. 1:9	208
Lament. 1:11	209
Lament. 1:20-22	209
Lament. 3:37-66	210
Lament. 5:1-3	212
Lament. 5:19-22	212
Daniel 2:18	213
Daniel 6:10-11	213
Daniel 9:4-19	213
Hosea 9:14	214
Joel 1:19-20	215
Joel 2:17	215
Jonah 1:14	216
Jonah 4:2-3	217
Matthew 8:31	224
Matthew 9:37-38	224
Matthew 14:23	225
Matthew 21:22	225
Matthew 26:36-44	226
Matthew 27:46	226
Matthew 27:50	226
Mark 1:35	227
Mark 5:10	227
Mark 9:24	228
Mark 11:22-26	228
Mark 14:32-39	229
Mark 15:34	229
Luke 1:13	229
Luke 8:31	231
Luke 18:1-8	232
Luke 22:39-46	234
Luke 23:42	234
Luke 23:46	234
John 12:27-28	235
John 15:16	236
John 17:1-26	236
Acts 1:13-14	237
Acts 1:24-26	238
Acts 4:23-31	238
Acts 7:55-60	239
Acts 9:11	240
Acts 10:31	240
Acts 27:29	242
Romans 1:8-15	243
Romans 8:23	244
Romans 15:30-33	244
2 Cor. 12:7-10	246
Philip. 4:6-7	250
1 Thes. 3:9-13	252
1 Tim. 5:5	255
Hebrews 4:16	257
Hebrews 5:7-8	258
Hebrews 10:19-22	258
Hebrews 13:20-21	259
James 4:7-10	259
1 Peter 5:6-7	261
1 John 3:21-22	261
1 John 5:14-16	262
Rev. 22:20-21	266

Praising God

Reference	Page
Genesis 14:20	6
Genesis 21:33	8
Genesis 24:26-27	8
Genesis 24:48	9
Genesis 24:52	9
Genesis 47:31	11
Exodus 4:31	12
Exodus 12:27	14
Exodus 15:1-18	14
Exodus 18:10-11	16
Deut. 3:23-25	21
Deut. 32:1-44	23
Judges 5:1-31	28
Judges 7:15	32
Judges 20:23-26	34
Ruth 4:14-15	35
1 Samuel 1:19	35
1 Samuel 1:28-2:10	36
1 Samuel 15:31	39
2 Samuel 6:14	41
2 Samuel 6:16	41
2 Samuel 7:18-29	42
2 Samuel 12:20	42
2 Samuel 22:1-51	43
2 Samuel 24:25	47
1 Kings 1:47-48	47
1 Kings 5:7	47
1 Kings 8:14-61	48
1 Kings 18:39	51
2 Kings 19:15-19	53
1 Chron. 16:7-36	54
1 Chron. 21:26	57
1 Chron. 23:30-31	57
1 Chron. 29:10-20	57
2 Chron. 6:	58
2 Chron. 20:18-19	62
2 Chron. 29:27-30	62
Ezra 3:11	64
Ezra 4:2	64
Ezra 7:27-28	64
Neh. 5:13	66
Neh. 8:6	67
Neh. 9:2-3	67
Neh. 9:5-37	67
Job 1:20-22	71
Job 42:1-10	76
Psalm 8:1-9	81
Psalm 9:1-20	82
Psalm 16:1-11	86
Psalm 18:1-50	87
Psalm 19:1-14	90
Psalm 21:1-13	92
Psalm 23:1-6	95
Psalm 24:1-10	95
Psalm 32:1-11	103
Psalm 33:22	103
Psalm 36:5-12	106
Psalm 40:1-17	109
Psalm 45:6	115
Psalm 46:1-11	115
Psalm 48:1-14	116
Psalm 57:1-11	121
Psalm 61:1-8	124
Psalm 63:1-11	125
Psalm 65:1-13	126
Psalm 66:1-20	127
Psalm 67:1-7	129
Psalm 68:7-10	129
Psalm 68:18-35	129
Psalm 71:1-24	134
Psalm 73:1-28	137
Psalm 76:6-10	140
Psalm 77:1-20	140
Psalm 85:1-13	146
Psalm 89:1-52	149
Psalm 92:1-15	153
Psalm 93:1-5	154
Psalm 97:8-9	156
Psalm 99:8	156
Psalm 101:1-8	156
Psalm 103:1-22	159
Psalm 104:1-35	160
Psalm 108:1-13	167
Psalm 115:1	170
Psalm 116:1-19	170
Psalm 119:1-176	172
Psalm 135:13	183
Psalm 138:1-8	184
Psalm 139:1-24	184
Psalm 144:1-15	189
Psalm 145:1-21	190
Psalm 146:1	191
Isaiah 6:3	192
Isaiah 12:1-6	193
Isaiah 25:1-5	194
Isaiah 25:9	194
Isaiah 26:1-21	194
Isaiah 63:7-19	198
Jeremiah 10:6-10	202
Jeremiah 11:5	203
Jeremiah 16:19-21	205
Jeremiah 17:12-18	205
Jeremiah 20:7-13	206
Jeremiah 32:16-25	208

Index

Lament. 5:19-22 212
Daniel 2:20-23 213
Micah 6:6 217
Habakkuk 3:2-19 218
Matthew 11:25-26 224
Matthew 14:33 225
Matthew 21:9-10 225
Matthew 28:9 226
Matthew 28:17 226
Mark 11:9-10 228
Luke 1:8-10 229
Luke 2:14 229
Luke 2:20 230
Luke 2:28-32 230
Luke 19:38 233
John 9:38 235
John 12:13 235
Acts 4:23-31 238
Acts 13:2-3 241
Acts 16:25 241
Romans 8:15 243
Romans 11:36 244
Romans 16:25-27 245
Philip. 4:19-20 250
1 Tim. 1:17 255
1 Tim. 6:16 255
2 Tim. 4:18 256
Hebrews 1:10-12 257
Hebrews 12:28-29 258
Hebrews 13:15 258
1 Peter 1:3 260
1 Peter 5:10-11 261
2 Peter 3:18 261
Jude 1:24 263
Rev. 1:6 263
Rev. 4:8 263
Rev. 4:10-11 263
Rev. 5:8-10 263
Rev. 5:12-14 264
Rev. 7:10-12 264
Rev. 15:3-4 265
Rev. 19:1-10 266
Rev. 22:17 266

Every Prayer in the Bible

Praying for Others
Reference .... Page

Genesis 17:18 6
Genesis 18:23-33 7
Genesis 20:7 7
Genesis 20:17-18 8
Genesis 25:21-23 9
Genesis 43:14 11
Genesis 48:15-16 11
Exodus 8:12 13
Exodus 8:29-30 13
Exodus 9:29 13
Exodus 9:33 13
Exodus 10:18 13
Exodus 32:10-13 16
Exodus 32:31-32 17
Numbers 11:2 18
Numbers 12:13 19
Numbers 14:13-19 19
Numbers 16:22 20
Numbers 21:7 20
Numbers 27:5 20
Numbers 27:15-17 20
Deut. 9:18-20 21
Deut. 9:20 21
Deut. 9:25-29 21
Deut. 21:6-9 22
Deut. 33:7 26
Deut. 33:11-16 26
1 Samuel 1:16-17 35
1 Samuel 2:20 37
1 Samuel 7:9 37
1 Samuel 8:6 38
1 Samuel 8:21 38
1 Samuel 12:18-19 38
1 Samuel 12:23 38
1 Samuel 15:11 39
1 Samuel 22:10 39
2 Samuel 12:16-17 42
2 Samuel 14:17 43
2 Samuel 24:17 46
1 Kings 13:6 50
1 Kings 17:20-21 50
2 Kings 4:33-35 52
2 Kings 6:17-18 52
2 Kings 6:20 52
2 Kings 19:4 52
1 Chron. 21:17 56
2 Chron. 6:12-42 58
2 Chron. 30:18-19 63
Esther 4:14 71
Job 42:1-10 76
Psalm 10:1-18 83

Psalm 12:1-8 84
Psalm 20:1-9 91
Psalm 72:1-19 135
Psalm 82:8 144
Psalm 125:4 182
Psalm 132:1-10 183
Jeremiah 28:6 207
Jeremiah 42:2-4 208
Ezekiel 11:13 212
Amos 7:2 215
Amos 7:5 215
Matthew 19:13 225
Mark 6:46 227
Luke 3:21 230
Luke 6:12 230
Luke 6:27-28 231
Luke 22:31-32 233
Luke 23:34 234
John 14:16 236
John 17:1-26 236
Acts 6:4-6 239
Acts 8:15-17 239
Acts 9:40-41 240
Acts 12:5 240
Acts 12:12 241
Acts 14:23 241
Acts 14:26 241
Acts 26:29 242
Acts 28:8 243
Romans 10:1 244
Romans 15:5-6 244
2 Cor. 13:7-9 247
Ephes. 1:15-23 248
Ephes. 3:14-21 249
Ephes. 6:19-20 249
Philip. 1:2-6 249
Philip. 1:9-11 250
Philip. 1:19 250
Col. 1:2-14 250
Col. 4:2-4 251
Col. 4:12 252
1 Thes. 3:9-13 252
1 Thes. 5:23-24 253
2 Thes. 1:11-12 253
2 Thes. 2:16-3:5 253
2 Thes. 3:1-2 254
2 Thes. 3:16 254
1 Tim. 2:1-4 255
2 Tim. 1:2-7 256
2 Tim. 1:16-18 256
Hebrews 13:18-19 258
Hebrews 13:20-21 259
3 John 1:2-4 262

Seeking God's Will

Reference......................Page
Genesis 15:8 6
Genesis 32:24-30 10
Exodus 3:11 12
Exodus 3:13 12
Exodus 4:1-2 12
Exodus 5:22-23 12
Exodus 6:12 13
Exodus 6:30 13
Numbers 11:21-22 19
Joshua 5:13-15 27
Joshua 7:6-9 27
Judges 1:1 28
Judges 6:12-13 31
Judges 6:15 31
Judges 20:18 33
Judges 21:2-3 34
1 Samuel 10:22 38
1 Samuel 14:37 39
1 Samuel 16:2 39
1 Samuel 22:10 39
1 Samuel 23:2 39
1 Samuel 23:4 40
1 Samuel 23:10-12 40
1 Samuel 28:6-7 40
1 Samuel 30:8 40
2 Samuel 2:1 41
2 Samuel 5:19 41
2 Samuel 5:23 41
2 Samuel 23:17 46
1 Chron. 14:10 54
1 Chron. 14:14 54
Job 7:17-21 71
Job 10:1-22 72
Psalm 10:1-18 83
Psalm 15:1-5 85
Isaiah 6:11 193
Jeremiah 5:3 202
Jeremiah 12:1-4 203
Jeremiah 14:19-22 204
Lament. 2:20-22 209
Ezekiel 9:8 212
Habakkuk 1:2-4 217
Habakkuk 1:12-17 217
Malachi 1:2 220
Malachi 1:7 220
Malachi 2:17 221
Malachi 3:7-8 221
Mark 1:23-24 227
Acts 9:5-6 239
Acts 10:14 240
Rev. 6:10 264

Thanksgiving and Gratitude

Reference	Page
1 Samuel 25:32	40
1 Samuel 25:39	40
1 Chron. 16:7-36	54
2 Chron. 7:3	60
2 Chron. 7:6	60
2 Chron. 20:21	62
2 Chron. 31:2	63
Ezra 3:11	64
Neh. 11:17	70
Neh. 12:31	70
Neh. 12:40	70
Psalm 30:1-12	100
Psalm 75:1-10	139
Psalm 106:1-48	162
Psalm 107:1-43	165
Psalm 118:25-29	171
Daniel 2:20-23	213
Daniel 6:10-11	213
Jonah 2:1-9	216
Matthew 14:19	225
Matthew 26:26	225
Mark 6:41	227
Mark 8:7	227
Mark 14:22	228
Luke 2:38	230
Luke 9:16	231
Luke 22:17	233
Luke 22:19	233
Luke 24:30	234
John 6:11	235
John 11:41-42	235
Acts 27:35	243
Acts 28:15	243
Romans 1:8-15	243
1 Cor. 1:2-9	245
Ephes. 1:15-23	248
Ephes. 5:19-20	249
Philip. 1:2-6	249
Col. 1:2-14	250
1 Thes. 1:1-3	252
1 Thes. 3:9-13	252
2 Thes. 1:3	253
2 Thes. 2:13	253
1 Tim. 1:12-14	254
1 Tim. 4:4-5	255
2 Tim. 1:2-7	256
Philemon 1:4	257
Hebrews 12:28-29	258
Rev. 11:15-18	265

Verses About Prayer

Reference	Page
Genesis 5:22-24	6
Exodus 17:10-12	16
Numbers 7:89	18
Deut. 4:5-8	21
1 Chron. 28:9	57
Psalm 50:7-15	116
Psalm 96:4-9	156
Proverbs 3:5-6	192
Proverbs 15:8	192
Proverbs 15:29	192
Proverbs 21:13	192
Eccles. 5:2	192
Isaiah 1:15	192
Lament. 3:25-26	210
Matthew 5:43-45	224
Matthew 6:9-13	224
Mark 2:18	227
Mark 9:28-29	228
Mark 12:40	228
Luke 5:16	230
Luke 9:18	231
Luke 9:28-29	231
Luke 11:1-4	231
Luke 12:22-31	232
Luke 18:1-8	232
Luke 18:9-14	232
Luke 20:47	233
Luke 21:36	233
John 14:13-14	236
John 15:7	236
Acts 2:42-3:1	238
Acts 10:2-4	240
Acts 10:9	240
Acts 16:13	241
Acts 16:16	241
Acts 17:24-27	242
Acts 20:36	242
Acts 21:5	242
Acts 22:17	242
Romans 8:26-27	244
Romans 12:12	244
1 Cor. 11:4-5	245
1 Cor. 11:13	246
1 Cor. 14:13-17	246
Ephes. 2:18	248
Ephes. 3:12	248
Col. 3:16-17	251
Col. 4:2-4	251
Col. 4:17	252

Every Prayer in the Bible — Index

1 Thes. 5:16-18 252
1 Tim. 2:8 255
Hebrews 10:19-22 258
James 1:5-8 259
James 4:2-3 259
James 4:7-10 259
James 5:13-18 260
1 Peter 3:7 260
1 Peter 3:12 260
1 Peter 4:7 260
1 Peter 4:11 260
1 John 5:14-16 262
Jude 1:20 263
Rev. 8:3-4 265

www.ingramcontent.com/pod-product-compliance
Lightning Source LLC
Chambersburg PA
CBHW071111160426
43196CB00013B/2537